Routine Decision-Making

Volume 74, Sage Library of Social Research

Sage Library of Social Research

Routine
Decision ~ Making:
The Future of Bureaucracy

Michael Inbar

Volume 74
SAGE LIBRARY OF
SOCIAL RESEARCH

SAGE PUBLICATIONS Beverly Hills London

For information address:

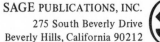
SAGE PUBLICATIONS, INC.
275 South Beverly Drive
Beverly Hills, California 90212

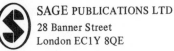
SAGE PUBLICATIONS LTD
28 Banner Street
London EC1Y 8QE

Printed in the United States of America

International Standard Book Number 0-8039-1152-1
0-8039-1153-x pbk.

Library of Congress Cataloging in Publication Data

Inbar, Michael.
  Routine Decision-Making: The future of bureaucracy.

  (Sage library of social research ; v. 74)
  Includes bibliographical references.
  1. Decision-making. 2. Bureaucracy. I. Title.
HD30.23.I5   658.4'03   78-26064
ISBN 0-8039-1152-1
ISBN 0-8039-1153-X pbk.

FIRST PRINTING

CONTENTS

PART IV: IMPLICATIONS

ACKNOWLEDGMENTS

American Association for the Advancement of Science for permission to quote from "Judgement Under Uncertainty: Heuristics and Biases" by Tversky A. and D. Kahneman, which appeared in *Science* Vol. 185, pp. 1124-1131, 27 September 1974, Copyright 1974 by the American Association for the Advancement of Science.

American Marketing Association for permission to reproduce Figure 18-1 from "A Method for Understanding Price Determinants" by Morgenroth W.M., which appeared in *Journal of Marketing Research,* August 1964, pp. 17-26, published by the American Marketing Association.

American Psychological Association for permission to reproduce Figure 2 and to quote from "Overconfidence in Case-Study Judgments" by Oskamp S., which appeared in *The Journal of Consulting Psychology,* Vol. 29, No. 3, pp. 261-265, Copyright 1965 by the American Psychological Association.

Harper and Row, Publishers, Inc. for permission to quote in Chapter XI from pp. 3-5 of "Introduction: Corporate America" by Hacker A. in *The Corporation Take-Over,* edited by A. Hacker, Copyright 1964 by Fund for the Republic, Inc.

R.E. Krieger Publishing Co., Inc. for permission to quote from "Comparison of Bayesian and Regression Approaches to the Study of Information Processing in Judgment" which appeared in *Human Judgment and Social Interaction,* edited by Rappoport L. and D.A. Summers, published by Holt, Rinehart and Winston, 1973.

McGraw-Hill Book Company for permission to quote from *New Patterns of Management* by Likert R. Copyright 1961 by the McGraw-Hill Book Company, Inc.

FOREWORD

In this volume I attempt to single out routine organizational decision-making as a significant topic of investigation and interest and to propose a rationale for modeling and, perhaps, computerizing certain processes of repetitive bureaucratic decision-making. The argument is interdisciplinary in nature, bringing to bear on the discussion findings and notions from sociology and psychology, and methods and perspectives from systems analysis and computer simulation. However, I do not assume an interdisciplinary background on the part of the reader. An inevitable result of this is that various parts of the book will appear pedestrian or superficial to readers with a professional background in one or more of the subdisciplines discussed. My hope is that at this price the discussion gains something in intelligibility for a wider audience of social scientists than would have been the case otherwise.

I have written this book over a period of several years. During this period of time I have become indebted to many people and institutions.

My first debt is to my mentor and friend J.S. Coleman and to the Johns Hopkins University, where some of the ideas presented in this book first took shape.

The Hebrew University of Jerusalem and the atmosphere of scholarship maintained in the department of sociology by J. Ben-David and S.N. Eisenstadt provided an environment conducive to preparing a first draft of the book with no need for a leave of absence. Additionally, having D. Kahaneman and A. Tversky as next door friends and colleagues proved to be an invaluable asset in finding my way through the literature on human information processing.

The Russell Sage Foundation, where I was a visiting scholar in 1975/1976, provided me with the means and the intellectual milieu necessary to put this book in final shape. In particular, I am indebted to its President, H.F. Cline, for his encouragements and support.

S.S. Boocock and B. Zablocki attended a month-long informal seminar at the foundation. Their questions and reactions in the seminar helped me greatly to clarify a number of ideas. W.L. Wallace read and criticized part of the manuscript. His comments have helped to make this book a better one than it would have been otherwise.

Also at the foundation, Ms. H. Silver read most of the manuscript and made valuable editorial comments. Ms. H. de Sterke typed several drafts of most of the chapters with unusual patience, competence, and editorial skill.

Ms. M. Curelaru, my long time friend, provided me with constant encouragements and helped me to ready the manuscript for publication.

Last but not least, I am indebted to the numerous scholars whose work is quoted in this book. The extent of this debt is reflected in the amplitude of quotations in the pages that follow.

PART ONE

THE PROBLEM

Chapter I

INTRODUCTION

Overview

This book deals with bureaucracy as a decision-making system. It is theoretical in the sense of what is called in French *un livre à thèse.*

Not all bureaucratic activities qualify as decisions, and many nonbureaucratic systems recurrently engage in decision-making. The discussion is therefore simultaneously narrower and broader than the concept of bureaucracy usually denotes.

In its pure form the essential characteristic of a bureaucracy is that it is by definition a system where problem solving and decision-making have been routinized. Indeed, if such processes are not routinized, we are not dealing with a true bureaucracy. Excluding the special case of crisis situations, a property of bureaucracies is, therefore, that the rules and procedures for the myriad of daily decisions are institutionalized. Moreover, through the operation of the principle of hierarchical accountability, these rules and procedures are constantly made explicit and often formalized. From these considerations, in particular the fact that decisions are routinized by the recurrent application of explicit rules and procedures, follows a very important proposition. Its essence is that a bureaucracy operating under normal conditions may be conceived of as a social computer.

In many ways this view is not new. As Max Weber put it:

The fully developed bureaucratic mechanism compares with other organizations exactly as does the machine with the non-mechanical modes of production. Precision, speed, unambiguity, knowledge of the files, continuity, discretion, unity, strict subordination, reduction of friction and of material and personal costs—these are raised to the optimum point in the strictly bureaucratic administration.

Its specific nature ... develops the more perfectly the more the bureaucracy is "dehumanized," the more completely it succeeds in eliminating from official business, love, hatred, and all purely personal, irrational, and emotional elements which escape calculation (Weber, 1946, pp. 214-216).

Weber intended this description to apply to the ideal type of bureaucracy. It represents the logical end product of one process of routinization of charismatic authority.

Weber's view, although acclaimed for its seminality, has been attacked on the grounds that bureaucracy is a complex social entity where informal structures and actual practices may significantly affect the aims and workings of the organization. This empirically based view has been cogently stated and documented by a number of students of formal organizations (Barnard, 1938; Simon, 1976; Gouldner, 1954; March and Simon, 1958; Merton et al., 1960; Whyte, 1961; Dror, 1968; Etzioni, 1975). As this literature indicates, in recent decades most theoretical and empirical work has been rather critical of, and has moved away from, Weber's early formulation. Indeed, in his *Dynamics of Bureaucracy*, Blau (1963) chose for the opening statement of his book the passages from Weber quoted above precisely to illustrate the extent to which modern thinking about bureaucracy differs from Weber's and his ideal type formulation.

I have quoted the same passages from Weber for exactly the opposite reason. Specifically, I shall argue that Weber's ideal type formulation is not an abstract model of bureaucracies, but a foresight of what they are becoming. This development is, I believe, inevitable because the forces of social rationalization of which bureaucracies are a product are today stronger than ever; moreover, the means to achieve the potential of rationalization inherent in Weber's model have now come into existence in the form of computers and operating systems.

In this light, one of the theses that I shall develop is that social decision-making—as recurrently carried out in large-scale formal organizations and bureaucracies—could, and indeed should, be improved by objectivizing part of the process. This may be both increasingly necessary and feasible. It may be necessary because recurrent social decisions that matter are more and more made in large-scale formal organizations and bureaucracies, whose methods of operation are imperfectly understood, and therefore faultily monitored. This may be feasible, because some inefficiencies—and many errors—in contemporary social decision-making may not be due to the *social* aspect of decision making. Rather, they may be held to stem from a conceptualization and a mode of organization of social problem solving which disregards some inherent characteristics of recurrent individual and social decision-making.

The argument rests on a fundamental proposition. It can be succinctly stated as follows: *for the study of bureaucratic decision-making it is theoretically and practically useful to focus on repetitive and routinized decision-making.* Empirically this implies that often—although by no means always—middle- and low-echelon decision-making will be the primary phenomenon of interest.

As we shall see, as a first approximation this focus appears to be as useful as, and does not seem to introduce more distortions in the study of the output of bureaucratic decision-making than, the strategic choice of the concept of a perfect market in the first stage of an economic study of price determination.

Viewed as a process, one can visualize bureaucratic decision-making along a continuum where policy-making constitutes one end and its routinized implementation by the lower echelons of the organization the other. It is probably fair to say that to date most of the extensive work done on bureaucracies has tended to focus almost exclusively on decision-making variables and processes related to the policy-making end of the continuum, rather than on its opposite—the process of routinized implementation.

I am inclined to believe that this is due to two causes. The first is that socio-political processes, and more particularly the power structures within which decisions are made as well as the salience of some unsolved problems and of crisis situations, exert a fascination that routine decisions lack. The second is that there appears to be a lack of awareness of the strong practical and theoretical reasons for focusing on the routinized aspect of problem solving, i.e., on what amounts to socially programmed decision-making (in intention at least). Deutsch expressed the same view when he suggested that "it might be profitable to look upon government somewhat less as a problem of power and somewhat more as a problem of steering" (Deutsch, 1966, p. XXViii).

In doing exactly this, however, this book departs from the prevalent focus of attention. The ultimate reason for the complementary focus advocated is its empirical usefulness and its theoretical implications for viewing the whole process of bureaucratic decision-making in a new light.

It is important to stress from the outset that this perspective should not be misunderstood. It does not deny the extreme importance of socio-political processes and of top level or unique decisions. Rather, it asserts that the bulk of bureaucratic activities is nonetheless carried out within stable power structures by its lower echelons and can be regarded as repetitive rather than nonrepetitive. The process of routinized decision-making is therefore merely held to be a dependent and independent variable of great importance for analyzing and understanding the effectiveness and possible future developments of bureaucracies.

The sheer quantitative aspect of routinized low-echelon bureaucratic decision-making is such that few would probably be willing to speculate about the exact percentage of variance that it accounts for in the daily output and performance of bureaucracies. Nevertheless, there is currently no theory of this process. As Wieck has noted of current theories about organizations in general:

> Theories are built on regularities among events, people, and relationships, not on sporadic, infrequent, explosive episodes. . . . [and yet] A large number of organization theories could legitimately be relabelled "theories of crises." This is so because many of them have more to say about the pathology of organizations than about their normalcy. Nobody seems to know much about how organizations operate in untroubled times; the day-to-day, routine existence of organizations is not given much attention. In the world of theories, organizations seem to hop along from crisis to crisis and to do nothing very interesting in between (Wieck, 1969, pp. 19, 34).

The same can be said, ceteris paribus, about daily bureaucratic decision-making. This book is in the final analysis an attempt to document both the feasibility and usefulness of filling the theoretical vacuum. It deals with what happens "in between," timewise and within given socio-political parameters. Whatever variance is explained by these variables lies outside the scope of this book. As we shall see, however, it appears that an information-processing approach can help to establish principles and means which are powerfully applicable to the task of explaining and controlling the considerable amount of residual variance of bureaucratic decision-making. The logic of the framework, then, allows one to speculate about the likely path of development of bureaucracies. This speculation is what gave the book its subtitle.

Concepts and Framework

To develop the specific theoretical framework, I shall use an interdisciplinary approach. In particular, I shall rely heavily on the concept of heuristic decision-making and use a systems viewpoint (an interdisciplinary background, however, is not assumed on the part of the reader).

Heuristic is an information-processing concept. This concept and the underlying information-processing paradigm together provide the cornerstone of the theoretical framework of analysis that I shall use.

Broadly speaking, a heuristic is an ad hoc mode of problem solving. As such it has both advantages and shortcomings. Its fundamental shortcoming is that—as opposed to, say, mathematical reasoning—it does not guarantee a valid solution to problems. Its advantages, on the other hand, include the fact that the procedure is applicable to situations where knowledge is uncertain or partial, that it can be applied when time or information-processing constraints limit to a few cues or variables the amount of information which can be processed, and above all, that it is demonstrably the predominant mode of actual decision-making in everyday life for men and organizations. This book might consequently have been given the title of *Bureaucratic Heuristic Decision-Making*. The term, however, has come to denote an individual and psychological level of analysis. Because the present volume deals with topics which are more social and molecular, is broader in scope, and presents a specific thesis about the future development of bureaucracies, a semantic distinction was felt to be in order. But semantics apart, what is attempted is to a large extent a generalization of the theory and perspective developed in the literature dealing with heuristic decision-making to the social level of analysis, i.e., to bureaucratic decision-making.

As a larger, often implicit framework, I shall further adopt a systems perspective (for reasons which will be elaborated shortly). Simon and Newell (1963) have suggested that the usefulness of a systems viewpoint for analyzing social settings depends crucially on two conditions. The first is that the system used as a theoretical paradigm be well developed and understood, much more so than the system of inquiry. The second is that the two systems be theoretically isomorphic.

The first condition is necessary if the systems approach is to be worthwhile. Should both the systems of reference and of inquiry be equally little understood, there is obviously little to be gained from using one as a theoretical model for the other. The second condition constitutes a prerequisite without which there is no guarantee that the analysis can leave the realm of analogical discourses. This happens, for instance, when societies or organizations are merely likened to known systems with, say, information and feedback properties. In such cases the specific isomorphisms between whatever actual system or organism is taken as a referent and the social setting under investigation are usually unspecified and, consequently, inferences from one system to the other must remain very general, at best, or simple metaphors, at worst.

Conversely, when a system of reference is both well understood and theoretically isomorphic with the system of inquiry, the stage is set for a more powerful process to unfold. In particular, empirical observations can be made, their implications worked out in the theoretical system of reference, and the validity of the inferences, in turn, verified in the real setting.

The systems approach to routinized decision-making and the cybernetic views that I shall either use or imply are guided by the foregoing concept of systems as a framework of analysis. This is made possible by the conceptualization discussed earlier, which views—correctly (by empirical standards, as we shall see)—routinized decision-making as the central datum to be explained in understanding the output of bureaucratic decision-making. The rationale behind this can be clarified by the following considerations.

Conceptually speaking, a decision-making process can be analyzed in terms of its factual and value premises (Simon, 1976), the procedures which are applied to the input, the nature of the output, and the feedback mechanism which allows one to ascertain the extent to which objectives have been achieved. This abstract scheme also describes the subtasks of decision-making. Because the scheme is recursive, subdecisions too involve value premises. Note, however, that as a rule their importance tends to diminish as a function of the level of subdivision of a decision-making task.

Related to this point, one can distinguish between two meanings of the term decision-making: goal setting and goal achievement. Goal setting has to do with the translation of aspirations and values into accepted social goals; goal achievement with their implementation. In many ways the two processes are difficult to tell apart. Aims affect the decision-making process, and problems encountered while it unfolds in turn affect aims. Nonetheless, the two notions are conceptually distinct. Goal setting is primarily a socio-political process; goal achievement, on the other hand, is more akin to problem-solving.

Quite clearly, the closer we are to the policy-making end of the decision-making continuum, the more value premises and goal setting can be expected to enter into decisions. Conversely, the closer we are to the routinized implementation end, the more values and socio-political considerations are irrelevant or illegitimate, and the more we can expect decisions to approximate the problem-solving model of information processing.

As a consequence of its focus, this book is primarily about the latter process, and one major advantage of this focus can now be made explicit. *By concentrating on routinized decision-making, a well-specified system—the computer as a paradigm of a cybernetic information-processing system—can readily be applied. This, in turn, makes possible the quasi-isomorphic use of a theory-specific methodology—simulation.* In particular, because, in ideal terms, a bureaucracy is a routinized (programmed) information processor, its theoretical yardstick is a programmed computer. Should the case warrant it, therefore, parallels are potentially establishable, down to the detail required by the real system and with the precision afforded by our working understanding of computers and programming.

As we shall see, this advantage, in combination with the heuristic approach, turns out to be of great theoretical and empirical power.

In this connection, it may be noted that to date most systems approaches have been used as potential tools for policy-making rather than for analyzing and monitoring the implementation process and repetitive decisions (Greenberger, Crenson, and Crissey, 1976, p. 30). As tools for policy-making, they have been criticized on various grounds (Shubick and Brewer, 1972; Brewer and Hall, 1972; Hoos, 1974; Inbar, 1976).

We shall see in Chapter 2 that many of these criticisms are valid and stem from the fact that the distinction between emergent solutions and structures, on the one hand, and their routinized counterpart, on the other—a distinction which parallels the difference between goal setting and goal attainment—has not been clearly made and/or adhered to in these applications. Consequently, systems analysis and simulation have often been applied to problems they are ill-suited to solve, while those for which they constitute a natural approach have largely been disregarded.

To avoid this pitfall, keep in mind that unless there is an explicit statement to the contrary, decision-making will always mean decision-making related to goal attainment. Goals and intentions—be they equality of educational opportunity, reduction of crime rates, or whatever—are always assumed to be exogenously determined. If they are not, the decisions fall outside the scope of this book. Using Weber's terminology, the perspective adopted raises the central question of the process by which the output of the policy-making process is enacted, that is, how *policies* are routinized; this question parallels the problem of the routinization of authority.

Scope and Aims

It should be made clear that neither the discussion of routine decision-making, the use of an information-processing approach, nor the adoption of a systems or cybernetic viewpoint in studying organizations, is new or original.

In fact, excellent discussions of the nature and importance of routine activities and decisions in organizations can be found in March and Simon (1958, pp. 139-150), and Wieck (1969). Similarly, systems analysis and the application of cybernetic ideas to the study of social systems have a long history and have generated a number of important contributions. Among these are Beer's *Cybernetics and Management* (1959); Deutsch's *The Nerves of Government* (1966); Quade and Boucher's *Systems Analysis and Policy Planning* (1968); and Steinbruner's *The Cybernetic Theory of Decision* (1974). The use of simulation and computer information-processing concepts for individual and organizational decision-making is not new either (Miller, Galanter, and Pribram, 1960; Cyert and March, 1963; Reitman, 1965; Feldman and Kanter, 1965; Crecine, 1969; Newell and Simon, 1972). Moreover, all the findings that I shall discuss are abstracted from the literature. By definition, then, the novelty in the following pages—if there is any—lies only in a specific combination of these perspectives for the problem at hand. In the final analysis, the usefulness of this book depends on the extent to which I have been able to blend and articulate naturally and effectively existing perspectives and methodologies. My effort will have been successful if the reader finds some implications of the theoretical perspective presented of interest, and, more importantly, if the theoretical framework or its inherent methodology are felt to have been conveyed in an instructive and usable manner.

The thesis about the probable future of bureaucratic organizations is likely to be controversial. Before turning to the discussion itself, it is therefore useful to clarify it as much as possible.

Coleman has noted that certain sciences—biology, for instance—could not have developed on earth before our planet had reached a certain stage of development. In a similar vein, to build a theory of industrialized societies, artisans' or manufacturers' shops are rather premature units of observation. By the same token, I shall argue that the clerical form of implementation of the bureaucratic function is likely to be a very poor choice for building a theory of routinized implementation of policies. Just as early factories turned out to be transient structures, so, in all probability, are clerical bureaucracies. Their well-documented problems and distortions may be as relevant to what is in the offing as child labor has become to industrialized countries. The impending development is best illustrated by a modern trend which makes explicit the innermost logic of many bureaucratic operations— replacing an employee with computerized rules, as in the case with the automated tellers which have now begun to appear in some banks.

The mechanization of routine blue-collar tasks has brought about far-reaching production and social changes in industrialized societies, and even in the most advanced societies these changes have not yet run their full revolutionary course. While it is true that in the final analysis men have been displaced rather than replaced, the process has nonetheless brought about tremendous changes in problems and modes of social organization. I believe that a similarly momentous transformation is about to start in earnest for routinized social decision-making, with untold consequences not only for white-collar work but for society as a whole.

The means to mechanize bureaucratized decision-making are now available, and my argument is that they will undoubtedly be applied. The choice, I argue, is not between improving the present form of bureaucracies and speculating about changes. It is between deliberately directing the coming revolution or risking its many pitfalls. These pitfalls, in my view, do not lie in the danger of applying untried or easily criticized methods for mechanizing routine human decision-making. The problem is exactly the opposite. It is precisely because some of the major conceptual and technical problems in starting this process have now been solved in theory and practice—however preliminary—that the time has come to face squarely the problems of application. The critical mass of knowledge exists, but as yet in somewhat compartmentalized disciplines; now is the time, therefore, to attempt to come to grips with a process that we have the power to disregard, but probably not to avoid.

In terms of perspective, however, the book is not about the process of transformation itself. That is to say, its thesis is not about the impact of computers on organizations or on decision-making in the usual sense; rather than being on change, the focus is on the full-fledged operation of selective processes of computerized bureaucratic decision-making. Put differently, the issues addressed include the question of why this kind of automation must come about—especially in those processes of organizational decision-making which are not naturally self-correcting; the consideration of conceptual and software means of implementation; and a discussion of concrete steps and methodologies for actual application. At issue are the types of organizational changes which are necessary if the computerized implementation of routine decisions is to become a functional social technology, in the same sense that different social contexts are necessary to a barter and to a market economy. In short, what is considered is the technical end product as it can be designed today with existing knowledge. The process of change-over itself, however, is not examined—it is taken for granted. Nonetheless, the discussion hopefully provides some guidelines for taking advantage of the organizational and social degrees of freedom that the paths which lead to the anticipated future of bureaucratic decision-making currently have.

In sum, this book and its argument are limited in many ways. Hopefully, they point out a direction. However, should they do this successfully, all or most of the road remains to be explored.

Organization of the Book

The discussion is divided into four parts. In the second chapter of the first part the systems viewpoint is introduced. In particular, the notions of the systems that I shall use are clarified; this is done by using the critique of systems analysis as a background for the discussion.

Part II summarizes some aspects of human information processing relevant to the task at hand. It constitutes the cornerstone for the elaboration that follows. Specifically, the legitimacy of looking at man as an organizational servomechanism, the handling of the problem of discretionary decisions, the validity of conceiving of bureaucracies as programmed cybernetic information processors, and the feasibility and perhaps even unavoidability of doing so crucially depend on this discussion.

Part III confronts some theoretical and empirical views about the nature of recurrent problem solving and decision-making in clerical bureaucracies and about the parameters set forth for the development of these functions by certain conceptual and methodological advances. The theoretical and empirical power of the approach in actual applications to bureaucracies is then documented.

Part IV reviews and draws some implications from the paradigm which has emerged. Potential, useful future developments of the approach are considered.

Chapter 2

SYSTEMS ANALYSIS: CRITIQUE AND REDEFINITION

Systems analysis, as the term is generally used in the social sciences, is a somewhat ill-defined concept. As I have noted in the Introduction, it is also an approach which has been criticized. Because the systems view and systems analysis are important parts of the perspective to be developed, they must be examined in detail at the outset. For this purpose, I first propose to consider in general some of the shortcomings of the systems viewpoint which are repeatedly mentioned in the literature. This will be followed by an attempt to redefine the approach for the task at hand. The chapter is organized accordingly; the first part deals with some blatant weaknesses of systems analysis as presently conceived; the second offers a reconceptualization adapted to the purpose of this book.

The Shortcomings

Critics are not necessarily the most qualified persons to define an approach. They are, however, a strategic source of information to achieve a sense of what is viewed as being controversial.

Of all the critics of systems analysis, Hoos (1974) is probably the most comprehensive in terms of the applications reviewed. Her conclusions are as far-reaching as her survey is encompassing: she hardly sees any feature of systems analysis as having a redeeming value for policy or decision making.

Because she is also exceptionally articulate in her indictments, I have chosen to summarize her views as a background for the discussion which will follow. Most of the additional references in the first part of the section are also taken from her essay.

As seen by Hoos, then, the fundamental problem with systems analysis is that it constitutes an example of unwarranted technology transfer.

To begin with, the whole enterprise is ill-defined. Thus, although the word system has over a score of classes of meanings, which range from the pertinent to the funny, she notes that "Proponents of the systems approach, for all their claims to precision, have so far neglected to specify which of [these] definitions they espouse. To judge by an almost universal predilection for the plural form, that is, the *systems* approach, one can only surmise that, in their ecumenism, they embrace all meanings" (Hoos, p.17).

Of course, this imprecision does not hold true in the case of purely electrical or mechanical systems. This, however, is not due to the quality of the verbal definitions found in engineering, which may range in specificity from "a collection of matter, parts or components which are included inside a specified, often arbitrary boundary" (Shearer et al., 1967, p.3), to "a device, procedure, or scheme, which behaves according to some description, its function being to operate on information and/or energy and/or matter in a time reference to yield information and/or energy and/or matter" (Ellis and Ludwig, 1962, p.3). Rather, the clear meaning of physical systems is anchored in their operationalization, which in one text is described as involving the following steps (Shearer et al., 1967, p.103):

(1) define the system and its components;
(2) formulate the mathematical model;
(3) determine the system equations;
(4) solve the desired output;
(5) check the solution;
(6) analyze or design.

In other words, in essence, systems analysis "seeks to identify an optimum objective for a given system and so to order the organization of the components and their interactions as to achieve a desired and presumably desirable goal" (Hoos, 1974, p.8). The system, however, must be described in terms of variables which are both quantified and commensurable. The solution, e.g., the optimization of goal achievement, is then obtained by mathematical techniques, for instance, linear programming. But wittingly or unwittingly, concepts, approaches, and techniques have a tendency to degenerate when they are transplanted from engineering, where they rest on clear and noncontroversial substantive processes and agreed-upon mathematical techniques, to disciplines where quantifications, formalizations, and the use of specific mathematical methods are more expressions of a set of arbitrary decisions than reflections of a process of rigorous thinking.

The dilution of meaning in social science applications has helped to give an aura of omnipotence to systems analysis. Thus, it is widely believed that a methodology which is used by the military and which has helped to put man on the moon is readily applicable to whatever baffling social problem awaits a solution, be it crime, education, urbanism, etc. This view is well illustrated in an introductory speech to a bill. This Senate speech, entitled "A Space Age Trajectory to the Great Society," ran in part as follows:

> Mr. President, why can not the same specialist who can figure out a way to put a man in space figure out a way to keep him out of jail?
>
> Why can not the engineers who can move a rocket to Mars figure out a way to move people through our cities and across the country without the horrors of modern traffic and the concrete desert of our highway system?
>
> Why can not the scientists who can cleanse instruments to spend germ-free years in space devise a method to end the present pollution of air and water here on earth?
>
> Why can not highly trained manpower, which can calculate a way to transmit pictures for millions of miles in space, also show us a way to transmit enough simple information to keep track of our criminals?
>
> Why can not we use computers to deal with the down-to-earth special problems of modern America?
>
> The answer is we can—if we have the wit to apply our scientific know-how to the analysis and solution of social problems with the same creativity we have applied it to space problems (Senator Gaylord Nelson, 1965).

In short, systems analysis awaits its overdue application to a score of social problems. Obviously this view disregards the fact that transfers of approaches from one discipline to another are often anything but a simple proposition. More importantly, the proposed transfer of methodology from engineering and from the military, where systems analysis was first developed, also assumes a degree of success on the very home ground of these fields, which is open to question. In fact, as Hoos notes, even in engineered systems, "the outcome of compromise among such factors as performance, reliability, cost, schedule, maintenability, power consumption, weights, and life expectancy . . . is a good deal less foolproof than the naive are led and inclined to believe." To take just one example, "the Ballistic Missile Early Warning System was engineered to detect incoming ballistic missiles through the electronic sensing of the energy they reflect. But its designers apparently forgot that large, distant objects, such as the moon, can reflect as much energy as can smaller, nearer ones. When, early in its operational life, BMEWS detected "incoming ballistic missiles," only a lack of confidence in the system blocked the reflex of a counterstrike, which would have precipitated one of the greatest tragedies in history—all because an untested electronic system had been relied on to launch nuclear missiles as a reaction to moonbeams." More generally, "Sober examination of some methodological disagreements now appearing as articles and book reviews in the professional journals causes one to reflect that it may not be an altogether unmixed blessing that the technique still remains to a considerable extent at an abstract level and has not been embraced as the planning tool to quite the total extent recommended by its creators" (Hoos, pp. 24, 25, 38).

In short, even on its home ground, systems analysis is not a panacea. In the social sciences, Hoos believes that present applications are not only occasionally faulty, but defective in principle. Her indictment rests on the contention that the approach is plagued by a misconception of aims and by a misrepresentation of achievement. Each of these criticisms deserves serious consideration.

MISCONCEPTION OF AIMS

One of the aims of systems analysis is to allow the replacement of a typically fragmented and piecemeal approach to social problems with a methodology which stresses comprehensiveness and integration; the focus is to be on problems conceived as wholes. As a result of such a perspective, public policy can be expected to become a manageable enterprise whose problems may be susceptible to rational solutions. In the case of one large-scale federal application—PPBS (Planning-Programming-Budgeting System)—this view took the specific form of the following list of objectives:

(1) Identify our national goals with precision and on a continuing basis;
(2) Choose among those goals the ones that are most urgent;
(3) Search for alternative means for reaching those goals most effectively at the least cost;
(4) Inform ourselves not merely on next year's costs, but on the second and third, and subsequent years' costs of our programs;
(5) Measure the performance of our programs to insure a dollar's worth of service for each dollar spent (PPBS, Congressional Hearings, 1967, p.1).

The problem, however, is that "These five items typify the confusion between what PPBS *is* and what it *does,* what it has accomplished and what someone hopes it will accomplish." In fact, these objectives were presented two years after the introduction of the methodology as *actual achievements* (Hoos, 1974, pp.68-69).

In terms of aims, such a view of what systems analysis can do, let alone what it has done, constitutes an utter misconception. Thus, in engineering, a systems approach can help optimize goal achievement, *given* a set of components, resources, and constraints; conversely, *given* a goal, the best paths to achieve it (in some agreed-upon sense) can be determined. But when neither goals nor means are given or agreed upon, there is obviously nothing in the methodology to bridge an ignorance gap, especially not one which involves the little understood but sovereign process of socio-political evaluation.

Yet such gaps are bravely bridged each time a system comes into existence. The process starts with the transfer of the frame of mind which is inherent in the systems approach in engineering; the systems analyst formulates as well as solves the problem. Because social scientists usually disagree about what the problem is, the analyst faced with a social problem is free to mistake his ignorance for objectivity, and should the case warrant it, his mathematical facility for understanding.

Most of the time this freedom is taken advantage of. The reason is that systems analysis as a discipline is dominated by engineers and economists who have acquired systems skills and experience in aerospace and defense programs. Cuts in these programs in the midsixties created for many of them a problem of job relocation. For others, "The most common career progression is the one based on a college degree in electrical engineering with postgraduate work in business administration, somewhere punctuated by a slight exposure to political science or sociology" (Hoos, 1974, pp. 66-67). Some social scientists, too, haunted as they are by the "softness" of their discipline, are at times only too eager to jump on this new system bandwagon. In so doing, they can vicariously keep a flattering company and benefit from the prestige that the use of a technical vocabulary confers. Indeed, "by its attribute of being all things to all people, the methodology has proved a vehicle for all who would ride" (Hoos, 1974, p. 40).

But nothing in the background of the community of self-appointed systems specialists (or "policy planners," as some have chosen to call themselves) qualifies them as experts on matters of social choice. It is not surprising, therefore, that the very problems that systems analysis was supposed to solve are generally either distorted or bypassed.

The problems are bypassed when preoccupation with technicalities deflects attention from the issues. Because systems analysis rests its claims on its quantitative approach, quantitative methods often become central issues. These issues, in turn, become topics in themselves, which are highly regarded by academic journals. In sociology, for instance, "The professional journals reflect this orientation, with a preponderance of articles concerned with technical niceties"; in economics, "The field of economic theory continues to become more and more the province of the mathematically anointed," due, in part, to the interest generated by the system equilibrium hypothesis. More generally, "Concern for purity of model and rules of the game often yields a result which is little more than a tautological exercise, satisfying only to the precious" (Hoos, 1974, pp. 29, 34, 38).

What is under dispute is not the importance of methodological advances; the issue is one of relevance. As Duncan (1969) has noted, the present problem with social measurement is not so much that we do not have the methodology to deal with what we can measure, but that we have little idea about what we *ought* to be measuring. In this respect, methodological problems and their solution are valuable contributions. They are, however, as relevant to the present aims of systems analysis as opening a bank account would be to solving the problem of lack of income. And, indeed, many of the analysts who do not engage in methodological virtuosity or escapism, as the case may be, produce systems analyses which, if not fraudulent, are generally distorted to the point where they are about as valuable as would be an overdrawn check.

Two related characteristics of systems analysis account for this state of affairs. The first is equating what is relevant to what is measurable. In order to be taken into account, facts must be in quantitative form, by nature or by arbitrary assignment; "Certain elements are amenable to this type of treatment. Thus, they become the crucial items in the calculation, even though they do not encompass or are not relevant to the real-life questions that should be faced" (Hoos, 1974, p. 138). The type of analyses that is thus generated is illustrated by the case of the supersonic transport which was debated a few years ago.

> Because speed is the major, if not the sole, contribution to the traveler of this controversial and costly aircraft, one of the research contractors participating in the study of the economics of the SST program unearthed the intelligence that a $20,000 per year executive would be willing to pay $10 for each hour of travel saved. Incidentally, none of the calculations included time lost as 1800-mile-per-hour giants circled over crowded airport runways or when, after landing, the 275 incoming passengers sought to retrieve their luggage and secure surface transportation. . . .
>
> Omitted from the cost calculations were such items as the sonic boom, noise pollution, and the possible degradation of environmental quality. . . . No one knows the likely effect of the booms on those exposed to it. Studies have been made and tests of acceptability conducted, but . . . the human subjects were young, healthy, and prepared. The startle effect was not assessed. There was no consideration for infants, the aged, or the nervous. The claim that only poorly constructed buildings are affected by sonic booms provides little comfort to the owners and occupants. And in this respect, it might be

worthwhile to mention that many schools and hospitals are included in this category . . . booms weaken structures, a possibility that may elude precise calculation but certainly does not escape the sober consideration of persons living in tornado belts, and along mighty geographical fault lines (Hoos, 1974, pp. 143-144).

The second, related, characteristic of systems analysis is that those factors which do enter into the system are reduced to some common denominator: "[the] assessment, because it must be compatible and comparable with other measures applied, is, of course, quantitative, and almost invariably in dollar terms" (Hoos, 1974, p. 133). It is with this measure as a criterion that cost-benefit and cost-effectiveness analyses are carried out on whatever social problems are of interest. The point, however, is that even this reductionist approach to social problems involves unsolved difficulties which are easily overlooked. A congressional committee report pinpointed a few of them:

> The lack of professional agreement on certain basic analytical issues, such as the appropriate public interest rate for discounting long-lived public investments; the development of shadow prices when outputs are not marketed; the evaluation of expenditures with multiple objectives; and the evaluation of public expenditures in regions or periods of less than full employment. (U.S. Congressional Report, 1970, pp. 8-9.)

In short, if systems analysis is conceived as an endeavor whose aim is to solve problems by setting social objectives—as it sometimes is by implication (Hoos, 1974, p. 130)—the enterprise amounts to a confusion in the Biblical sense. In socio-political terms, it is an illegitimate activity because "The point cannot be stressed enough that *discriminatory value judgments prevail throughout systems analytic procedures.* Who is the Paul being paid, and the Peter getting robbed, whose benefit becomes whose cost is not a question of indisputable accounting but rather a highly subjective interpretation" (Hoos, 1974, p. 131). Such judgments are clearly the prerogative of elected representatives, not of self-appointed experts.

If, on the other hand, systems analysis is seen as an application of engineering and, even more so, of economic concepts and methods to social problems in general, one ought to consider the warnings of some of the greatest economists against misconceived aims *in economics itself,* let alone in related disciplines:

> Deeper understanding eludes a technique which approaches life as a game, with its payoff strategies calculated according to minimax or maximin criteria or, perhaps, conceived as a excercise in satisficing. What may be a thoroughly satisfying model in the technical sense may

be completely unacceptable as a guide to real-life planning. The lack of congruence between the model that satisfies and the problem that baffles is not new. Keynes expressed it clearly in his famous critique "Professor Tinbergen's Method" in 1939: "If only he [Professor Tinbergen] is allowed to carry on, he is quite ready and happy at the end of it to go a long way towards admitting with an engaging modesty, that the results probably have no value. The worst of him is that he is much more interested in getting on with the job than in spending time in deciding whether the job is worth getting on with" (Hoos, 1974, p. 128).

And more recently:

Construction of abstract "models" intended to describe in mathematical terms the complex interrelationships governing the process of economic growth has become one of the favorite occupations of economic theorists. Unfortunately, the lack of factual knowledge of conditions existing in the real world forces the model builder to base many if not all of his general conclusions on all kinds of *a priori* assumptions, chosen for their convenience rather than for their correspondence to observed facts (Leontief, 1968, p. 32).

In short, even in economic matters, systems analysis is often of debatable value. Forcing the method on social problems which are arbitrarily simplified so as to be compatible with cost-benefit analyses may yield an output, however, it is more likely than not to be of the GIGO type.[1] Everything may be given a dollar value, as Bernard Shaw once wittily demonstrated.[2] That everything should be given such a value, or that solutions to social problems should be primarily gauged in economic terms, however, is likely to be a misconception. It is a fact of life that many contemporary problems are social and political in nature. It may be intellectually interesting to know what their solution might be *if* they were economic instead. Conceiving them in earnest as such, however, is as misguided as is Kaplan's drunkard who, as the story goes, was "searching under a streetlamp for his house key, which he had dropped some distance away. Asked why he did not look where he had dropped it, he replied, 'It's lighter here!' " (Kaplan, 1964, p. 11).

MISREPRESENTATION OF ACHIEVEMENT

Aims which are political rather than scientific in nature, and conceptualizations which express a "drunkard's search" for solutions, have yielded predictable results. These, however, are not always presented for what they are. The reason is not a lack of awareness on the part of the analysts. Indeed, "It is interesting to note the extent to which the plethora of little journals has become the repository for the conveniently shelved conscience of today's experts" (Hoos, 1974, p. 77). Footnotes and qualifications, which their authors proceed to ignore as they draw the "implications" of their studies, fulfill an apparently similar function.

Be this as it may, systems analysis as it is currently practiced has another fundamental shortcoming. As a result of one of its inherent characteristics, the much-heralded aim of replacing a discredited piecemeal approach by a methodology which stresses the total aspect of social problems is utterly misleading. "Identifying, quantifying, and relating service objectives with the costs and benefits of various courses of action have forced concentration on the measurable elements rather than the whole. Called 'piece-meal fragmentation' when old-line bureaucrats approached their task this way, the technique is called 'sub-optimization' when professional analysts juggle the parts they can handle" (Hoos, 1974, p. 138). And indeed, suboptimization is the order of the day; as for optimization itself, it is always mentioned as a task to be achieved in the future, generally with additional research funds. For the present, however, the simple fact is that "sub-optimization serves as a useful rationalization for failure or inability to grasp and grapple with large wholes" (Hoos, 1974, p. 147). The result is not only analyses which are narrow in focus (i.e., restricted to economic variables), but also fragmented, and, as we have seen earlier, even then, biased in their approach by unrepresentative value judgments. Hoos gives numerous examples to illustrate these weaknesses. The following are some illustrations from substantive fields of application.

Welfare. In accordance with middle-class values, many cost-benefit analyses rest on a specious dichotomy between work and welfare, as though the choice between these two options were always voluntary. The employability of many if not most of the welfare recipients, however, has yet to be demonstrated. Furthermore, even if the vocationally handicapped could all be employed, the outcome might amount to a solution of the musical chairs type. Indeed, those who are currently marginally employable would be likely to be pushed out of the labor market and replace on the welfare rolls those who had just left it. The point is that efficiency in one subsystem can be commensurably disruptive to other parts of the system.

Law enforcement. Controlling crime means different things to different people. To some it means essentially detecting and apprehending criminals. In such a case, an analysis may concentrate on patrolmen, helicopters, courts of justice, etc., which should be made available to a law enforcement system. To others it is a social problem, which must be dealt with at the level of its familial, cultural, and economic roots. Present criminal justice information systems stress apprehension; in so doing they express the " 'police' mentality of the system's designers" (Hoos, 1974, p. 216). More generally, distorting value judgments pervade the whole enterprise. For instance:

When commitments to California penal institutions were scrutinized, the major portion of offenders was found to be male, between 14 and 29 years of age, Negro or Mexican-American, poorly educated, unemployed, and from heavily populated, low-income geographical areas. Analyzing the statistics, the analysts thought they had discovered "criminal characteristics" that set the offenders apart from the population at large. In actual fact, experienced criminologists contend that persons behind bars bear greater resemblance to those outside than to their fellow inmates. . . . Ironically, the system of criminal justice which was designed on this shaky basis caught those sectors of the society which were least protected and most needed protection from and by law. The proverty syndrome—poor education, lack of employment, a slum address, a dark skin—became within the system engineers' conception of that term, the accepted "indicators" of propensity for a life of crime (Hoos, 1974, pp. 210-211).

As is well known, however, the selective (generally discriminatory) enforcement of law sends to jail an unrepresentative sample of the population of criminal offenders. All a model based on such a sample can do, therefore, is to help identify the "criminal characteristics" of the offenders who tend to get caught. The issue of lawbreaking itself, including white-collar crime, is conveniently bypassed.

The military illustrates with particular strength the danger of complete artificiality. In this respect, war games are especially informative. They are a particular form of systems analysis which is conducted within an hypothetical framework—the scenario:

"The scenario," as its name implies, is a sketch of the make-believe. . . . A sequence of speculative outcomes to hypothetical queries, the scenario is intended to describe the various possible conditions under which the system being studied may be assumed to operate at the present or some future date. . . . It may be full of fury, with strategic nuclear war spreading destruction and destroying neatly calculated portions of the human population; it may reflect only the scenario writer's strange love for horror stories. It may signify nothing so far as sound basis for military planning is concerned. But persuasive it is, for it has been arrived at through "systematic solicitation of expert opinions," *expert* here being the honorific term bestowed on all who would play the particular war game (Hoos, 1974, p. 57).

Education is a field where most of the weaknessess of systems analysis can be found simultaneously. In one variant, the applications take the form of computer-assisted instruction. However, "From the psychological point of view the one-way communication of a machine stunts the growth of skill in interpersonal relations. . . . The widespread phenomenon of new social arrangements, outside the traditional forms, marks in essence, the emergence of *ersatz* primary groups, which may provide a clue to the way in which deficiencies within our educational and other systems right themselves through extreme and not always wholesome means." Furthermore, "There is no evidence that the costly and cumbersome systems save money now nor that they ever will" (Hoos, 1974, pp. 169, 165).

In most of its other forms of applications to education, systems analysis has the shortcomings which are by now familiar. In the first place, the analyses are almost invariably reductionist, i.e., are expressed in terms of economic rewards. Moreover, even then they do not always qualify as cost-effectiveness analyses because "The typical response to frustration at failure to achieve a workable cost-effectiveness formula in education as elsewhere leads to preoccupation with and fixation at the level of development of a cost model." These models are little more than a glorified form of bookkeeping; they merely process information. This adds little to our understanding of the problems, and nothing to their solution. And yet,

> Notwithstanding their limitations, cost models are being developed and used as a basis for education planning. The University of California's activities are typical. There is the "student flow model," intended to indicate the university's "retention rate." It tells the number of students accepted, matriculated, and graduated. It counts the courses taken, the hours of credit. It tallies "dropouts." But, with all this intelligence, it does not indicate whether the latter really left college or merely transferred to another institution of higher learning, a crucial difference to anyone seeking to understand student needs and the educational process. The "faculty flow model" has as inputs the "economic" and "social" characteristics of the present academic staff. By what judgment the latter are defined and by what reason the former are construed to be a university's business are not clear. What is definite is that the operation of the model is expected to yield "optimal hiring strategy." We need pause only briefly to wonder about the analysts' criteria for significant "social" characteristics (race? color? political affiliation? party behavior? conviviality?). . . .
>
> Cost considerations and plant utilization probably influenced the decision to institute a quarterly, four-term calendar. . . . The possibilities that compacting of courses into a quarterly system or holding evening classes might interfere with other activities of the student's life or adversely affect the teaching-learning process were not taken into account. If number of bodies processed in the academic mill is the prime consideration, then shortening, hastening, and compressing the curriculum does wonders for the "productivity level" (Hoos, 1974, pp. 151-152 and 160-161).

On the other hand, genuine cost-benefit models are at times developed. In such cases, the operationalization of benefits is almost invariably expressed in terms of labor force characteristics. The results of such analyses do not differ, however, from what we have just seen in respect to either value or meaningfulness. These analyses too are fragmented and biased by value judgments, in particular concerning the cui bono issue. Thus in one illustrative case, "The authors recognized that their 'tangible benefit' criterion did pose a special problem with respect to the education of women. Carried to its extreme, it could deprive little girls of instruction even in reading and writing just as it did their great-great-grand-mothers in the Old World. Moreover, emphasis on earnings, popular in benefit analysis, could lead to many courses for plumbers, whose training pays off early and well, and few for physicians, who spend at least twenty years in school before earning a penny." More generally, the very attempt to subject education to a cost-benefit analysis is a misconception. The reason is that

Gearing education to the proximate needs of the economy represents not only a skewed view of the society's value system; it also is a serious distortion of the role of education in civilized society. The "customer oriented" goal of supplying a labor force disregards individual needs, interests, opportunity, and rights. A regressive step on the scale of civilization, it comes at the very time when advancing technology has dwarfed man's role in the production process, when automation has deprived him of whatever emotional and psychological satisfaction he once could have derived from work, and when reduction of hours and mandatory retirement have already provided him with more leisure than he knows how to enjoy. . . . What appears very likely is that the full and productive life of the future will have to be achieved with little reference to, if not in spite of, the means by which the daily bread is earned (Hoos, 1974, pp. 155, 158).

In sum, systems analysis is misconceived in its goals and worthless in its applications. As these illustrations suggest, it has failed in education as it has in all other applications where the concepts and methods of engineering and economics have been used as a paradigm in social problem solving. Rather than being germane to the problems, the results produced by the analyses cast light on what the solutions to social problems might be if life were a game, if human groups behaved like mechanical systems, or if their components strived for economic rewards only. But man not only plays and seeks and fights for economic rewards; he also strives in earnest and kills for love, power, dignity, freedom, and for countless other reasons.

The essence of the failure of the technology transfer is that in social matters, what is perceived as resources and constraints, let alone as goals, is fundamentally a value judgment. There are no known solutions which await a methodology by means of which they can be integrated and optimized, unless untenable assumptions are made. In other words, systems analysis is a misguided effort, because, even disregarding a host of other shortcomings, as a technique of social problem solving it recklessly attempts to introduce through the back door arbitrary solutions to the currently untractable problem of a welfare function.

Management of Information. The approach has also failed in its restricted MIS form (Management of Information Systems). There are two major reasons for this. The first stems from the "Common and erroneous assumptions . . . that lack of relevant information constitutes a critical deficiency for managers, and that more information will improve their decision making." The second is that "Implicit in the technical conception for the information system is the presupposition that facts, data, or information exist in pristine state and need only be captured as input" (Hoos, 1974, pp. 195, 198). The problem with such views is that they implicitly take over "the assumptions of a past society where information rather than attention was the scarce resource" (Simon, 1976, p. 296).

As a result of these misconceptions, many information systems are based on huge data banks, whose contents are indigested, and if not useless for one reason or the other, at least not used. When they are, they yield results of the type and quality discussed above in the law enforcement example.

The value of information systems is also open to questions on additional grounds. One has to do with the unsolved problem of invasion of privacy. Another is that there is a tendency to assume that the information on file is complete and accurate. This assumption, however, is at best debatable. In medical applications, for instance, "Unique identification of each individual so that relevant items of information refer to one and the same person is a problem for which current technology has no solution. There [is] no guarantee that actual data have not been attributed to the record of the wrong person or omitted from that of the right person." Furthermore, "There is little demonstrable proof that doctors accomplish their professional mission more effectively with computerized files" (Hoos, 1974, pp. 175-176). A related danger is that inaccuracies are made permanent. In this respect, even temporary mistakes can have far-reaching consequences because of the trust which is placed in the computerized handling of data. The Food and Drug Administration's restrictions on the use of saccharin is a case in point. "The margin of safety imposed was grossly inconsistent with other additive regulations because the advisory committee of the National Academy of Science had based its calculations on data in which, it was later discovered, a misplaced decimal point had remained unnoticed" (Hoos, 1974, p. 198).

More generally, information systems make possible—and may induce—centralization of authority. This, together with the availability of cradle-to-grave records, raises chilling possibilities. These range from what Hitler might have done with such a technology to the consideration that "Even under the most benevolent regime the possibilities for misuse, through intent or sheer ignorance, are enormous" (Hoos, 1974, p. 226). For instance, a few years ago agents of a federal agency tried to gain access to the circulation records of libraries in several large cities, a move which was opposed by the American Library Association.

> The rationale for this monitoring was to search out the names of persons who had taken out books on explosives. Information was sought because of the proliferation of bombings across the country. The professional librarians, aware that police may have neither time nor talent for discrimination, realized that a roster of suspects could easily be expanded, especially in a climate of political suspicion (Hoos, 1974, p. 221).

In summary, then, Hoos' critique covers the whole gamut of applications. This critique is a good illustration of the case which can be made against systems analysis as currently practiced; this includes projections of future trends, for example, Forrester's (1969) work on urban problems, because futurology as a systems approach "attacks the future in much the same way as it deals with the present" (Hoos, 1974, p. 237).

I believe that many of the points made by Hoos are valid. At the same time, a few of them may require some qualification. For instance, as we are reminded by Stinchcombe (1968), and also for that matter by Hoos (1975) herself, we should not forget that methodological ability does not imply theoretical ineptitude, any more than mathematical incompetence guarantees social acumen (for an engineering view on this issue, see White and Wright, 1975). Furthermore, the dangers of misuses should be distinguished from the intrinsic value, or lack of it, of the instrument. A knife can be used to prepare a meal or to murder; at times it is used for both. From time immemorial, knowledge has similarly been used for constructive and destructive purposes, generally for both. The fact that systems analysis might be misused is a different issue from the criticism that it is a meaningless or misleading methodology. Keeping this distinction in mind is probably the only way to avoid blurring the very real issues which are at the heart of the controversy.

Simulation

As a transition to the discussion of this problem, and more generally of the points that I consider to be of particular importance in the criticisms that we have reviewed, it is useful to consider an additional aspect of systems analysis not yet discussed—simulation. This will make possible the introduction of distinctions upon which the operational redefinition to be presented in the last section can build.

Simulation is the systems analyst's methodology par excellence. It is the analyst's equivalent of a set of differential equations in that it allows him to follow the behavior of whatever system cannot presently be described completely by an analytically solvable set of equations. Thus, as Newell and Simon put it, computer simulation "is quite analogous to explaining the path of a planetary system by a system of differential equations. The differential equations determine what will happen next (during the next 'infinitesimal' interval of time) as a function of the exact state of the system at the beginning of the interval. The program determines what the mechanism will do next as a function of its exact state at the moment—this state being dependent, in turn, on the previous history of the system and on its current environment." For instance, in the concrete example of the simulation of the human thought process, the analogy yields the following parallels:

> [T]ape-record some human subjects who are thinking aloud while solving problems (make observations of the phenomena); try to write a computer program that you think will simulate the human protocols (formulate some differential equations); realize the program on a computer, and determine what behavior path it would follow when confronted with the same problems as the human subjects (integrate the equations numerically); compare the simulated with the actual behavior (compare the predictions with the data); modify the program on the basis of the discrepancies that are discovered (modify the euqations). Repeat until you are satisfied with the fit   (Newell and Simon, 1971, p. 154).

From a different and more pragmatic point of view, simulation is often defended on other grounds. The justification is seen as resting on the notions of complexity and convenience. Because the justification applies to systems analysis as well, it is useful to scrutinize this rationale.

The notion of complexity is held to justify three types of simulations. These may be called *calculating simulations, mirroring simulations,* and *dynamic formalizations.*[3]

The complexity argument has two variants. The first rests on the premise that when a model is complex, it may be difficult or impossible to work out its implications. In such a case the role of the simulation is to *compute* outcomes under specific conditions. The observation that a simulation is no better than the assumptions built into it does not constitute a criticism of this type of simulations. The reason is that those who run them are usually very confident in all the details of the theory simulated. Simulations of pure or derived physical processes, e.g., wind tunnels, lunar flights, etc., are cases in point.

The second variant takes two related forms. These can be summarized as follows:

(1) Social phenomena are extremely complex. To study them it is essential to simplify and abstract the main characteristics of social processes. Indeed, "there are always more relevant variables than any observer or any theory could conceivably take into account at any time. Through simulation, such processes may be simplified, measured, and manipulated, so that . . . extraneous disturbances [may be] eliminated, and the process observed comprehensively, precisely, and more or less at the will of the investigator" (Zelditch and Evan, 1962, p. 49). Here, simulations, as simplified representations, are seen as a useful means for overcoming the confusing complexity of social processes. These are what was referred to above as *mirroring simulations.*

(2) The second form places less emphasis on simulations as finished products and more on the *activity* of building a simulation. In this case, the main benefit is held to be the sharpening of one's formulations which necessarily occurs during the process of designing a simulation. As Guetzkow (1962, p. 88) puts it: "Although it is but one of alternative ways of building models about the operation of social systems, its operating character demands a greater clarity in formulation than is often necessitated in literary and mathematical formulations. To construct an operable representation one must specify variables with some precision and then interlock the variables with some exactitude." Thus, for instance, it is one thing to say that, theoretically, problem solving involves such stages as preparation, incubation, illumination, and verification, and quite another thing to specify exactly what is involved in each stage so that a computer can simulate the process (cf., Hovland, 1962). Here, then, the perplexing complexity of social processes is seen as usefully tackled by the activity of designing a simulation, whatever its ultimate value as a product may be. A simulation in this sense is an exercise in *dynamic formalization.*

As to the convenience argument, it rests primarily on the observation that simulations allow one to experiment at will with alternative courses of action. In particular, such experiments do not have to depend on rare events (Inbar, 1969), or on considerations of safety, morality, or practical feasibility, which often constrain real experiments (Rasor, 1969).

Quite clearly, however, these advantages accrue only to the extent that one has succeeded in building a valid simulation. Experimenting with simulations in whose theoretical structure and details we have less than complete confidence, i.e., with mirroring simulations or dynamic formalizations, entails the above advantages only insofar as the results of the runs have heuristic or insight value.

Herein lies one aspect of the problem of most simulations. Their ultimate goal is explicitly or implicitly to achieve the status of calculating simulations in order to give policy- or decision-makers the advantages of convenience just discussed. Present-day simulations, however, are probably best characterized as being mirroring simulations at most. Logically, therefore, they are merely a step on the road to their goal. This is generally acknowledged by the designers; unfortunately, as we have seen, they usually proceed to disregard their own warnings.

Another problem, in some sense more fundamental because it is conceptual, is related to the hierarchical view that taking calculating simulations as an ultimate goal implies. Because such simulations are taken as the ideal form, the criterion of validity and usefulness which is appropriate in their case tends to be generalized. This generalization, however, is often inappropriate, as the following considerations indicate.

For purposes of validation, calculating simulations are by their very nature a two-entity concept. The two constituent entities are the referent structure which is being modeled and its representation, the simulation. The criterion of validity in such a case is quite properly the referent structure itself.

A moment's thought, however, shows that as a general conceptualization this view is imperfect. The reason is that a third element is always involved. This additional element is the designer and his image of the referent structure that he has or wishes to simulate. The two situations are diagrammed in Figure 2.1.

An important implication of Figure 2.1 is that while situation A allows and requires only one type of validation—the referent structure validation just mentioned—B points to the existence of several criteria of validation, according to the goals or combination of goals which were sought. These include: the objectivization of a researcher's or decision-maker's subjective representation, in order to follow its implications; the objectivization of this representation to examine its fit with reality; or an attempt to represent adequately the real referent system—in effect the situation discussed in reference to Figure 2.1.A.

This conceptualization, which rephrases the distinction between the three types of simulation discussed earlier, is also appropriate in classifying any systems analysis;[4] indeed, a simulation implies a systems analysis, and any genuine systems analysis can readily be translated into a simulation, as in fact it usually is. Figure 2.1 therefore suggests criteria of evaluation which are appropriate for both the systems approach and its inherent methodology.

One derivation from the preceding discussion is that the overlap between man's representation of a social referent structure and the actual structure itself, which must be assumed to transform Figure 2.1.B into Figure 2.1.A, is currently most likely to be an unrealistic assumption. Consequently, systems analysis should not be expected to produce valid results in most social science applications, as Hoos convincingly shows that it does not. This, it will be recalled, is due to a number of shortcomings, which can be classified under the following major headings:

(1) Value-laden formulation of the problems (i.e., questionable choice of social goals and debatable evaluation of means, e.g., "optimum" hiring policies in universities);

(2) artificial conceptualization of processes (by means of arbitrary assumptions or procedures, e.g., scenarios, to fill ignorance gaps);

(3) narrow focus (brought about by concentration on limited variables, e.g., economic costs and rewards);

(4) limited scope (i.e., segmented view of the problems and disregard for dysfunctional effects on other parts of the system);

(5) potential misuses.

The point of the foregoing discussion is that it is now possible to relate to these weaknesses in a more balanced manner than was previously the case. Specifically, Figure 2.1 suggests that systems analyses and simulations which lack validity or usefulness in the usual sense of the terms may nonetheless be extremely valuable. This, however, is only so as long as the cardinal sins of confusing goal setting with goal achievement and computing systems and simulations with noncomputing ones are avoided. When these pitfalls *are* avoided, however, the very shortcomings of the systems approach suggest that objectivizing the latent (and possibly distorted) models and assumptions upon which natural decision-making is based may be a most useful endeavor. Phrased differently, there appears to be room for the systems approach to help formalize what is known and believed, to facilitate drawing the implication of premises, and to contribute to the improvement of communication

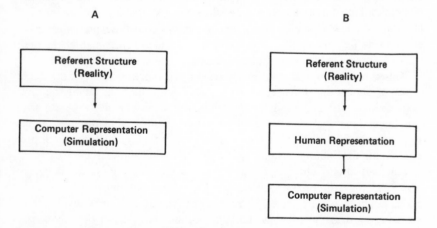

Figure 2.1: TWO MODELS OF SIMULATION

(cf., Simon, 1976, pp. 306-307). At the same time, it is obvious that the methodology cannot provide missing knowledge or by itself bridge ignorance gaps about social processes; neither can it determine trade-offs nor somehow replace the political process in the choice and evaluation of social goals and means. On these points I believe that Hoos is quite correct in her unmitigated critique.

These considerations make it possible to turn from what systems analysis cannot or should not do—which has been our topic until now—to potentially more promising applications.

A Reconceptualization

The views presented in the preceding section suggest that, in general terms, there are two kinds of useful approach for systems analysis.

The first is to explicitly conceive of the systems approach as an experimental activity whose heuristic value rests in the process of feedback which it affords between the designer, the environment, and the system or the simulation. For such work, a legitimate criterion of usefulness is the improved representation of man's view of the referent systems that modeling affords. The proper ultimate goal of this process is the construction of systems as perfectly validated in terms of the referent structures as possible. Currently, however, the case for such systems analyses would seem to rest first and foremost on the progress of man's representations that they afford through objectivization. Should it be the case that, for a particular topic or substantive area, imperfect systems analyses are not useful or efficient for improving communication or for bettering man's representations, a rationale for engaging in systems analysis and/or simulation building for decision-making in such areas would seem to be largely lacking. Indeed, few people would currently consider using most available systems analyses for serious decision-making, and mediocre claims of validity are not likely to salvage the situation; rather, they are likely to blur the picture and, in general, discredit the value of all systems analysis and simulation efforts.

The second useful approach is to analyze or simulate social processes for which human representations are demonstrably valid, or for which such representations are in themselves the legitimate data of interest. The latter condition is often met in disciplinary discourse because human representations and theories are the stuff of which science is made. In regard to the former, I shall argue that in the social sciences, the prerequisite already holds in the case of institutionalized systems of rules for decision-making. The reasons are many, but are reducible to the observation that such systems are man-made for man-conceived purposes. Conceptually, therefore, any discrepancy between a systems analysis and the referent structure becomes manageable, in principle at least. This follows from the fact that in the case of artificial and purposeful systems, people, rather than nature, are the anchor and ultimate locus of control of the system. As a result, discrepancies between a systems analysis based on limited human knowledge—in this case the knowledge of the responsible persons in charge of the system—and the actual mode of operation of the system itself, do not necessarily invalidate the model.

To clarify this point, consider the ways in which a systems analysis of the type considered may lack validity. The first is rather trivial. The designer may have poorly retrieved the formal rules and procedures which constitute the system. This, of course, is easy to remedy. The second assumes that the rules have already been properly retrieved and are demonstrably incorporated into the model. In such a case, a discrepancy between the analysis and the operation of the actual system may have two sources. The first is that other or additional rules than those publicized are, in fact, applied. In such a case, the formal rules and procedures are misleading, and probing questions are in order. One is related to who is being misled; another is whether or not this is intentional. Quite clearly these are significant issues, which may even raise problems of social control; an important contribution of systems analysis is that it can help to focus and clarify them.

Another source of possible discrepancies is related to the fact that rules and procedures are applied by people who might be inconsistent. This, however, is not a problem of validity, but rather one of reliability. Furthermore, it is a problem located in the referent system, and one on which systems analysis can cast valuable light. In particular, it raises the issue of the process of diffusion of errors, a central problem in any system, but one which has largely gone unstudied in human organizations (for an exception, conceptually at least, see McPhee, 1963, pp. 26-73).

In short, I would argue that systems analysis and simulation are useful at least as a scientific methodology, i.e., for theory building and communication, and for practical applications to selected social systems—among them bureaucracies.

Because my aim in this chapter is not to defend systems analysis in general, but to show why the approach may be justified for one specific purpose, I shall not discuss its additional useful applications. Nonetheless, before leaving the subject of such applications, a substantive example might be useful. It will clarify some of the points made above with regard to the insight and scientific value of systems analysis as an analytical tool and as a means of communication in nonbureaucratic contexts.

Parenthetically, then, consider the following controversy: some anthropologists believe that the empirical frequency of cross-cousin marriages found in a number of societies reflect an a priori social norm, or at least a personal preferential bias; others hold that these marriages result from certain territorial and residential constraints, and that kinship rules are unnecessary to explain the phenomenon. The two views were subjected to a systems analysis by means of simulations. Jeanne and John Gullahorn have examined the two simulations, and the following are excerpts of their report.

Representing the former position, Kundstadter and his associates model the effects of variations in demographic variables on the operation of an ideal pattern of marriage preference. . . . Their model incorporates the following assumptions:

1) All women marry according to age-specific probabilities.
2) Women can marry starting at age five, but they do not begin reproducing until age eleven. Marital fertility probabilities change with age, starting at .05 at age eleven and declining to zero at age forty-five.
3) Only married females reproduce.
4) Marriages are monogamous; however, widowed individuals can remarry.
5) The ideal marriage partner for a man is his mother's brother's daughter; for a woman, her father's sister's son.
6) The search for an ideal mate begins early in childhood (age two for girls, five for boys). If no matrilateral cross-cousin is available at the time of marriage, a mate is randomly chosen from unmarried individuals with whom marriage is not restricted either by incest taboos, eliminating primary relatives, or by exogamy proscriptions, eliminating patrilineal relatives up to three generations removed from the concerned party.

Findings: . . . Operating under the described maximal conditions for ideal-type liaisons, the model generates an average rate of 27% for matrilateral cross-cousin marriages. . . . According to the experimental condition simulation runs, therefore, a population presumably could achieve a 25-30% rate of cross-cousin marriages by consistently adhering to the preferential rules incorporated in the model. These findings thus raise the question of why observed frequences of cross-cousin marriages are so low in actual societies whose members profess such marital preference. . . .

Following a different theoretical approach . . . Gilbert and Hammel hypothesize that cousin marriage rates can be accounted for without specifying a preferential marriage rule phrased in kinship idiom. . . . The Gilbert and Hammel computer model involves patrilateral parallel cousin marriage in an Arab society, manipulating territorial rules in an effort to demonstrate that the occurrence of such cousin marriages constitutes an "epiphenomenon" of the interrelationship among the input variables. . . .

In the program, a village from which a husband will be chosen is randomly selected; then a village from which a wife will be drawn is

selected according to the probability of the husband making an endoga-
mous marriage. . . .

If the marriage is permissible according to the implemented territorial and incest rules, any genealogical relationship between the spouses
is recorded, and the two individuals are removed from he lists of
eligibles and placed onto a married couple list. . . .

Findings: . . . Operating with territorial preference parameters estimated from Arab ethnographic data, the model generates an average of
only four to five percent of father's-brother's-daughter marriages, as
contrasted with the reported Near Eastern rate of nine to twelve
percent. Given the estimated inputs, therefore, only about half the
frequency of patrilateral parallel cousin marriages can be accounted for
on the grounds of territorial preference. In discussing possible reasons
for the discrepancy between their model's output and the real-life data,
Gilbert and Hammel suggest that finer territorial divisions might generate a higher incidence of cousin marriage. On the basis of their modeling efforts, they further echo the simulator's plea for additional numerical information which currently is seldom available in published
ethnographic reports.

Comparisons: . . . Unfortunately, it is impossible to compare systematically the endeavors by Kundstadter et al. with those of Gilbert and
Hammel, since the alternative theoretical formulations were represented
in separate programs involving different social systems and different
types of cousin marriages.

. . . clarification and resolution of competing formulations might be
achieved by developing a modularized general computer model to
simulate marital choices. In one simulation run, the processes implied
by prescriptive or by preferential kinship-choice rules would be implemented; in another run these routines would be replaced by others
operationalizing the alternative hypothesis concerning territorial and
residential preferences. Then the output of each run could be compared
with ethnographic data regarding rates of cross-cousin marriage (Gullahorn and Gullahorn, 1970, pp. 21-25).

This example clearly shows how useful a systems analysis can be in order
to follow the implications of one's theories. It also illustrates the potential of
the methodology for intra- and inter-disciplinary communication, provided,
of course, that more attention is paid than is presently the case to questions
of compatibility between formulations. In short, for scientific purposes, as
opposed to policy-making applications, the systems approach is already a very
valuable tool. Problems arise only when contributions to the clarification of
an issue, in terms of the premises involved or their consequences, is confused
with the belief that the issue has been settled by the results of the analysis.

Returning now to our main concern, in the case of bureaucracies, the
situation is quite different from the one just considered. Here the funda-

mental assumption is that issues are settled, and that premises and consequences are no longer debated. If it were otherwise, there would be no reason for routinizing procedures and solutions for the handling of problems; indeed, if the solutions are not trusted in all their significant details, their systematic and repetitive application—which is what bureaucratization implies—has no justification.

These considerations suggest that artificial and purposeful systems of rules—i.e., those whose legitimacy derives from man's sovereignty rather than from his nature or from transcendental beliefs—can be appropriately subjected to a systems analysis. Indeed, such entities have the social status of a means—and only that of a means; in a crimeless society there would be no room for a police force—unless such a force were believed to be either natural or divinely ordained. In other words, a bureaucracy, like a police force, has a function. Moreover, this function has not to be inferred, it is known. At most, various classes of actors (within and without the system) hold different views about what this function is or should be—a question which is researchable.

The point is that as a decision-making entity a bureaucracy is a system with objectives. These are socially expected to be optimized by the persons in charge of the organization; such persons are accordingly held responsible for the system's performance.

In clerical bureaucracies the system's organization and performance stem in part from the need to accommodate the human and social demands of the agents who carry out its routinized operation. Additionally, the mode of organization reflects the need to attend to the routinization of policies, i.e., the necessity to translate principles into standardized procedures for decision-making and, at times, to review and modify them.

Concentrating for the time being, however, only on the segment of the bureaucratic structure which is defined by the body of rules, procedures, and criteria which are routinized at any one point in time, and among them on those which are used to deal with the problems of the agency's clients, a number of remarks are of interest.

First, because a bureaucracy is an artificial and purely instrumental system, its attempts to achieve and maximize certain objectives must be the expression of what is, in the final analysis, a full-fledged or ad hoc implicit or explicit systems analysis. Because of this, the workings of a bureaucracy may be expected to incorporate any or all of the weaknesses of systems analysis, namely, a value-laden formulation of problems, arbitrary assumptions, a narrowness of focus, a disregard for consequences, and misuses. When these are found in a bureaucracy, they result from the rules, procedures, and criteria which are recurrently applied to the clients. These shortcomings may stem from the indifference, ignorance, powerlessness, or ill will of the persons in charge of the bureaucracy, or they may be due to unnoticed incremental changes in the workings of the system or its environment. But whatever the case, the important point is that these weaknesses can be scrutinized by means of an objective systems analysis.

It is noteworthy that when such analyses are carried out, the table is turned around and the shoe is put on the official's foot, rather than on the analyst's. This happens because both inherently and as a result of its source of social legitimacy a bureaucracy must be modelable on the basis of its rules, procedures, and criteria: if this is not the case, something is wrong with the bureaucracy or the analysis. But, as noted earlier, in the latter case the analysis can be at most *technically* at fault, a shortcoming which can be easily remedied. Once the bureaucratic rules, procedures, and criteria are demonstrably incorporated into a model, any remaining discrepancy between its operation and the output of the actual system, let alone its intended output, puts the burden of the justification on the shoulders of the persons who are in charge of the system which has been modeled. This, it will be recalled, follows from the logic of systems of rules, which are socially defined as being exclusively instrumental.

In short, routinized artificial systems which are created for an instrumental purpose and within which responsibilities are clearly defined, appear to constitute a strategic topic for systems analysis. It should be noted that such systems differ in an essential way from natural systems, e.g., nations. In the latter case the question of means and goals is almost impossible to determine with any satisfactory degree of accuracy, either logically or consensually. This fact leaves the analyst with intractable problems of validation. The application considered differs also from the attempt discussed earlier to provide solutions to certain socio-political problems; the difference in this case is similar to what distinguishes the formulation of policies from their review. To put it differently, instrumental systems which are routinized are modelable because the results of the analyses can be validated against the actual systems' intended purposes, which are ultimately the only source of legitimacy for the routinization. It should be emphasized that a systems analysis so conceived has nothing to do with problem solving—it is exclusively descriptive. But because, as we shall see, this task can be achieved with great accuracy, the possibilities for research, problem solving, and policy-making are intriguing indeed.

With the substantive topic and the aims thus restricted to artificial systems of rules and to producing (in a first stage) validated descriptions rather than solutions, the systems approach appears to constitute a valid and useful approach, on an abstract level at least.

WHAT IS A SYSTEM?

Before leaving this level of discourse, one more conceptual task remains to be handled. We must consider in greater detail than has been the case until now what exactly is meant by a system. As already noted, the term has a variety of meanings. In the following pages it will be used in two senses.

The first derives from its cybernetic meaning. Cybernetics, as defined by the American College Dictionary (1970, p. 301), refers to the "scientific study of those methods of control and communication which are common to living organisms and machines, especially as applied to the analysis of the operations of machines such as computers." It is exactly in this sense that the term will be used here; the perspective, however, will be reversed. In particular, the applications will be to organizations, while computers, or rather the more encompassing notion of an operating system, will constitute the theoretical framework of reference. In terms of Simon and Newell's criteria, it is probably noncontroversial that operating systems are currently much better understood than are formal organizations. As for the requirement that formal organizations be isomorphic with operating systems—in important respects, at least—this is what the present book will attempt to show as part of its wider thesis.

Additionally, the cybernetic paradigm involves a key nonimplementation specific concept, that of servomechanisms. Conceptually, servomechanisms are decision-making devices which process raw or elaborated information through processes of feedback for the purpose of maintaining whatever constant performance is of interest. In this sense a computer can itself play the role of a servomechanism in a wider cybernetic system. More generally, classical examples of servomechanisms are the thermostat and the Watt governor for steam engines. The essence of a servomechanism is that it does not solve problems or make decisions according to the analytical paradigm of decision-making, a consideration of extreme importance. Rather, its decision-making ability rests on the notions of *critical variables,* and of their *tolerable range of variation.* As an example, consider the case of the Watt governor. The device is made of two masses (e.g., steel balls), linked by arms to a central shaft (see Figure 2.2). Its operation as well as its fundamental dissimilarity with analytical decision-making have been discussed in detail by Steinbruner. His discussion of the core idea begins with a description of the Watt governor:

> The shaft of the governor is attached to the shaft of the engine and rotates as a direct function of the speed of the engine. The swinging arms of the governor are attached to the throttle of the steam engine such that as the arms swing outward they begin to close the throttle and as they swing inward they open it. As the speed of the engine

increases the balls on the governor swing outward by centrifugal force and close the throttle, thus decreasing the speed of the engine. As the engine slows down, the balls swing toward the shaft by gravity, thus increasing the speed of the engine. The overall effect of the governor is to keep engine speed within a particular range, and the relationships within the system (mass of the balls, length of the arms, etc.) can be adjusted to insure that this range is the desired one. Once set properly, the Watt governor successfully makes decisions regarding the speed of the engine.

The decision-making capacity of the Watt governor, it has been recognized, exists in the fact that it sets up a structured feedback loop between the speed of the engine and the degree of throttle opening. It serves to focus decisions about throttle openings on a single variable

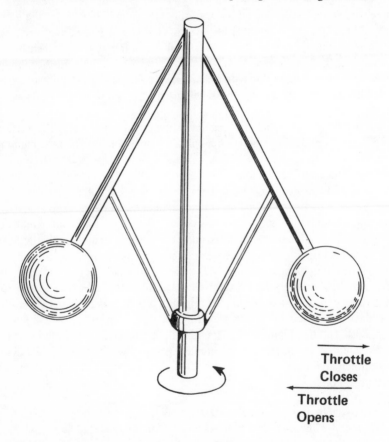

Throttle
Closes

Throttle
Opens

Figure 2.2: THE WATT GOVERNOR FOR STEAM ENGINES
(after Steinbruner, 1974, p. 52)

(speed), which is itself a function of the throttle's action. Obviously, in this decision mechanism there is no explicit model calculating the effects of engine speed and relating these to basic preferences to derive an optimal speed. If such calculations are done they are done completely outside the mechanism by an industrial engineer. . . .

As seen from within the system, the decision process of the servo-mechanism avoids the preference ordering, the explicit calculations of alternatives and outcomes, and the optimizing process which form the core of the analytic paradigm. . . . The Watt governor is an extreme case of the simple cybernetic decision-maker, but as such it illuminates the divergence in assumptions (Steinbruner, 1974, pp. 51-53).

As Steinbruner further notes, for the cybernetic paradigm to be used with full power, the system to which it is applied must be conceived as closed. This assumption is at best problematic in most social situations. For our purpose, however, even more problematic is the assumption that clerical bureauc-racies—let alone computerized ones—process, or will ever process, information according to such nonanalytical principles. Currently, such a notion may sound like an absurd proposition. Nonetheless, it is both in the specific and general sense just outlined that the cybernetic approach will be used. Hope-fully the application will appear to be much more warranted and much less of an heresy after the discussion in Part II.

The other sense in which I shall use the term system is heuristic. It follows the usage recommended by Merton (1959, especially pp. 50-84). In essence this usage advocates analyzing social systems in terms of the conscious motivations for social behavior contrasted with their objective consequences. The major tenets of Merton's paradigm which will be of interest to us are that systems are viewed as entities in which there are always functional alterna-tives in goal achievement, i.e., there is a range of possible actions which will bring about the same goal. Conversely, as a rule, actions have multiple consequences; these can be overt (manifest) or covert (latent), and be func-tional or dysfunctional; in fact, they are usually simultaneously both, but to various degrees and with different time lags for different parts of the system.

Merton's paradigm was intended for the study of natural systems. It has been so used by Blau (1963) for the study of the dynamics of bureaucracy, dynamics referring in this case to the process of continuous transformations that a bureaucracy undergoes. The approach is well suited for such a task, because a view that systems correct their deficiencies by actions which are postulated to have simultaneously functional (corrective) and dysfunctional (need-generating) consequences, is in essence dialectic, and is naturally adapted to the study of the open-ended adaptive aspect of systems.

As I have noted earlier, I shall not be dealing with problems of change. For the most part, therefore, Merton's ideas will be used in a much simpler way than the paradigm affords. In particular, in the case of the instrumental systems with which we are concerned, conscious motivations and objective consequences will be reduced to the task of determining the fit between legitimate functions and consequences, and between intentions and realizations. The heuristic value of the approach, however, will come into its own when functions and dysfunctions are considered for the human components of the anticipated complex man-machine system which will be analyzed, and for its interfacing with society at large.

Conclusion

As we have seen, the possible pitfalls of applying systems analysis to real world situations are both serious and numerous. The discussion suggests, however, that in the case of instrumental systems of rules for recurrent decision-making, these shortcomings may reach a vanishing point. This follows from the fact that, by definition, the output of such systems must be retrievable from the workings of their rules, procedures, and criteria—a retrieval task which does not involve special value judgments or unsuperable problems of validation. Modeling and simulating the routinized aspects of the operation of bureaucracies appears therefore to be theoretically and practically feasible, and potentially useful. In particular, it should yield a more integrated view of this aspect of the workings of a system and thus enhance both our understanding and our monitoring ability.

A strong case can therefore be made for applying the systems approach to the study of routinized decision-making in bureaucracies. This would be unqualifiably so were it not for the apparent unrealism of the information-processing assumptions that the chosen cybernetic systems approach implies. This problem is further compounded by a seemingly even more formidable obstacle. As every student of bureaucratic organizations knows, in many cases the formal procedures do not specify rules and criteria, but simply state who is entitled to make which decisions. Together, the nonanalytic assumptions which underlie the cybernetic approach and the discretionary aspect of bureaucratic decision-making raise fundamental problems. Quite clearly, they could even render completely sterile the argument developed to this point, because if rules, procedures, and criteria can be modeled, and discretionary decisions cannot, very little has been achieved. It is undeniable that computerized bureaucracies which would bypass the issue of discretion—a process which has been called the life blood of bureaucracy—could not be conceptually considered as being a development of clerical bureaucracies; they would be largely unrelated to them and would therefore fulfill different functions and require a justification of their own.

Because my thesis is that there is no breach of continuity, and that clerical bureaucracies merely do what can already be done more efficiently, we must now confront these difficulties. Specifically, we must examine whether the problem of discretionary decisions is tractable, and whether the cybernetic assumptions which will be required are realistic and useful. Part II is devoted to these tasks. The reader is warned that the discussion is rather detailed and starts, at times, from basics. But I believe that this strategy is necessary if the premises which will be needed in Part III to outline the beginnings of a theory of computerized bureaucracies are to be firmly established, and irrelevant controversies avoided.

NOTES

1. Garbage in, garbage out.

2. At a dinner party he is once reported to have asked a lady whether she could possibly consider betraying her husband, say, for a million pounds. Well, she replied, if a man were willing to pay such a sum of money, who knows? The dialogue then went on: and for five pounds? Mr. Shaw! Who do you think I am? That madam, replied Bernard Shaw, is now established; what remains to be determined is your price.

3. This discussion is based in part on Inbar (1976).

4. For a related discussion, see Inbar and Stoll (1972, pp. 27-33), whose definition, however, of the term "model" is not adhered to in this book.

PART II

HUMAN INFORMATION PROCESSING

Chapter 3

THE IMPOSSIBLE TASK

We all hold an image about the manner in which people in general, and each of us in particular, reach decisions. What we expect from ourselves and from our social environment depends in large measure on this image. The task of this chapter is to examine how people actually process information and make decisions.[1] In so doing, we shall lay the groundwork for confronting the issue of discretionary decisions as well as for probing the extent to which the application of a cybernetic model to the problem at hand is warranted. I specifically consider some constraints on human information processing. The notion of human decision-making which emerges from this discussion is the basis for the elaboration which is undertaken in Chapters 4 through 7.

In any attempt to clarify the concept of man as a decision-maker, the first point which deserves attention is the fact that human information processing appears to be severely limited by memory capacity. This has been demonstrated in a variety of studies. To illustrate the nature of the limitations, it may be useful to discuss them in the context of a typical experiment which brings them out.

Consider the following task: subjects are instructed to read strings of digits or letters. Upon completion of the reading, they are asked to repeat them to the experimentor.

The standard finding in such experiments is that subjects generally perform correctly on strings of up to seven, sometimes ten items. If any other task, however simple, is interposed between the reading or hearing of the items, correct recall drops to about two items. Slight interruptions by the subjects' own thoughts have a similar effect.

What can one learn from such experiments? In the first place they would indicate that men do not have the means for storing more than minimal amounts of information. The very title of Miller's (1956) famous paper, "The magical number seven, plus or minus two," is a concise statement of the problem.[2]

Secondly, they point to the need for distinguishing between two types of memory. The reason lies in the fact that men do have enormous permanent or semipermanent storage capacity. This is evident if one considers man's life-long ability to store and retrieve information from his memory. The problem, therefore, must lie in what, in contrast to permanent or semipermanent storage capacity, has been called short-term memory. To quote Simon (1969, pp. 33-34): "The bottleneck of the experiment* must lie in the small amount of rapid-access storage (so-called short-term memory) available and the time required to move items from the limited short-term store to the large-scale long-term store."

It is noteworthy that there appears to be a striking similarity between long- and short-term memory on the one hand, and on the other a computer's main storage and processor. In this light, one of the limitations of human information processing appears to be the small working area capacity of his specialized part of memory where all data to be worked on—whether incoming or temporarily retrieved from long-term memory—must be held to be operated on.

Another limiting factor is the time required for moving items from the short-term to the long-term memory. Again, the exact value of this parameter varies with the task and the definition of an "item." The range appears to be from one to ten seconds, with five seconds being a modal value for durable fixation of elementary items (i.e., familiar basic elementary structures, for instance a digit or a simple word—e.g., "cat"). Experimentally, the evidence is as follows: When presented with few stimuli which do not overload the capacity of the short-term memory, subjects have no recall problem, even if the presentation is rapid (one second per item, or even less). This leads to the inference that short-term memory is rapidly accessible. On the other hand, if the quantity of stimuli grows beyond about seven unrelated items, requiring a clearing of the short-term memory for additional processing, the items are not properly recalled, or not at all, if presentation time falls much below five seconds per item.[3] Hence the inference that five seconds is about the time required for transfer and fixation from short-term to long-term storage. It

---

*A different task from the one just described.

should be stressed that neither in the literature nor a fortiori here are the values of the size and time parameters believed to be very exact. They are only rough orders of magnitude. But as such, their existence is very well documented (see, e.g., Gregg and Simon, 1967).

An additional constraint is the internal representation of stored information. An example will clarify the nature of the problem. Suppose a subject is asked to memorize the following stimulus, a magic square (taken from Simon, 1969, pp. 43-46).

$$
\begin{array}{ccc}
4 & 9 & 2 \\
3 & 5 & 7 \\
8 & 1 & 6
\end{array}
$$

Now the stimulus is removed and the subject is asked a series of questions, the answers being timed. The questions are of the following nature: What numeral lies to the right of 3, to the left of 1? What numeral lies just below 5? What numeral is diagonally above and to the right of 5? The questions are arranged in increasing order of difficulty, as measured by the growing time it takes subjects to answer them.

The question is the following: Why should the tasks be increasingly time-consuming? Obviously, if the information stored in memory were organized in the matrix form of the visual stimulus, we would not expect any large time differences in task performance. In the light of the evidence, however, one is led to the hypothesis that the internal mode of organization of stored information is not matrix-like. An alternative mode of organization—list structures—turns out to be compatible with the experimental results. In list structure representation, the stimulus would be stored in memory according to the pattern illustrated in Figure 3.1.

Such a representation would make the experimental results perfectly understandable. Indeed, the first question, What numeral lies to the right of 3? is easily answered by searching sequentially the sublists. The other questions, however, say for instance, What numeral lies just below 5? require a matching of sublists, item by item. Such a task is evidently more complex and time-consuming than the preceding one.[4]

List name	Name of sublist 1	Elements of sublist 1	Name of sublist 2	Elements of sublist 2	...etc.	
Magic Square	Top Row	4-9-2	Middle Row	3-5-7-	Bottom Row	8-1-6

Figure 3.1

Let us now pause briefly and take stock of the findings we have reviewed. If one takes into account the size and time constraints of human information-processing, as well as the fact that the slightest interruption or interference destroys the subject's trains of thought, a dismal image of man as an information processor emerges. Mentally, he appears to be a peculiar biological computer, characterized by slow, limited, and serial information-processing capability. Furthermore, his list structure organization of information, while having the substantial advantage of being space-saving, is not necessarily always the most useful representation for solving problems.

Consider now one of the simplest real-life tasks which man sometimes confronts, playing games.[5] Take, for instance, the following puzzle (Simon, 1969, p. 26).

$$DONALD$$
$$+ GERALD$$
$$\rule{3cm}{0.4pt} \quad D = 5$$
$$ROBERT$$

The goal is to replace the letters by numerals, from 0 through 9, so that the result is a correct addition.

A systematic solution can be found by considering all the 10!, ten factorial, ways in which ten numerals can be assigned to ten letters. One of these assignments is the solution, to the extent that there is a solution. This analytical approach, which exhausts all the possibilities, is sometimes referred to as the *comprehensive decision model* (Feldman and Kanter, 1965). A program designed to perform this task would require about ten hours to generate and test each of the $10! = 3,628,800$ possibilities to find the solution. This is under the assumption that each assignment takes one-tenth of a second. (The present generation of computers might require less than this amount of time to examine each possibility, and complete the task significantly faster.) In any case, if, as in the puzzle we consider, one assignment is already given, the time required shrinks by a factor of ten, to one hour in our example.

Compare now this performance with man's capability. If we assume conservatively that man needs about one second to generate and test an assignment, one is led to the conclusion that finding a solution by the comprehensive method would require several man-years of work, assuming a forty hour week. Note that this estimate does not take into account the fact that he would be slowed down by the need to keep track of where he was and what assignments he has already tried, a most taxing requirement as soon as the number of such assignments would become greater than the "magical number seven." Paper and pencil would be of help; such material aids would permit a more functional representation of the data than list structures. In addition, writing down partial results would allow a more efficient use of the short-term memory by making rapid and recurrent visual scanning of the data possible. But, clearly, the task would nonetheless remain prohibitive.

If we consider next the case of a more complex game, for instance chess, we enter the realm of the impossible. It is estimated that a comprehensive examination of all the possibilities of a game of chess requires a number of computations in the order of 10^{120}. Such a task cannot be carried out by any known computer, even if it were running uninterruptedly for millions of years (Shannon, 1950; 1950b), let alone by man.

A fundamental question thus arises. In view of the extremely stringent constraints which limit man's information-processing capability, how does he solve problems of more than trivial complexity? For despite the theoretical impossibility, he does play chess in real time, and sometimes very well. Moreover, he behaves adaptively in the countlessly more complex situations he confronts daily. Shopping, for instance, is routinely done in minutes or hours, despite the number of choices to be made which far exceed the twenty options available at the beginning of a game of chess.

One thing appears to be clear. Except, perhaps, for some simple laboratory tasks involving at most a couple of dichotomous or trichotomous choices, man cannot and does not solve problems by anything resembling the comprehensive strategy. This fact has an immediate implication if we note that no other strategy can guarantee that a chosen course of action is the best path to a goal. Quite clearly, if one does not generate and inspect the whole decision tree of a problem, the solution, or another solution, may have been overlooked. It follows that whatever alternative strategy man actually follows, he cannot be sure of the quality of his decision *for his own purposes.* Whatever the noncomprehensive strategy which is used, it must amount to a sampling of the problem space. Under these conditions, and without some knowledge of the decision-making strategy and of the nature of the problem, the probability of having found the correct solution, or a good solution, is an open question. Insofar as most people do not have such conscious knowledge, the objective quality of any decision which cannot readily be validated is unassessable, including by and for oneself. From these considerations it appears that the usual belief that in decision-making there is always some possibility of making a mistake, is probably grossly misleading. In truth, the situation is more likely to be the other way around. On a priori grounds it would seem that for any nontrivial problem, it is an *error-free decision which is accidental.* To what extent and how generally this conclusion holds true is the topic of the next two chapters.

NOTES

1. The discussion draws heavily on Simon (1969).

2. Since the publication of this classic paper, numerous studies have shown that this parameter of memory size must be qualified according to the types of tasks and the definition of the term "item." However, as *an order of magnitude of size,* the basic conclusion has remained unchallenged.

3. For related items, transfer and fixation time appears to be curtailed by two-thirds (Simon, 1969, p. 38).

4. For additional empirical evidence of the list-structure characteristics of human information storage, the reader is referred to McLean and Gregg (1967).

5. Simplest, because the rules are clear, the alternatives few in number and spelled out, the pay-offs given. By comparison with even routine social situations, the most complex games—for instance chess—are trivially simple.

Chapter 4

THE NOTION OF HEURISTICS

Heuristics is the generic term commonly used to refer to the class of all noncomprehensive strategies of problem solving. Formally, a heuristic is a "rule of thumb, strategy, method, or trick" (Slagle, 1971, p. 3), used to attempt to discover solutions to complex problems. We have seen that whether man is aware of the fact or not, it turns out to be the only strategy available to him for nearly all the problems he confronts. A similar conclusion holds true in the case of computers when their task is to solve relatively complex problems, as the chess example has illustrated. The field of artificial intelligence is concerned, among other things, with precisely the task of devising heuristics for game-playing computers. By the very nature of the programming task, the scientists engaged in this kind of work have spelled out in detail in a number of cases the specifics of such heuristics. In so doing they have contributed several concepts which are of general interest. It is useful to examine closely a couple of them.

Consider the task of playing a game of checkers. A computer—once the rules to represent and generate legal positions have been programmed—must select a move each time it is its turn to play. What are the steps involved in this selection?

The first decision must deal with the size of the problem space which will be examined, as by definition not all the possibilities will be considered. This is the depth problem, that is, how many levels of branchings will be considered, or, alternatively, how many moves ahead will be examined. Related to this decision is the problem of allocation of effort. Will the computer look into all the possibilities existing in a given situation at a shallow depth, or concentrate on a few of them at a greater depth? The power of the heuristic will, in part, depend on the functionality, for any given problem, of these decisions.

A second question is how to evaluate the positions generated during the analysis. If the positions examined were all final positions—win, draw, or loss—there would not be any difficulty. Any reasonable set of weights, say, 1, 1/2, and 0, would be adequate and allow a straightforward choice. However, final positions are limiting cases encountered only toward the end of a game. The bulk of the choices have to be made from positions whose exact relationship to the final outcome is unknown. This leads to the concept of an *evaluation function*. All heuristics have such a means to evaluate the quality of intermediate positions. As one might suspect, the elements which enter into the evaluations, i.e., into a given evaluation function, are arbitrary. Indeed, without having solved a problem in extenso, the value for goal attainment of any intermediate situation must be a matter of enlightened guess.

To illustrate the concrete form of evaluation functions, the following is a miniature example taken from checkers (Slagle, 1971, pp. 19-20).

$$f = 6k + 4m + u$$

In this equation k stands for the king advantage, m for the man advantage, and u for the undenied mobility advantage. By undenied mobility advantage is meant the total number of squares that one's pieces can move on the board without being jumped. Thus, if in a position to be evaluated, the computer has two more kings, two men fewer, and three units of undenied mobility, the evaluation function assigns the value $6 (2) + 4 (-2) + 3 = 7$ to the position. The arbitrary nature of both the variables and the weights which enter the evaluation function should be obvious.

This preliminary clarification enables us to turn now to a more elaborate example. Consider the game of ticktacktoe. The game is played on a board subdivided into nine cells. Two players alternatively place a mark (an X or an 0) in one of the unoccupied cells. A player wins if he has three of his marks in a row, vertically, horizontally, or diagonally. Without mistakes by any side the outcome is a theoretical draw. The game is simple, simpler than the puzzle discussed in the previous chapter. It is therefore relatively easy to program a computer to play it by using the comprehensive strategy of decision-making. Kemeny and Kurtz (1971, pp. 82-87), however, have written a heuristic-based program for illustrative purposes. The game's very simplicity makes it easy to follow with paper and pencil a complete run of this program. The details of the actual instructions are unimportant. For the purpose of hand-simulating a run, the following precisions are sufficient.

First, the nine cells of the board are identified in the following manner:

$$1 \quad 2 \quad 3$$
$$8 \quad 9 \quad 4$$
$$7 \quad 6 \quad 5$$

Second, winning is defined by a matrix. As we have seen, a player can win by filling one of three rows, one of three columns, or one of two diagonals. There are, thus, eight winning paths. These paths and the cells included in each one of them constitute the operational definition of winning; they are listed in a matrix, as illustrated in Table 4.1.

Third, a centralizing table is set up with the cells of the board as row entries, and for each cell the recapitulation—derived from the previous table—of the winning paths to which it belongs. (See Table 4.2.)

Fourth, for purpose of bookkeeping, the status of each cell is indicated by 0 if it is empty, 1 if it is occupied by the computer, and -1 if it is occupied by its opponent.

Fifth, there is (what amounts to) an exact replica of Table 4.1 with the eight winning paths as row entries, but with the number of the cells defining each path left out. This is the situation matrix illustrated in Table 4.3. The use of this matrix is as follows: After each move a -1 or a 1 replaces in the matrix the 0, which corresponds in each winning path to the cell just occupied by the player or the computer. It is thus possible to tell at any time if either player has won by simply summing the rows; if any row equals 3 or -3, one of the players has won.

TABLE 4.1: **Definition of a Winning Position**

Identification of Winning Paths	Cells Constituting the Winning Path		
I	1	2	3
II	8	9	4
III	7	6	5
IV	1	8	7
V	2	9	6
VI	3	4	5
VII	1	9	5
VIII	3	9	7

TABLE 4.2: Recapitulation of the Winning Paths to Which Each Cell Belongs

Cell Number	Winning Path to Which the Cell Belongs			
1	I	IV	VII	
2	I	V		
3	I	VI	VIII	
4	II	VI		
5	III	VI	VII	
6	III	V		
7	III	IV	VIII	
8	II	IV		
9	II	V	VII	VIII

Finally, there is the heuristic. It is made of three rules to be applied in the order in which they are listed:

(1) If you (the computer) can win on the next move, do so.
(2) If the player could win on his next move, block him.
(3) Otherwise, occupy the square of greatest strategic value.

Rule (1) is implemented by simply consulting the situation matrix just described. If any row sums to 2, the computer looks up the third cell included in that winning path and occupies it. Rule 2 is similarly implemented with reversed signs; if any row sums to -2, the computer occupies the third cell of the winning path. Rule 3 is really what the whole heuristic is about, and requires the use of an evaluation function. According to this rule, if no win or loss is in view, the computer must choose among the available cells the one to occupy. For this purpose it must rely on an evaluation

TABLE 4.3: The Situation Matrix

Identification of Winning Paths	Cells Constituting the Winning Path		
I	0	0	0
II	0	0	0
III	0	0	0
IV	0	0	0
V	0	0	0
VI	0	0	0
VII	0	0	0
VIII	0	0	0

function. Kemeny and Kurtz chose to build one based on the distinction between the static value and the dynamic value of a cell, the latter including the former.

The static value of a cell reflects its winning potential independently of any other consideration. Cell 9, for instance, can lead to a win in four different ways, by being part of a string of marks in a row, a column, or one of the two diagonals. Cell 8, on the other hand, can only lead to two wins by being part of a row or a column. The static value of a cell takes this into consideration and is simply the sum of the winning paths to which a given cell belongs. Thus, in our example, the static value of cell i is obtained as follows:

$(i = 9)$ $S_9 = 1_r + 1_c + 1_{d1} + 1_{d2} = 4$
$(i = 8)$ $S_8 = 1_r + 1_c = 2$

where S_i is the static value of cell i and the subscripts of the weights (r = row, c = column, $d.1,2$ = the diagonals) are reminders of the winning path to which they are due. Note that in this program the weights are the simplest possible—0 or 1. Note also that Table 4.2 contains all the information needed to determine the static values of the cells; by summing the number of Roman numerals listed in each row, one gets the static value of the corresponding cell.

The dynamic value of a cell rests on a straightforward consideration. If a player has already a mark in a winning path, the other cells constituting this path have an increased strategic value. Operationally, this is implemented in the following manner: The rows of the situation matrix are summed; if a row sums to zero, the corresponding winning path is either empty or already occupied by a mark of each player. In either case this path is regarded as less important than one which sums to $1, -1, 2$, or -2, because one of the players must already have a start in it (disregarding the case where a path is completely filled out). The dynamic value of a cell expresses this fact by adding to the cell's static value one additional point for each *nonzero* winning path to which the cell belongs. For instance, assume that the computer started a game by occupying cell 9, and that the opponent replied by occupying cell 7. The dynamic value of cell 1 is now five (rather than three, its static value). This result is obtained as follows:

$(i = 1)$ $D_1 = (1 + 0)_r + (1 + 1)_c + (1 + 1)_d = 5$

where D_i is the dynamic value of cell i. Going through the equation, we note that the weight for the column and diagonal winning paths to which cell 1 belongs have been increased by one point each. This reflects the fact that in each of these winning paths, there is already a mark. On the other hand, the row-winning path to which cell 1 belongs is still weighted one, a reflection of the fact that the row is still empty and does not contribute anything to the dynamic value of cell 1. (Note that the weight of a winning path is similarly increased by one, whether it is the computer or the player who has a start in it. Note also that the weight of a winning path is equally increased by one, whether its nonzero absolute value is 1 or 2.)

We are now in a position to go through a run of the game, providing as it develops a few specific computing rules left out at this stage.

The computer is programmed to allow the player to start. Assume that we, as the player, choose to begin the game by occupying cell 9. The computer will proceed to perform the following main operations: First, it will look up in the recapitulation matrix—Table 4.2—the winning paths to which cell 9 belongs. These are paths II, V, VII, and VIII. Next, it will fill out the situation matrix—Table 4.3—by entering a –1 in the appropriate paths (rows). The matrix then looks as shown in Table 4.4.

Now the computer invokes its heuristic, and begins by checking whether rule one or two is applicable. No row in Table 4.4 summing to 2 or –2, the rules are not applicable. The computer proceeds then to apply rule three. For this purpose it generates the value of each empty cell by means of the evaluation function. This is done by first looking up the recapitulation table (Table 4.2) and by attributing to each cell its static value—the sum of the number of winning paths to which it belongs. At this step, for instance, the value of cell 1 would be three, in accordance with its belonging to winning paths I, IV and VII. Next, the computer checks in Table 4.4 whether any of the paths entering the static value of a given cell has a row value different

TABLE 4.4: The Situation Matrix after the First Move

Identification of Winning Paths	State of Winning Paths after Occupancy of Cell:			Row Totals
	9			
I	0	0	0	0
II	–1	0	0	–1
III	0	0	0	0
IV	0	0	0	0
V	–1	0	0	–1
VI	0	0	0	0
VII	–1	0	0	–1
VIII	–1	0	0	–1

Note: According to the presentation format adopted in the text, the minus ones should appear in second position in each row, for cell 9 appears in second position in each row of Table 4.1. However, the program disregards the ordering of cells within each path, and Table 4.4 illustrates the actual computer's internal representation of the information.

from zero. For each such path, an additional unit of weight is given to the cell. In the case of cell 1, for instance, Table 4.4 shows that of the three paths which constitute the cell's static value, two (paths I and IV) still sum to zero, while one (path VII) is nonzero. Accordingly, one additional point is given to cell 1. As a result the dynamic value obtained for this cell is four. The set of dynamic values computed in similar fashion for each cell is as follows:

$$D_1 = (1 + 0)_r + (1 + 0)_c + (1 + 1)_d = 4$$
$$D_2 = (1 + 0)_r + (1 + 1)_c = 3 \qquad = 3$$
$$D_3 = (1 + 0)_r + (1 + 0)_c + (1 + 1)_d = 4$$
$$D_4 = (1 + 1)_r + (1 + 0)_c = 3 \qquad = 3$$
$$D_5 = (1 + 0)_r + (1 + 0)_c + (1 + 1)_d = 4$$
$$D_6 = (1 + 0)_r + (1 + 1)_c = 3 \qquad = 3$$
$$D_7 = (1 + 0)_r + (1 + 0)_c + (1 + 1)_d = 4$$
$$D_8 = (1 + 1)_r + (1 + 0)_c = 3 \qquad = 3$$
$$D_9 = \text{Not applicable, already occupied.}$$

The computer now proceeds to choosing the cell with the highest dynamic value as its move. In our case there are four cells, namely, cells 1, 3, 5, and 7, which fulfill this criterion, with a value of four. When such situations occur, the computer is instructed to choose the first cell on the list with the criterion value. In our case the first cell with value four is cell 1, and the computer returns this choice as its move. It also brings up to date the situation matrix by entering a one in the winning paths to which cell 1 belongs, paths I, IV, and VII.

Assume that we choose now to occupy cell 6 as our second move. The computer proceeds to enter the appropriate information in the situation matrix, in this case a minus one in winning paths III and V. The resulting matrix is shown in Table 4.5.

The computer now invokes its heuristic for choosing its second move, and finds that rule one is not applicable—no winning path sums to 2. Rule two, however, does apply; path V has a value of minus two, indicating that if cell 2 (which is the third cell constituting this path—see Table 4.1), is not immediately occupied, the computer will lose on the next move. Hence, without even examining the present dynamic values of the cells, the computer returns its second move, the occupancy of cell 2. The situation matrix is appropriately brought up to date with a 1 entered in winning paths I and V. At this stage the game itself looks as follows:

$$
\begin{array}{cc|c}
\triangle & \triangle & 3 \\
8 & \textcircled{9} & 4 \\
7 & \textcircled{6} & 5
\end{array}
\qquad
\begin{array}{l}
\triangle = \text{computer's mark} \\
\bigcirc = \text{player's mark.}
\end{array}
$$

TABLE 4.5: Situation Matrix after Three Moves, Two by the Player and One by the Computer

Identification of Winning Paths	State of Winning Paths after Occupancy of Cells:			Row Totals
	9	1	6	
I	0	1	0	1
II	−1	0	0	−1
III	0	0	−1	−1
IV	0	1	0	1
V	−1	0	−1	−2
VI	0	0	0	0
VII	−1	1	0	0
VIII	−1	0	0	−1

Note: For purposes of clarity of presentation the effect of each move on the filling up of the winning paths is presented in separate columns. Thus, column one gives the image of the situation matrix after our first move (occupancy of cell 9), column two is the additional information entered in the winning paths after the computer's reply (occupancy of cell 1), and column three is the effect of our latest move (occupancy of cell 6) on the present situation matrix.

Obviously, we, as the player, have little choice; we must now occupy cell 3, otherwise we would lose on the next move. Our move is entered by the computer in the situation matrix as a minus one in winning paths I, VI, and VIII, giving rise to the situation matrix shown in Table 4.6.

The computer is now faced with the task of choosing its third move. The reader may verify that the game has entered a loop and is now headed toward a draw. Indeed, again by rule two of the heuristic, the computer will return as its third move the occupancy of cell 7, which is the third cell of winning path VIII, whose present value is minus two. The game situation reached is then as follows:

$$\triangle \triangle ③$$
$$8\ ⑨\ 4 \qquad \triangle = \text{computer's mark}$$
$$\triangle ⑥\ 5 \qquad \bigcirc = \text{player's mark.}$$

In this position we have again little choice; our move must be the occupancy of cell 8, for otherwise we would lose on the next move. This move generates in the situation matrix a value of minus two for the winning path made of cells 8, 9, and 4. By a last application of rule two of the heuristic the computer will then occupy the third cell of this path, cell 4, and our final move, the occupancy of cell 5, will achieve nothing. The game ends in a draw.

There were several purposes to this example. In the first place the reader may have noted how difficult it was, at times, to follow the development of

TABLE 4.6: Situation Matrix after the Player's Occupancy of Cell 3

Identification of Winning Paths	State of Winning Paths after Occupancy of Cells:					Row Totals
	9	1	6	2	3	
I	0	1	0	1	−1	1
II	−1	0	0	0	0	−1
III	0	0	−1	0	0	−1
IV	0	1	0	0	0	1
V	−1	0	−1	1	0	−1
VI	0	0	0	0	−1	−1
VII	−1	1	0	0	0	0
VIII	−1	0	0	0	−1	−2

the game, this, despite its extreme simplicity and the fact that at the end it even became trivial. Nonetheless, it is probably toward the end of the game, when the degrees of freedom have shrunk to two or three, that the visual aids became more important. At this point the experience of most readers is likely to have been that their already filled up short-term memory could not accommodate the few additional bits of information needed to complete the game. This is exactly what the previous chapter would have led us to expect.

Secondly, having gone through a concrete example, we are now able to distinguish between three conceptually different components of heuristics. These are the side conditions, the evaluation procedure, and the satisfaction criterion. Each may contribute a potential loophole to the juxtaposition of rules and procedures that is the essence of any given heuristic. It may be felt that this characterization is somewhat derogatory and in any case does not apply to the simple, elegant, and well-integrated little heuristic that we have just seen. Theoretically, however, that is exactly what a heuristic always is. The subjective good feeling that a specific heuristic may give has no bearing on the matter; on the contrary, it is all the more misleading as we shall shortly see.

Let us consider what the functions and weaknesses of each component are. The first component—the side conditions—fulfills the role of a warning light which can be switched on. Rules one and two are such side conditions in our example. When they are applicable, the whole decision procedure is short-circuited and a top priority action or set of actions is taken. The advantage of having side conditions incorporated in a heuristic is twofold. First, this is time-saving; each time a particularly useful or dangerous situation arises, no time is wasted examining the set of moves which would usually be considered.[1] Secondly, it is a safeguard—although not a foolproof one—against the inherent weaknesses of the two other components. Turning to the side condition's own weakness, it is as follows: Should they be inappropriate or incomplete (as they are likely to be in any large-sized, imperfectly understood problem space), the cut-off of the complete application of the heuristic that they cause may do more harm than good. Indeed, left to its own devices, the evaluation function might have found a better move and led to a qualitatively superior decision.

The second component is the evaluation procedure embedded in the evaluation function. As we have seen, it is at the heart of the heuristic. Without side rules a heuristic may lose some of its efficiency, but without an evaluation function, there is no heuristic at all. Its weakness derives from the sui generis complete arbitrariness of both the weights and the variables which enter into it. Unless stringent conditions—which will be discussed later—are met, there are no reasons to believe that mistakes should not be the characteristic output one ought to expect from such constructs. The poor performance of chess-playing computers recurrently demonstrates this fact as soon as they are matched with players who can take advantage (with their own more powerful heuristics) of the many inadequate moves produced during a computer's game.

The third component of heuristics—the satisfaction criterion—is related to the evaluation function. It provides a decision procedure to choose among the values returned by the evaluation function. In general, the first stipulation is to select the move with the highest value. When this is not possible, additional rules apply. We have encountered such a situation in our example when four cells were returned with a dynamic value of 4 each. In this and similar situations, the satisfaction criterion provides a decision rule to cut off the search among the evaluated alternatives as soon as a position with a *satisficing* value is found. The term has been coined by Simon (1957, p. 204), and refers to a satisfactory solution as opposed to an optimal one. In our example cell 1 was the first cell with the satisficing value of four, and was thus returned by the computer as its second move. In relatively complex problems—for instance a chess game—the satisfaction criterion plays an even more important role than may appear from the ticktacktoe example. In such games the problem space is so large, and the conceptualization of the problem so unsatisfactory, that rather than determining in advance how many positions the evaluation function will examine before proceeding to choose the one with the highest value, the heuristic is sometimes more flexibly instructed to pursue the search until a position with at least a given absolute or relative satisficing value is found. The particular value or form chosen for the satisficing rule reflects one's theoretical understanding of a problem space and the time and effort constraints within which one works. The weakness of the satisfaction criterion lies in its insensitivity to the unexamined aspects of the positions with equal values to which it is applied, and to its blindness to the values of positions not yet generated. In other words, as we shall immediately see, the satisfaction criterion in association with a weak evaluation function can constitute a very vulnerable combination. This is an important short-coming, and as pointed out above, one of the functions of the side rules is to safeguard against it. To illustrate how important this safeguard can be, the following is an example of how the computer would play the ticktacktoe game without its side rules. Assume that the following position has been reached:

$$
\begin{array}{ccc}
\triangle_1 & \triangle_2 & 3 \\
8 & \bigcirc_9 & 4 \\
7 & \bigcirc_6 & 5
\end{array}
$$

$\triangle$ = computer's mark
$\bigcirc$ = player's mark.

In this position the reader may verify that the situation matrix would look as shown in Table 4.7.

In this situation it is the computer's turn to move. By assumption the computer will disregard the critical value of path II and proceed to generate the dynamic values of each cell in order to decide on its second move. For our present purpose only two values are of interest, those of cells 3 and 8. Cell 3 has a dynamic value of six, in accordance with its static value of three, plus one point for each of the winning paths to which it belongs, which are all currently nonzero (paths I, VI, and VIII). Cell 8, on the other hand, has only a dynamic value of four, in accordance with its static value of two, plus one point for each of the two winning paths to which it belongs, which are both currently nonzero (paths II and IV). The reader may verify by generating the dynamic values of the other cells that cell 3 remains in this position the cell with the highest dynamic value. In other words, by application of the satisfaction criterion, the computer will return the occupancy of cell 3 as its second move, and immediately lose upon our occupying cell 8.

TABLE 4.7: Situation Matrix Before the Computer's Second Move

Identification of Winning Paths	State of Winning Paths after Occupancy of Cells:			Row Totals
	9	1	4	
I	0	1	0	1
II	−1	0	−1	−2
III	0	0	0	0
IV	0	1	0	1
V	−1	0	0	−1
VI	0	0	−1	−1
VII	−1	1	0	0
VIII	−1	0	0	−1

This example highlights the limitations of the separate components of a heuristic. Taken together, a particular combination of such components may be an efficient construct. But it is important to stress that whether it is or not is always an empirical question. As already noted, no matter how tight or logical a given heuristic may look, it is theoretically a simple juxtaposition of fallible rules and procedures. Consequently, it may and, in fact, *will* make *systematic* errors, under circumstances not well covered by the conceptualization of the problem space or by the architecture of the heuristic. The ticktacktoe game is again a case in point. The computer will always lose to the player if a loophole in its heuristic (the complete one, not the truncated version we have just discussed) that the reader may have noticed, is taken advantage of.

The reader may verify that if he starts the game by occupying one suboptimal cell, say cell 7, the computer will return as its first move the occupancy of cell 9, which has in this position the highest dynamic value—a value of five. If the player now occupies as his second move cell 3, the computer will return as its own second move the occupancy of cell 1. This cell shares at this point a dynamic value of six with cell 5; however, being the first on the list, it is chosen by application of the satisfaction criterion. By occupying now cell 5 as his next move, the player forces a win. The computer is helpless in the face of the double threat created by the player's move to win by occupying either cell 4 or cell 6. (The reader may find it interesting to work out for himself a modification of the heuristic so that at least this loophole is avoided.)

This example completes the review and the discussion of the logic and anatomy of a heuristic which was the topic of this chapter. At this point a few general comments may be in order.

In the first place it should be noted that in the ticktacktoe example, the simplicity of the problem space allowed us to check rather easily the effectiveness of the heuristic. Whenever this is possible, remedial steps can be taken by perfecting one or more components of the heuristic itself, or by reconceptualizing the problem space, or both. The simpler the problem space and the better our understanding of it, the easier the performance of the task will be. Even in such cases, however, a good feeling might be dangerously misleading, as we have just seen. The reason is that heuristic problem-solving remains always by its very logic an inherently fallible procedure. Moreover, the more complex the problem, the more fallible it will be, for due to man's information-processing capability, the size and complexity of heuristics should be expected to remain more or less constant (that is, relatively tiny and simple), while problem spaces and pitfalls grow exponentially with the problem's complexity.

Secondly, at the end of the last chapter I raised the possibility that in terms of the solutions afforded by a problem space of any nontrivial size, a correct decision might be regarded as a chance occurrence. We shall see in the next chapter that there are reasons to believe that for natural human problem-solving this is indeed the case under numerous and specifiable conditions. For spelled-out, objectivized heuristics of the kind we have discussed in this chapter, however, the situation would seem to be somewhat different. If one judges by the performance of the ticktacktoe heuristic, it would appear that for any reasonable heuristic, it is, at worst, the probability of a wrong decision which is unknown. Furthermore, by the very fact that such heuristics are spelled out, they can be systematically improved even if the probability of a wrong decision remains theoretically unknown (as opposed to empirically approximated). In this perspective it may be parenthetically noted that scientific work may be looked upon as an attempt by a community of persons to construct objective heuristics for problem solving in various substantive areas. Interestingly, Kuhn (1964) developed a similar view on the basis of historical considerations. In any case, this conceptualization suggests that societies in general and disciplinary communities in particular, may affect the efficiency of problem solving of their members. In particular, cultures and subcultures may provide variously adequate and explicit models and rules for setting up evaluation functions and for structuring heuristics in different problem areas.

Returning now to our main concern, and to the extent that theories can be looked upon as scientific heuristics, they would seem to differ from the ones used by individuals in at least two respects. The first is the extent of their validation and the methods used for this purpose; this leads in some problem spaces to the development of algorithms, which are often in origin heuristics whose problem-solving steps have been formalized and constitute a logically demonstrable solution to appropriate problems, especially mathematical ones. The second, central to the present argument, is their degree of complexity, which puts them usually outside the range of man's unaided information-processing capability.

This last consideration suggests that when the scientific process of building empirical heuristics (i.e., predictive theories) for a given problem space starts, the important question may not be the degree of the heuristic's validity, but rather the quality of the process by which it can be improved. Indeed, the likely degree of validity of an early heuristic is derivable from the nature of such constructs, and from the constraints put on their size and complexity by the human information-processing capability. By any standard the theories must be poor; not surprisingly, the history of science lends support to the view that this is generally the case (Kuhn, 1964). The crucial question, then, is how can early versions of heuristics be efficiently improved? From the present perspective, a major bottleneck is man's information-processing capability. Part of the answer must therefore lie in the quality of the information-processing aids used for objectivizing and spelling out the conceptualization of the theory. Writing down theories constituted such an information-processing aid at a certain stage of the history of science. Introducing mathematical formulations was another. It may be that for the problem space at hand (i.e., institutionalized social decision-making), significant progress may require still another one. I shall later argue that this is likely to be the case, and that systems analysis by means of computer modeling and simulation, may have both theoretically and empirically some of the required characteristics to fulfill such a role.

This argument will rest on the characteristics of formal and natural heuristics, and their mutual relationship in the simulation-mediated process of developing and testing theories of routinized social information processing and decision-making. This discussion will rest on the premise of the quasi-universality of human heuristic problem solving, a characteristic uniquely shared for the problem at hand by both the empirical systems of interest and those who investigate them. Because of the nature of the premise, it is important to ask before leaving the topic whether, in addition to the compelling theoretical reasons reviewed in Chapter 3, there are also empirical grounds for the axiomatic use of the notion of heuristics which is contemplated. This is the question which I address in the next chapter.

NOTE

1. In computer work this has mainly the advantage of elegance. For man, however, this can constitute a substantial gain in the light of the slowness of his information-processing capability.

Chapter 5

HUMAN HEURISTICS

The empirical evidence in support of the view that human problem solving is heuristic in nature is of two kinds: circumstantial and direct. Man not usually being aware of his decision processes, the evidence in both cases rests on the consequences we would expect from this mode of problem solving. Foremost among the expected consequences are the constant errors which should accompany decision-making under problem conditions, which defeat the heuristic's architecture, that is, the anticipated errors are of the type that the ticktacktoe heuristic would make against a player who had understood its structure and who would start the game by occupying one of the four diagonal cells. As we have seen, the computer would always lose to this player unless its heuristic were mended, and even then it would start losing again as soon as other possible loopholes in it were taken advantage of. One difference between the two types of evidence is that in the case of the direct evidence the specific aspect of the heuristic which is taken advantage of is specified in advance. In the case of circumstantial evidence it is not, at least not in man. We shall discuss first the circumstantial evidence.

Circumstantial Evidence

The circumstantial evidence is made of both numerous and disparate experimental results. The first class of findings to be discussed consists of speculative generalizations from animal research.

GENERALIZATIONS FROM ANIMAL RESEARCH

Imprinting is probably the most intriguing example of the evidence provided by this type of research. By imprinting is meant the following phenomenon: In certain species, the young identifies as its mother whatever object is present in its vicinity at a critical time. For mallard ducklings, for instance, this critical time is an exposure of about ten minutes to a moving and adequately-sized object between exactly twelve and seventeen hours after hatching (Hilgard, 1957, pp. 122-125). Outside this critical six-hour period, no mother attachment occurs. Within it, however, the young will as readily identify as its mother whatever mother object is present, the mother herself, a wooden model, or a shoe.

In terms of the organism as a problem-solving entity, the phenomenon of imprinting appears to have all the characteristics of a heuristic. In particular, it would seem that the problem space generated by the task of identifying one's mother is biologically tackled by means of an evaluation function involving the notions of proximity, size of object, movement, and duration of movement. A satisficing value of these variables leads to mother identification. The procedure has a safeguard: before and after the critical time interval side condition, the operation of the heuristic is cut off. Characteristically, the whole procedure is open to systematic errors under problem conditions which take advantage of the limitation and inadequacy of the heuristic.

A *releaser* is another type of heuristic. It is aimed at problems of aggression (as in the case of dogs and wolves, who can inhibit further attack by a dominant conspecific by exposing their throat), or of recognition, for instance, of threats or of appropriate sexual partners. (For specific examples, including the discussion of the ease with which heuristics of the releaser type can be defeated, the interested reader is referred to Hilgard (1957, pp. 122-125), and Berelson and Steiner (1964, pp. 39-43); for still other examples, e.g., the thirst and hunger cut-off mechanisms, see Lindsay and Norman (1972, pp. 605-609).)

These and similar mechanisms are naturally far removed from human cognitive problem solving. However, they are perhaps not as alien to man himself as one might be inclined to think. Lorenz (1966), for instance, believes that group identification and nationalism are best explained by assuming an imprinting or an imprinting-like mechanism in adolescence. John Money, the authoritative Johns Hopkins' sexologist, concludes on the basis of his research that gender identification and behavior are neither deterministically inborn nor learned, but imprinted, although the details of the heuristic (which is probably hierarchical) and the critical age (which seems to last several years) are still imperfectly understood (Money, 1970). In line with this view is the fact that, with animals, aberrant imprinted adult sexual behavior of the most extreme kind has already been repeatedly obtained in the laboratory (Hess, 1959, p. 140).

The importance of these examples and considerations does not lie, of course, in what they can tell us about human heuristic problem solving. Rather, it lies in what they suggest about heuristics as a biological device. In particular, whether homo sapiens is or is not a heuristic problem solver, the procedure is widely found in living organisms. This does not imply that we should expect to find it in man, and in particular at the cognitive level. However, it does mean that should we find it at this level, this is not an unusual or emergent evolutionary solution to the task of providing organisms with the potential for solving problems which far exceed—even in the simplest of instances—their information-processing capability.

HUMAN PERCEPTIONS AND FEELINGS

A second body of circumstantial evidence is related to human non-cognitive decision-making. The evidence includes findings from research on perception and attitudes. These topics are among the most extensively studied by psychologists and psycho-sociologists. In the present state of knowledge it is difficult to summarize accurately the findings without engaging in a review of the literature, which is far beyond the scope of this chapter. Suffice it to mention that as a broad generalization, it may be said that both perceptions and attitudes exhibit characteristics which are reminiscent of those expected from the operation of heuristics. For instance, perception clearly involves a very limited and selective sampling of the environmental cues. These cues, in turn, are organized according to simple principles. Under conditions which take advantage of the simplicity and limitations of these principles, systematic misperceptions can be induced (see, for instance, the summary of findings by Berelson and Steiner, 1964, pp. 104-121). In similar fashion, attitudes appear to be organized according to simple and fallible principles, e.g., balance theory, sometimes leading the puzzled observer to the conclusion that man is essentially an irrational creature (Heider, 1958; Festinger, 1957; Zajonc, 1960; Fishbein 1967; Fishbein and Aizen, 1975).

NORMATIVE DECISION-MAKING

The third type of circumstantial evidence is directly related to our concern. It rests on the failure of a whole tradition of research to fit a normative model of decision-making to the behavior of subjects in even simple laboratory tasks. Two experimental paradigms of this type of research will illustrate the nature of the evidence.

The first paradigm is known as the *light-guessing experiment*.[1] In this experimental paradigm the subject is seated before two bulbs and is asked to predict which one will light on each trial. In the basic variant of this experiment, one light goes on at each trial with a constant probability over blocks of trials. That is, if the blocks are made of twenty trials, and if the probabilities are .80 and .20, in any block of trials one light will illuminate sixteen times, and the other four times, in random order. In every experimental session there are several blocks of trials. Typically, after some experience with the task, the subjects reach an accurate estimate of the relative frequency with which the two lights illuminate and are able to verbalize it.

Now as to the problem. Given the nature of the task, and after the subjects have established a stable and correct estimate of the relative frequencies, one would expect that the number of correct predictions would be at least 80%. Any subject can ensure for himself this level of performance by adopting the following simple problem-solving strategy: always predict that the light with the highest probability will illuminate. Yet this is not the level of performance reached by the subjects. Rather, they tend to choose each light with the same probability with which the bulbs illuminate. As a result, the theoretical expectation of success is only .80(80) + .20(20) = .68. The empirical results are in line with this theoretical base line. The problem-solving strategy leading to these results is known as the fallacy of *distribution matching*. That is, people make decisions as if every instance of a distribution were a holographic image of the whole distribution (Kahneman and Tversky, 1972). We shall gain more insight into this phenomenon when we discuss the direct evidence pertaining to human heuristic problem solving, and in particular the local representativeness principle.

The second example illustrates the paradigm of research associated with the Bayesian school of thought. Consider the following problem used by Ward Edwards in some of his experiments. The problem is presented to the subjects as follows:

> I have two canvas book bags filled with poker chips. The first bag contains 70 green chips and 30 white chips, and I shall refer to this as the *predominantly green* bag. The second bag contains 70 white chips and 30 green chips and I shall refer to this as the *predominantly white* bag. The chips are all identical except for color. I now mix up the two bags so that you don't know which is which, and put one of them aside. I shall be concerned with your judgments about whether the remaining bag is predominantly green or not. Now suppose that you choose 12 chips at random with replacement from this remaining bag and it turns out that you draw eight green chips and four white chips, in some particular order. What do you think the odds are that the bag you have sampled from is predominantly green? (Quoted by Raiffa, 1970, p. 20.)

The answers to the problem vary across populations of subjects. Typical answers are that the odds are slightly in favor of the bag being predominantly green, the estimates reaching a high of .70 in the case of statistics students

(Raiffa, 1970, p. 21). Actually, the probability that the bag is predominantly green is much higher—.967. This discrepancy between the estimates and the actual probability—always underestimates (except in the case of cascaded inference, see Shulman and Elstein, 1975, p. 23)—is a standard experimental outcome. In their extensive review of the literature, Slovic and Lichtenstein (1973, p. 59), summarize the situation as follows:

> The primary finding [of Bayesian research] has been labelled *conservatism*. Upon receipt of new information, subjects revise their posterior probability estimates in the same direction as the optimal model, but the revision is typically *too small*; subjects act as if the data are less diagnostic than they truly are. Subjects in some studies (Peterson, Schneider, and Miller, 1965; Phillips and Edwards, 1966), have been found to require from two to nine data observations to revise their opinions as much as Bayes' theorem would prescribe for one observation. Much of the Bayesian research has been motivated by a desire to discover the determinants of conservatism in order that its effects might be minimized in practical diagnostic settings. A spirited debate has been raging among Bayesians about which part of the judgment process leads subjects astray.

While this debate has been going on, an increasing number of psychologists have begun wondering whether on fundamental grounds this and other normative approaches are at all fruitful for investigating actual human decision-making. Indeed, already in the midsixties it became obvious that years of research, which can only be characterized as brilliant in conception and design, had led to essentially negative results. The possible explanations for the mismatches between normative models and actual decision-making recurrently turned out to generate more problems, or more fundamental ones, than those they were intended to solve. Thus, for instance, a crucial issue in the light-guessing experiment is that of utilities. It could be that the subjects' matching strategy expresses their boredom with having to always give the same answer, that is, the argument is that the subjective value of a choice is made of more than the monetary reward for correct answers. The advantage of such an explanation is that a revised normative model can be fitted to the experimental data. Its disadvantage, however, is that, at times, manipulating utilities introduces formidable problems for the fitting of models of decision-making. In the light-guessing experiments, for instance, a revised model yields, under certain conditions, predictions of the probability of a choice greater than one. This particular problem can be taken care of (Ofshe and Ofshe, 1970, p. 15); however, one then often runs into other difficulties, felt by some to be untractable. A distinguished student of game theory—another decision-making paradigm involving utilities as a central concept—summarizes his review of these difficulties by stating that as a prescriptive theory of actual decision-making, the game theory approach is faced by "severe, and in our opinion, insuperable limitations" (Rapoport, 1966, p. 202). After review-ing the possible explanations for the conservatism discrepancy as well as other biases which, if man is held to be a Bayesian problem-solver, albeit at best a fallible one, must be dealt with, Slovic and Lichtenstein (1973, p. 94) conclude: "The evidence to date seems to indicate that subjects are process-ing information in ways fundamentally different from Bayesian . . . models."

Direct Evidence

It is against this background that some researchers started to approach the study of actual decision-making from a completely different perspective. The core idea of this alternative approach is to renounce attempting to explain the discrepancies between normative models and actual behavior. Rather, the search is for a kind of model which would be compatible with the accumu-lated evidence, and which, instead of explaining away the discrepancies, would clarify their theoretical origin and predict their occurrence under specified circumstances. Heuristic problem solving is such a model, and the research generated by this approach provides us with the direct evidence mentioned at the beginning of the chapter. To anticipate, it may be noted that from the very start, this line of inquiry was rewarded with a series of striking empirical successes, which are in sharp contrast with the history of frustrations and failures of the normative approaches.[2]

THE SYSTEMATIC STUDY OF HEURISTICS

The most influential work on heuristic problem solving in recent years is probably that done by D. Kahneman and A. Tversky, a team of psychologists who joined forces in the late sixties. At the time of the constitution of the team, Tversky had established his reputation as a Bayesian student of deci-sion-making, while Kahneman had established his as a student of perception. Within but a few years, they have verified the existence of at least three major heuristics which appear to be universal in their operation for at least certain classes of problems.

Kahneman and Tversky's views are well summarized in the following introduction to the draft of one of their papers:

Most important decisions are based on beliefs concerning the likelihood of uncertain events such as the outcome of an election, the guilt of a defendant, or the future value of the dollar. These beliefs are usually expressed in statements such as "I think that . . . ," "chances are . . . ," "it is unlikely that . . . " etc. Occasionally beliefs concerning uncertain events are expressed in a numerical form as odds or subjective probabilities. What determines such beliefs? How do people assess the likelihood of an uncertain event or the value of an uncertain quantity? The theme of the present paper is that people rely on a limited number of heuristic principles by which they reduce the complex tasks of assessing likelihood and predicting values to simpler judgmental operations. In general, these heuristics are quite useful, but sometimes they lead to severe and systematic errors.

The intuitive assessment of probability resembles the assessment of perceptual quantities such as distance or size. These judgments are all based on data of limited validity, which is processed according to heuristic rules. For example, the apparent distance of an object is determined in part by its clarity. The more sharply the object is seen, the closer it appears to be. This rule has some validity, because in any given scene the more distant objects are seen less sharply than nearer objects. However, the reliance on this rule leads to systematic errors in the estimation of distance. Specifically, distances are often overestimated when visibility is poor because the contours of objects are blurred. On the other hand, distances are often underestimated when visibility is good because the objects are sharply seen. Three features of this example are worth noting. (i) People are not generally aware of the rules that govern their impressions: they are normally ignorant of the important role of blur in the perception of distance. (ii) People cannot deliberately control their perceptual impressions: a sharply seen hilltop looks near even if one has learned of the effect of clarity on the perception of distance. (iii) It is possible to learn to recognize the situations in which impressions are likely to be biased, and to deliberately make appropriate corrections. In making a decision to climb a hill, for example, one should consider the possibility that the summit is further than it looks if the day is perfectly clear.

A similar analysis applies to the assessment of likelihoods and to prediction of values. As in the perceptual example, people apply heuristic rules to their fallible impressions. Here too, people are rarely aware of the basis of their impressions and they have little deliberate control over the processes by which these impressions are formed. However, they can learn to identify the heuristic processes that determine their impressions, and to make appropriate allowances for the biases to which they are liable" (Tversky and Kahneman, 1973, pp. 1-2).

What some of these allowances might be, and in particular the role of systems analysis and computer simulations in them, is a topic to which this chapter will be put to use later. Presently, it is useful to consider in some detail the specifics of the heuristics documented by Kahneman and Tversky.

Representativeness is the first such heuristic. The authors suggest that it is operative when subjects are confronted with the class of problems illustrated by such questions as: "What is the probability that object A belongs to class B? What is the probability that event A originates from process B? What is the probability that process B will generate event A?" (Tversky and Kahneman, 1974, p. 1124).

A valid answer to questions like these must take into consideration certain aspects of the problem, like the shape of the population of events, the variance, the sample size, etc. When this is the case, powerful statistical problem-solving algorithms are available. In most cases, however, people do not have either the time, the information, or the knowledge required for applying the algorithms. What happens then? That is, how do people, including statistically sophisticated scientists, solve everyday problems of the type illustrated above? The empirical evidence is that they rely on a simple heuristic, the essence of which is that judgments of likelihood are reduced to judgments of similarity, i.e., people "select or order outcomes by the degree to which the outcomes represent essential features of the evidence" (Kahneman and Tversky, 1973, pp. 237-238).

Under the assumption that such a specific heuristic is operative, it can be predicted that systematic judgmental errors will occur when one manipulates the elements of a problem which affect the probability of an outcome, but are irrelevant to the judgment of similarities. That is, in fact, the result that Kahneman and Tversky have obtained in a series of experiments. Their findings clearly show that variations in similarity determine the judgments of likelihood, in complete disregard of such variables as prior probabilities, sample size, randomness, etc., which are apparently not part of the evaluation functions of the subjects' heuristics. To illustrate the nature of the experimental evidence, consider the following task of attribution.

An individual, Mr. X, is described as being "meticulous, introverted, meek, solemn," and a set of occupations, "farmer, salesman, pilot, librarian, physician," is given. The subjects are now asked to evaluate the likelihood that Mr. X is engaged in each of these occupations, and to rank-order the occupations according to this likelihood.

On the basis of the representativeness heuristic the subjects should assess the similarity of Mr. X to the stereotype of each occupational role, and rank-order the occupations by the degree to which Mr. X is representative of these stereotypes. For a valid decision, on the other hand, the subjects should consider other factors, or additional ones, such as the probability of the outcome. In the illustration, the fact that there are more farmers than librarians in the population at large should affect the subjects' answers, unless, of course, the representativeness heuristic is indeed operative, because prior probabilities are irrelevant to the similarity of Mr. X to the stereotypes considered. In other words, one of the consequences expected from the representativeness heuristic is that prior probabilities will be neglected. This has been shown to be the case. Moreover, the evidence indicates that the heuristic is also operative when prior distributions are not left implicit. Tversky and Kahneman (1974, pp. 1124-1125), have summarized one such experiment and the far-reaching implications of its results as follows:

> Subjects were shown brief personality descriptions of several individuals, allegedly sampled at random from a group of 100 professionals— engineers and lawyers. The subjects were asked to assess, for each description, the probability that it belonged to an engineer rather than to a lawyer. In one experimental condition, subjects were told that the group from which the descriptions had been drawn consisted of 70 engineers and 30 lawyers. In another condition, subjects were told that the group consisted of 30 engineers and 70 lawyers. The odds that any particular description belongs to an engineer rather than to a lawyer should be higher in the first condition, where there is a majority of engineers, than in the second condition, where there is a majority of lawyers. Specifically, it can be shown by applying Bayes' rule that the ratio of these odds should be $(.7/.3)^2$, or 5.44, for each description. In a sharp violation of Bayes' rule, the subjects in the two conditions produced essentially the same probability judgments. Apparently, subjects evaluated the likelihood that a particular description belonged to an engineer rather than to a lawyer by the degree to which this description was representative of the two stereotypes, with little or no regard for the prior probabilities of the categories.
>
> The subjects used prior probabilities correctly when they had no other information. In the absence of a personality sketch, they judged the probability that an unknown individual is an engineer to be .7 and .3 respectively, in the two base-rate conditions.

It may be noted that this experiment included also a third condition. In this experimental treatment the subjects were given personality sketches utterly irrelevant to the lawyer and engineer occupational stereotypes. As we shall immediately see, the results of this treatment, disturbing as they are, are not without resemblance to (at a more molecular level) the digit memorization findings discussed in Chapter 3. That is, they are consistent with the type of faulty information processing one would expect from the existence of a small-sized, short-term memory requiring the clearing of existing information to accommodate even small amounts of newly incoming knowledge. Tversky and Kahneman (1974, p. 1125) summarize this part of the experiment as follows:

> The subjects used prior probabilities correctly when they had no other information. . . . However, prior probabilities were effectively ignored when a description was introduced, even when this description was

totally uninformative. The responses to the following description illustrate this phenomenon:

> Dick is a 30-year old man. He is married with no children. A man of high ability and high motivation, he promises to be quite successful in his field. He is well liked by his colleagues.

This description was intended to convey no information relevant to the question of whether Dick is an engineer or a lawyer. Consequently, the probability that Dick is an engineer should equal the proportion of engineers in the group, as if no description had been given. The subjects, however, judged the probability of Dick being an engineer to be .5 regardless of whether the stated proportion of engineers in the group was .7 or .3. Evidently, people respond differently when given no evidence and when given worthless evidence.

To investigate further the representativeness heuristic, Kahneman and Tversky have run a whole series of experiments.[3] The major findings to date can be summarized as follows:

(1) The representativeness heuristic hypothesis has also been established by direct assessment against replication of Bayesian type studies.

To illustrate the nature of the evidence, it is necessary to recall a derivation from a feature of many Bayesian problems (a feature which was also present in the Bayesian task described earlier). A property of such problems is that they involve a symmetrical binomial distribution. Whenever this is the case, the posterior probability depends only on the difference between the number of chips of each color observed in a sample (Edwards, 1968, p. 23). That is, given two samples, say a sample of 5 red chips and 1 blue chip, and a sample of 15 red and 11 blue chips, the support for the hypothesis that the sample was drawn from the predominantly red bag is exactly the same in both cases. However, according to the representativeness hypothesis, this is not at all the response one should expect to get from the subjects. The reason stems from the fact that the sample "in which the proportion of red chips is 5/6, seems to provide much stronger evidence for the hypothesis that the majority is red than the second sample, in which the proportion of red chips is only 15/26" (Kahneman and Tversky, 1972, p. 447). Of course, 5/6 is much more representative of red dominance than is 15/26.

(2) Whatever variables in addition to similarity might enter the heuristic used for completely assessing likelihoods, sample size is not one of them; neither is sample distribution, a fact already widely observed and reported in the literature as the "gambler's fallacy," and now reproducible in the laboratory under conditions derived from the logic of the representativeness heuristic (Kahneman and Tversky, 1972. See, in particular, their discussion of "local representativeness").

(3) It has been established by using as subjects participants to meetings of the Mathematical Psychology Group and the American Psychological Associa-

tion that the representativeness heuristic is also operative in the case of sophisticated researchers (Tversky and Kahneman, 1971).

(4) Lastly, Tversky and Kahneman (1974, p. 1126) note that the confidence people have in the accuracy of their predictions depends in some measure on the degree of representativeness attained in the prediction, that is, on the quality of the match between the selected outcome, for instance an occupation, and the input, for instance the description of a person. There is a whole literature on choice and judgment, including formal approaches, based on a notion of similarity akin to the one that we have just discussed which would tend to support this view (Restle, 1961; Tversky, 1972.) But whether or not this is generally true, there appears to be a specific "confidence" heuristic available for this type of judgment. More significantly, it apparently relies primarily on the notion of familiarity.

This is demonstrated in a study which deserves more than passing attention. The author (Oskamp, 1965) set out to investigate whether an increased degree of confidence in one's conclusions necessarily reflects an increased degree of their accuracy. For this purpose, he performed an experiment with thirty-two psychologically experienced subjects, including a number of professionally active clinical psychologists, who were given the task of studying a typical "case." The material was handed out in four stages, according to the following procedure:

> Stage 1 contained only the following brief demographic information about the case, in order to test for the "psychological chance" level of predictive accuracy (Patterson, 1955):
>> Joseph Kidd (a pseudonym) is a 29-year old man. He is white, unmarried, and a veteran of World War II. He is a college graduate, and works as a business assistant in a floral decorating studio.
>
> Stage 2 added 1-1/2 single-spaced typed pages of material about Kidd's childhood, through age 12. Stage 3 (2 pages) covered his high school and college years, and Stage 4 (1.3 pages) covered army service and later activity up to age 29 (Oskamp, 1965, p. 262).

To establish the accuracy of the judges, a multiple-choice test was constructed. The subjects filled out four identical copies of this test, one after each stage; they also indicated for each alternative circled on the test the degree of confidence they had in their answers (there were twenty-five questions, each followed by four wrong alternatives, and one correct one, in random order). The results of the experiment are reproduced in Table 5.1.

The major findings are easy to summarize: the level of accuracy does not vary significantly with increased information; furthermore, it never rises significantly above the 20% level of accuracy one would expect from random choices. At the same. time, however, confidence steadily increases as a function of quantity of information, that is, with the degree of familiarity with the case. Of course, as with all experiments, one should be careful about unwarranted generalizations. A number of tasks have clearer cues attached to their correct performance than do clinical evaluations. Objective accuracy and confidence need not therefore always be mismatched. But that they can be is a possibility we have come to expect from the operation of heuristics. The fact that several classes of problems are structurally of the clinical diagnosis type is, therefore, a consideration which must be kept in mind.

Availability. The second general heuristic documented by Kahneman and Tversky is availability.[4] The term refers to the ease with which instances or occurrences can be brought to mind. The heuristic is used when decisions or judgments require memory retrievals. It explains such fallacies as the pernicious "illusory correlation" which does not spare specialists working in their field of expertise, even when they are confronted with strong contradictory evidence (Chapman and Chapman, 1967; 1969; Tversky and Kahneman, 1973, p. 19). Again, the heuristic is usually an adequate procedure (for such tasks as the assessment of frequencies or likelihoods) "because instances of large classes are recalled better and faster than instances of less frequent classes" (Tversky and Kahneman, 1974, p. 1127). However, one can easily conceive of conditions under which the heuristic will lead to systematic errors. For instance, one should expect that "when the size of a class is judged by the availability of its instances, a class whose instances are easily retrieved will appear more numerous than a class of equal frequency whose instances are less retrievable." To illustrate:

> In an elementary demonstration of this effect, subjects heard a list of well-known personalities of both sexes and were subsequently asked to judge whether the list contained more names of men than of women. Different lists were presented to different groups of subjects. In some of the lists the men were relatively more famous than the women, and in others the women were relatively more famous than the men. In each of the lists, the subjects erroneously judged that the class (sex) that had the more famous personalities was the more numerous (Tversky and Kahneman, 1974, p. 1127; Tversky and Kahneman, 1973b).

In addition to salience, there are a number of additional circumstances which can be expected to defeat the heuristic (Tversky and Kahneman, 1974, pp. 1127-1130). These include the ease with which relevant instances can be constructed from memory or their "imaginability," and what Tversky and Kahneman call "the effectiveness of a search set." It is instructive to examine how such a search set affects problem solving.

TABLE 5.1: Performance of 32 Judges on the 25-Item Questionnaire
(Reproduced from Oskamp, 1965, p. 264, Table 2)

Measure	Mean Score				F	P
	Stage 1	Stage 2	Stage 3	Stage 4		
Accuracy (%)	26.0	23.0	28.4	27.8	5.02	.01
Confidence (%)	33.2	39.2	46.0	52.8	36.06	.001
Number of changed answers	–	13.2	11.4	8.1	21.56	.001

N.B.: The significance tests are about fluctuations over the four stages, not about differences from a chance base rate.

The effectiveness of a search set becomes a consideration when one tackles problems having the following structure: assume that you sample at random a word with three or more letters from the English language. Is it more likely that the words start with an r, or that an r is the third letter? Empirically, Tversky and Kahneman found evidence indicating that:

> People approach this problem by recalling words that begin with r (road) and words that have r in the third position (car) and assess the relative frequency by the ease with which words of the two types come to mind. Because it is much easier to search for words by their first letter than by their third letter, most people judge words that begin with a given consonant to be more numerous than words in which the same consonant appears in the third position. They do so even for consonants, such as r or k, that are more frequent in the third position than in the first (Tversky and Kahneman, 1974, p. 1127; Tversky and Kahneman, 1973b).

We have already seen how the notion of a short-term memory provides insights for interpreting some findings related to the representativeness heuristic. Presently, in the context of the availability heuristic, the consequences expected from a list structure mode of information storage inevitably come to mind. Viewing man as a biological computer is thus clearly more than a rhetorical device. The point of this remark is that certain expectations which are theoretically derived from the nature of information processors in general have demonstrable empirical usefulness. Because some of these expectations are largely invariant across at least certain classes of information processors, the inherent similarity begins to illustrate one of the uses which can be made of artificial information processors as theoretical models for anticipating and dealing with certain types of information-processing problems and activities, including, as we shall see, in bureaucracies.

Anchoring. The third major heuristic investigated by Kahneman and Tversky is anchoring. For the sake of brevity I shall leave to the reader the pleasure to find out about its specific operation in the authors' original report (Tversky and Kahneman, 1974, pp. 1128-1130). In broad terms, the heuristic deals with the phenomenon of conservatism and inertia observed by many Bayesian investigators. Consider the problem of having to estimate within five seconds one of the two forms of an identical product, namely, 8 x 7 x 6 x 5 x 4 x 3 x 2 x 1, or 1 x 2 x 3 x 4 x 5 x 6 x 7 x 8. Under the assumption that people extrapolate from an initial value (the anchor), widely different results should be expected according to whether one estimates one or the other form of the product. Indeed, empirically, Tversky and Kahneman (1974, p. 1128) obtained the following median estimates: 2,250 for the group who estimated the factorial in its decreasing form (8 x 7 x 6 . . . etc.), and 512 for the group who estimated it in its increasing form (1 x 2 x 3 . . . etc.). It may be worth noting that the correct answer is actually 40,320. Clearly, the pervasive effect of the constraints imposed by man's information-processing capability on the quality of the answers is again in evidence.

Additional Support for Heuristic Decision-Making

The foregoing constitutes but an illustration of the empirical literature pertaining to heuristic decision making.

Yet, limited and selective as the discussion was, it is probably fair to say that the evidence reviewed strongly supports the contention that in most situations the classes of decisions involving (at least) evaluations and judgments of likelihoods are based exclusively on heuristics. The reader who might still nourish doubts on the matter or on the generality of the phenomenon will find additional evidence in the treatment of the problems of intransitivity of choices provided by Tversky (1969) and in Ornstein's experiments on the experience of time (Ornstein, 1969). But rather than reviewing here these studies (or a large number of others that the reader will find in the references quoted throughout this chapter), I would like to conclude the present empirical discussion with two little studies to which I shall have occasion to refer in later discussions.

The first study is that of de Groot, the authoritative student of decision-making by chess players. The particular problem faced by de Groot (1966) was the following: The performance of certain chess masters and grand masters appears so impressive to the observer that it could be argued that it is indicative of mental powers (in particular a memory, or a short-term memory) which are either of an unknown qualitative order, or else quantitatively different from those we have learned to expect from men on both theoretical and empirical grounds. To investigate this possibility, the following kind of experiment was performed. Chess positions taken from actual games were shown for five seconds both to poor chess players and to masters and grand masters (each position involved some twenty pieces). The subjects were then asked to reconstruct the positions they had just seen. The results were striking. While the masters and grand masters hardly made any mistake at all, the poor players were hardly able to locate correctly any of the pieces. This outcome is clearly consistent with "a special endowment" hypothesis. Now, however, a control condition was added. The experimenter showed to the same subjects new chessboards (with on each one the same number of pieces as before), but this time *the pieces were arranged at random.* The results were again striking: while the poor players remained equal to themselves—as poor performers as they had been in the previous condition—the performance of the masters and grand masters was now indistinguishable from that of the other group. In short, the previous finding had vanished; the ability of the two groups to reconstruct the positions was now practically identical.

This experiment, replicated with similar results by Chase and Simon (1973), strongly suggests that the major difference between the two groups resides in their conceptualization of the information, rather than in their information-processing capability. In particular, it is noteworthy that in the control condition the latter is perfectly consistent with what we have come to expect. This would indicate that, together with better evaluation functions, "chunking" (a technical term for the process of information conceptualization through list formation), is an important means for improving heuristic decision-making within the constraints of man's information-processing capability.

The second study is that of Parkinson (1957), and illustrates his "law of triviality." It provides an opportunity to illustrate the different expectations and criteria of assessment which follow from the heuristic versus the comprehensive approaches to decision making. The study consists of the description of a committee's review of a list of proposed expenditures (see Table 5.2).

In accordance with the "law of triviality" there is an inverse relationship between the complexity (and in this case the importance) of a decision, and the time spent at arriving at a conclusion. From a comprehensive point of view, the result is both anomalous and ironic. From a heuristic point of view, on the other hand, the result is anything but striking. By now the reader will undoubtedly have developed the expectation that man has no choice but to reduce the complexity of a decision to his information-processing capability. Whenever this is not possible, avoidance, ritualism, or any of a number of maladaptive psychological reactions can be expected to occur. In other words, such occurrences as reported in Table 5.2 are not only lacking in surprise value, but, from a heuristic point of view, if anything is criticizable it

TABLE 5.2: A Committee's Deliberations

Agenda Item	Estimated Cost	Total Time of Deliberation in Minutes	Final Disposition
Atomic reactor	$10,000,000.00	2½	Plans approved without change.
Bicycle shed	$2,350.00	45	Plans approved with a modification that achieved a $300 savings
Refreshments at meeting	$4.75 (per month)	75	Final decision deferred pending procurement of additional information.

Reproduced from Moore, 1968, p. 208; source: Parkinson, 1957.

is the expectation that it could be otherwise. This illustration highlights the fact that the two approaches are not merely different; they have implications which are worlds apart, just as do the corresponding analytical and cybernetic models of decision-making discussed in Chapter 2.

We are now in a position to turn to a discussion whose implications turn out to bear directly on the vexing problem of repetitive intuitive and discretionary decision-making.

NOTES

1. The paradigm was established by Humphreys (1939).

2. This should not be taken to mean that these approaches are without interest or value. Quite the contrary. For a discussion of their advantages and usefulness as formal theories, as standards of comparison, and as hypothesis generators, see, for instance, Rapoport (1966, 1970) and Slovic and Lichtenstein (1973).

3. See, Tversky and Kahneman (1973; 1974).

4. In calling representativeness, availability, (and later anchoring), heuristics, I am following the terminology adopted by Kahneman and Tversky. It could be argued, of course, that all three are really some of the variables which enter into the evaluation function of what could be a general heuristic that men use for assessing likelihoods in natural settings. However, dwelling on the pros and cons of conceptualizing representativeness, availability, and anchoring, as independent (sequential or hierarchical) heuristics, rather than as components of the evaluation function of a single heuristic, would not add anything to the present argument.

Chapter 6

THE PREDICTABILITY OF HUMAN DECISION-MAKING

Subjectively as well as objectively, the decision-making process is viewed as being extremely complex. And yet, the preceding theoretical and empirical discussions suggest that the process is amenable to a surprisingly simple operational conceptualization.

One of the advantages of a new perspective, as well as one of its tests, is its ability to generate new expectations and hypotheses. One such hypothesis is that, should the simple operational conceptualization that has been discussed be valid, the process of decision-making should be easy to capture and reproduce, at least to a degree commensurate with the functional simplicity of the heuristic conceptualization. Moreover, because heuristics can be expected to vary less in sophistication than problem spaces vary in complexity, human decision-making in natural settings should be relatively easy to model and predict.

To put this expectation to the test outside the laboratory, a sufficient amount of relevant data is necessary. One situation where this condition obtains is when role incumbents engage in recurrent decisions which are recorded. This occurs regularly in bureaucracies, and frequently among professionals. Clinical diagnoses are decisions which meet the necessary criteria. They are of particular interest for the present purpose because their lawfulness has been systematically studied by Brunswik and the school of thought that he originated. Brunswik's approach is unrelated to the notion of heuristics; rather, it rests on a view of the task of decision-making which is embedded in the *lens model* (see Figure 6.1). As we shall see in this chapter, however, the results of these studies strikingly corroborate the expectations raised by our previous discussion.

As conceptualized in the lens model, the judgmental task rests on the notion of cues—the variables X_1 X_2, ... X_n—which stand in some relationship to a true state of nature (operationally defined by a criterion), and to the response or evaluation of the decision-maker. For instance, if the task is to predict school achievement, the X_i's can represent the students' I.Q., S.E.S., etc. The true state, the students' actual grade-point average (Y_e), is conceptualized as bearing a "true" ecological relationship r_{ie} to the cues. On the subject's side, the response or judgment of the decision maker (Y_s) is related to the various cues by rules of utilization expressed quantitatively by the

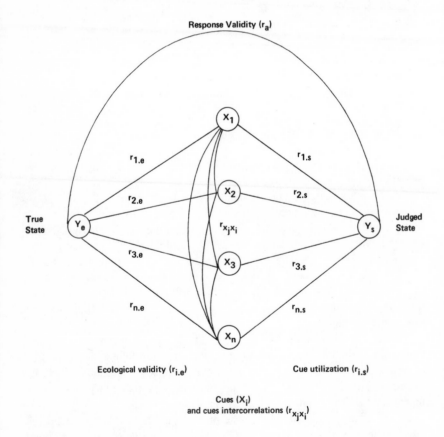

Figure 6.1: THE LENS MODEL

$r_{i,s's}$. The degree of fit between Y_e and Y_s, between the true state of nature and the estimated or predicted one, reflects the validity of the judgment.

The advantage of such a model is that it can be readily applied to concrete situations if one is willing to make linear assumptions about the nature of the relationships existing between the cues and the true state of nature, and even more so, between cues and judgments or decisions. The latter assumption may seem especially questionable in the light of most people's personal experience about the contextuality and configurality of judgments, and the fact that professionally skilled and experienced decision-makers reject the linear assumption out of hand (Hoffman, 1968). Nonetheless, the mathematical parsimony with which the parameters of the lens model can be estimated by means of a linear multiple regression, and the availability of numerous computer programs to perform the computations, are powerful incentives for considering accepting the linear assumptions. The rationale for such a step has been called *paramorphism* (Hoffman, 1960). Given an input—the cues—and an output—the judgment—the argument is that one may fruitfully attempt to establish a lawful relationship between them without assuming in any way that the actual and modeled relationships are isomorphic. If the relationships embedded in the model make it possible to functionally reproduce the output of the actual system, the paramorphic representation of the process has proven useful.

It is from this essentially apologetical position that the multiple regression tradition of research started in the late fifties and early sixties.[1] To illustrate the type of studies carried out within this intellectual framework, consider the clinical task of having to diagnose neurotic and psychotic patients by means of their MMPI profiles. If we use the scale scores of the subparts of these personality inventories as the cues, and the judgments as our dependent variable (the judgments being expressed as a dichotomy, 0-1, or as scale values of estimated intensity of sickness, for instance 0 through 11), we can attempt to capture the decision process if a sufficient number of judgments are recorded. Under the assumption of linearity, a multiple regression analysis of these data will give us the size of the b's and of the correlations relating any single cue to the decision; it will also provide us with the multiple correlation between the set of cues and the decision, that is, with a measure of the decision's predictability. Such a task was actually carried out on a data bank at the Oregon Research Institute. The data bank is made of 861 diagnoses by 29 clinical psychologists. Procedurally, each psychologist diagnosed the same 861 MMPI profiles of actual patients (for which independent information on their mental health was also available). In other words, the data include 29 independent sets of 861 decisions per judge. Hence, the decisions having been recorded, the cues constituting the information being known, and a criterion for the true state being available, the analysis implied by the lens model can be performed with a straightforward regression analysis under the aforementioned assumption of linearity. A number of detailed reports have been published on the results of various studies performed on this data bank (Meehl, 1959; Meehl and Dahlstrom, 1960; Goldberg, 1965; Wiggins and Hoffman, 1968; Goldberg, 1968; Goldberg, 1970). I shall limit myself here to a review of some selected findings.

The first finding has to do with the degree of predictability of the clinical judgment, and, in particular, its reproducibility with linear assumptions. In the case of the data we are considering, it should be noted that "the differences between psychotic and neurotic profiles are considered in MMPI lore to be highly configural in character, so that an atomistic treatment by combining single scales linearly should theoretically be a very poor substitute for a configural approach" (Meehl, 1959, p. 104). Yet, the results after over a decade of research and replications are astounding. Indeed, it turns out that the decisions are *almost completely reproducible*. The overall conclusion which imposes itself is, in the words of a prominent student of the Oregon data bank, that "a simple linear model will normally permit the reproduction of 90-100% of (the clinical judges') reliable judgmental variance" (Goldberg 1968, p. 491). This finding, which strikes one as verging on the impossible, naturally gave rise to a number of replications with different judges and tasks. Slovic and Lichtenstein (1973, pp. 43-44) reviewing the empirical evidence to date, summarize the situation as follows:

> Examination of more than 30 of these studies illustrates the tremendous diversity of judgmental tasks to which the model has been applied. The tasks include judgments about personality characteristics (Hammond, Hursch, and Todd, 1964; Knox and Hoffman, 1962); performance in college (Dawes, 1970; Einhorn, 1971; Newton, 1965; Sarbin, 1942) or on the job (Madden, 1963; Naylor and Wherry, 1965); attractiveness of common stocks (Slovic, 1969) and other types of gambles (Slovic and Lichtenstein, 1968); physical and mental pathology (Goldberg, 1970; Hoffman, Slovic and Rorer, 1968; Oskamp, 1962; Wiggins and Hoffman, 1968); and legal matters (Kort, 1968; Ulmer, 1969). In some cases, the stimuli were artificial and the judges were unfamiliar with the task. Typical of these is a study by Knox and Hoffman (1962), in which college students were asked to judge the intelligence of other students on the basis of grade-point average, aptitude test scores, credit hours attempted, and so on; and a study by Summers (1968), in which students were asked to rate the potential for achieving minority group equality as a function of legislated opportunities and educational opportunities. At the other extreme are studies of judgments made in complex but familiar situations by skilled decision makers who had other cues available besides those included in the prediction equation. For example Kort (1968) modeled judicial deci-

sions in workmen's compensation cases using various facts from the cases as cues. Brown (1970) modeled caseworkers' suicide probability estimates for persons phoning a metropolitan suicide prevention center; the cues were variables such as sex, age, suicide plan, etc., obtained from the telephone interview. And Dawes (1970) used a linear model to predict the ratings given applicants for graduate school by members of the admissions committee.

In all of these situations the linear model has done a fairly good job of predicting the judgments, as indicated by R_s values in the .80's and .90's for the artificial tasks and the .70's for the more complex real-world situations.

Thus, what started as a shy and insecure attempt turned out to be a tremendously powerful approach to reproduce role decision-making, that is, repeated judgments under recurring circumstances. It proved able to capture and make explicit the weighting policy of decision-makers, whatever the actual process by which they actually reach it may be. Paradoxically, the very strength and consistency of the findings have generated what Goldberg (1969, p. 528) has called a "detective hunt for configural predictor models." The reason is that in spite of the evidence to the contrary, there are compelling reasons to believe that, as a process, human decision-making is nonetheless interactive (see, for instance, Hoffman, 1968; Einhorn, 1970; de Bono, 1971). However, the results to date of this search have shown that while as a *process* decision-making is indeed very likely to be interactive in nature, little improvement, if any, in predictive accuracy can be expected from configural models (Slovic and Lichtenstein, 1973, pp. 45-49)—a fact which stands to reason when one considers that almost all the explainable variance is already accounted for by a simple linear model.

The second finding builds on the preceding one. If, as a paramorphic black box, a simple linear regression can act as a functional subrogate for what decision-makers typically describe as a complex interactive process, one might well start wondering how *simple* the lens model and its multiple regression operationalization can afford to be before they become inefficient. Empirically, this amounts to the question of the number of cues which are really needed to reproduce the judges' decisions. In the MMPI task discussed above, the clinical judges were presented in each case with eleven subscores of the subparts of the MMPI. If decision-makers so grossly misperceive the functional simplicity of their judgment, could it be that they also misperceive the number of cues they actually take into consideration in a decision? This can be checked in two ways: first, by using in the regression equation less cues than were available to the decision-maker; and second, by asking the judges to list the cues they believe they have taken into consideration, and also to describe the relative weights they have used for each cue. The second approach would also allow to assess the judges' insight into their own policy. Actually, both procedures have been used. The findings of a number of these studies have been summarized as follows:

> Across a number of studies, varying in the number of cues that were available, three cues usually sufficed to account for more than 80% of the predictable variance in the judges' responses. . . . One type of error in self-insight has emerged in all of these studies. Judges strongly overestimate the importance they place on minor cues (i.e., their subjective weights greatly exceed the computed weights for these cues) and they underestimate their reliance on a few major variables. Subjects apparently are quite unaware of the extent to which their judgments can be predicted by only a few cues (Slovic and Lichtenstein, 1971, p. 684).

As a possible explanation for these findings, Slovic and Lichtenstein subscribe to the hypothesis advanced by Shepard (1964, p. 266): "Possibly our feeling that we can take into account a host of different factors comes about because, although we remember that at some time or other we have attended to each of the different factors, we fail to notice that it is seldom more than one or two that we consider at any one time." A study by Olshavsky (1971) lends support to such an interpretation.

Whatever the case may be, we are faced, once more, with what appears to be an iron law. Note that in the present case the dwarfing consequences of our information-processing capability are contrary not only to intuition, but also to the deepest beliefs of professionally skilled decision-makers in their field of expertise. (For the one exception known to date to the findings discussed, see Libby, 1976a; and the two rejoinders: Goldberg 1976; Libby 1976b.)

One more result of the research reviewed in the context of the lens model remains to be mentioned. The finding is related to the issue of the validity of the decisions. Specifically, when one formalizes the cue-utilization procedure of a judge, the resulting model (i.e., the parameters of the multiple regression) generates decisions which are *more valid than are the judge's actual decisions from which the model was derived in the first place.* The research procedure used to establish this result is straightforward. A given data bank is randomly split into two subsamples. A model of the judge's decision-making is then constructed on one of the subsamples. Next the model is used to generate decisions for the second subsample, using the cues of this subsample as input. Finally, the available criterion is used for computing the validity coefficient of the artificial decisions, and this coefficient is then compared to that of the judge's actual decisions. In the MMPI study discussed above, for example, the result across the 29 judges was that "in 86% of the comparisons the model was more accurate—on the remaining half of the cases—than was the clinician" (Goldberg, 1970, p. 428). This paradoxical finding holds true not only when the task is subjectively perceived as being configural, but also when it is objectively so (Yntema and Torgerson, 1961). A likely explanation for this phenomenon is that man applies somewhat erratically his own decision-making procedure, and thus is less than perfectly reliable. Under this assumption a machine with perfect memory, and with no attention failures or "states of mind," can be expected to apply more efficiently the very same model of decision-making used and invented by man, provided that this model has any degree of stability and validity. As the reader will have recognized, this reasoning is simply a rephrasing of the proposition of measurement theory which relates the concepts of reliability and validity. In our case, the findings that we have discussed are consistent with the assumption that man has the ability to invent decision-making procedures with some degree of validity and stability. Hence, the seemingly paradoxical finding should have been expected on purely theoretical grounds. In fact, it has been, in a number of writings (see Yntema and Torgerson, 1961, p. 24; Cronbach and Glaser, 1965, p. 164); moreover a speculative implication advanced in one such writing (Dudycha and Naylor, 1966, p. 127) may even be worth more attention than the tongue-in-cheek phrasing may appear to suggest.

> Humans tend to generate "correct strategies" but then, in turn fail to use their own strategy with any great consistency. . . . One is left with the conclusion that humans may be used to generate inference strategies but that once the strategy is obtained the human should be removed from the system and replaced by his own strategy!

It should be mentioned that in addition to the lens model there is a number of other simple and efficient paramorphic models of information processing reported in the literature (see, for instance, Osgood and Tannenbaum, 1955; L.R. Anderson and Fischbein, 1965; N.H. Anderson, 1971). A few successful attempts have also been made with models having various degrees of implicit or explicit isomorphic claims. For instance, Hernes (1971), using Coleman's matrix model of collective decision-making (Coleman, 1973), has been able to predict assessments of influence among the M.P.s of a Norwegian party on the basis of two conceptual cues—interest and control of resources—the correlations between actual and modeled evaluations running into the .80s; Gross, Mason, and McEachern (1958) have developed a contingency model of school superintendents' decision-making in role conflicts (it involves three conceptual cues), which reproduces the decisions actually reached in 264 out of the 291 role conflicts investigated (91%); a replication of this study by Ehrlich, Rinehart, and Howell (1962) achieved similar results with only one—although different—cue variable. There are also attempts at representing the process of decision-making as a full-fledged branching process, that is, as a step-wise implementation of a complex sequence of operations similar in its form and logic to the run of a computer program (see, for instance, Newell and Simon, 1972; Scurrah and Wagner, 1970). Not surprisingly, the form taken by such models is that of a bona fide flow chart. (The data for this type of modeling is a "think aloud" protocol of the decision-maker's thought process while engaged in the decision-making activity; a sequence of decision rules is then abstracted from the protocol and programmed.) It may be noted that one such model has been developed for the MMPI task discussed above, and is comprehensively reported in Kleinmutz (1963). This particular model has sixteen sequential steps (decision rules) mirroring the subject's decision procedure. For our purpose it is noteworthy that the most complex decision rule used at any single step by the subject was in the form of $Y = X_1 + X_2 - 2X_3$ and that he essentially trichotomized the values of each variable (Kleinmutz, 1963, p. 11).

In short, whatever the black box assumptions on which a variety of decision-making models are built, it is clear that they lead to empirical findings which are in striking agreement about the boundary properties of human information-processing capabilities. In particular, it is noteworthy that recurrent decisions can be modeled with a surprising degree of parsimony and accuracy, whether the decision-makers are aware of it or not.

NOTE

1. For an extensive review of the literature related to this research tradition, see Slovic and Lichtenstein (1973).

Chapter 7

THE COMPLEXITY OF HUMAN INFORMATION PROCESSING

One danger of the perspective that has been developed in the previous chapters is that the extreme complexity of the human thought process—about which I have inserted reminders at various points of the discussion—may have been somewhat blurred. This chapter is intended to help avoiding any possible misunderstanding. Indeed, it could be argued that it is precisely because human information processing is so complex that recurrent decision making may be paramorphically so simple.[1] The selective discussion of the complexity of the thought process which is the topic of this chapter should help clarify this apparent paradox. The discussion will also provide the opportunity to introduce some concepts of information processing which are shared by man and computer systems. The degree to which these concepts are applicable to formal organizations will be discussed in Part III.

At the outset, it is useful to sharpen the issue. As will be recalled, a number of the studies that we have examined were laboratory-type studies. That is to say, they reflect the level of performance that one can expect from man when he is able to concentrate on whatever task is at hand. We have noted in Chapter 3, however, (in the context of the digit memorization task), that even slight interruptions or interferences with task performance result in a drastic lowering of man's already very bounded information-processing capability. In other words, the results that we have reviewed are likely to represent an overestimate of man's actual information-processing capability, if we assume that problem solving in many everyday life situations might be less shielded from interferences than is the case in the laboratory. Note that at this point this means facing the possibility of having to lower our sights from an already low estimate of about three cues or chunks of information-processing utilization, which, as the findings reviewed suggest, would seem to be a modal value. Obviously, there is little room for reducing still further our already shrunken expectations. Nonetheless, this might be necessary, at least to some extent.

The reasons for this necessity lie in the nature of man and his environment. This can be seen by noting that everyday problem-solving situations are indeed not shielded from interference. Unlike a computer—whose needs are attended to, and which does not strive to survive—man must be able to cope with potential threats to his well-being and safety. Operationally, this means that somehow he must continuously attend to danger and needs signals from his outer and inner environments. As we have seen, however, the evidence is that man is a *serial* information processor, by which is meant that he cannot attend but one task at a time.[2] The contradiction between the existential requirements for continuous information processing and the evidence that man cannot engage simultaneously in several tasks, leads therefore to a paradox. While the constant processing of environmental cues presumably takes place, man does nonetheless engage in a variety of problem-solving activities which are often unrelated to any immediate environmental concern.

The paradox, however, need not be as real as might seem at first sight. In fact, it can easily be dealt with, if one adopts a time-sharing view of the human information-processing activity.

Such a view has been taken by Simon (1967). In order to follow the argument with a shared frame of reference, it is useful to review some general characteristics of the referent model, computer time sharing. Spencer (1970, p. 1) describes the computer time-sharing concept as follows:

Time-sharing is the simultaneous use of a computer by several users. . . . The time-sharing concept is based on the principle that there is enough capacity in a computer system for multiple users, providing that each console is active only a small fraction of the time. Each user of a timesharing system has the illusion that he is the only person using the system. . . . How does a time-sharing computer system take care of several users simultaneously? Each one has control over the computer for a specified quantum of time. The computer picks up orders from one user, works on his problem, say for 1/20 of a second, and stores the partial answer. It then moves to the next user, receives his orders, works on the second problem for 1/20 of a second, and moves to the third user, etc. When a problem is completed, the answer is printed on the user's console. The computer system accomplishes this work so fast that the user feels the system is working for him full-time.

Quite clearly, if we replace the word "users" by the words "needs" or "tasks," time sharing provides us with a model which is compatible with the serial information-processing constraints, and with the kind of "simultaneous" performance required. The applicability of this model to man requires only that some functional means and parameters be both available and adequate for the system to be operative. It is useful to examine what these requirements are; in so doing we shall get a glimpse at the mind-boggling complexity of human information processing.

As pointed out by Simon (1967), there are two major prerequisites for a time-sharing information processor: a *noticing mechanism* and an *interrupt system*. The function of the noticing mechanism is to determine when conditions have arisen which require that ongoing programs be interrupted. The noticing processes must go on in parallel with whatever information-processing task is being performed, "although this parallelism may be realized, in fact, by the high-frequency time-sharing of a single serial processor" (Simon, 1969b, p. 109).

The second requirement is that the noticing mechanism be able to activate an interrupt system having the capability of: (a) interrupting an ongoing program; (b) setting aside this program and the partial results achieved; and (c) calling a new program.

In computer time-sharing such tasks are performed by a meta-program known as the *supervisor* or *executive*. The supervisor (which is also part of non-time-sharing computers, although in simplified form) automatically takes over the execution of any incoming task by breaking it down into subtasks and supervising their execution. This includes the decoding and encoding of any incoming message, the setting up of the program called for by the job, and the required time and memory space allocations for its execution—all this automatically, and before the program actually starts to run. The supervisor also handles the interrupts, which may be hieararchical. That is, if a low priority interrupt is being serviced, a higher priority one can preempt it and receive immediate attention. Thus, there may be interrupts within interrupts. On the other hand, interrupts with similar degrees of priority which occur in rapid succession are put on a queuing list and serviced in the order of their arrival.

The complex tasks of interpretation, organization, and bookkeeping, and the numerous and relatively time-consuming shifts and transfers of information in memory required by these operations are at the heart of the possibility and efficiency of time sharing: while this house-keeping aspect of information processing is taking place for one program, the processor is free to execute the operations readied in the meantime by the executive for another one. As one might suspect, the exact mode of operation of the executive is, as a rule, unknown to the general programmer; the supervisor is conceived as operating automatically and as being part of the machine itself.

Turning now to man, it appears that many of the functions of the supervisor are carried out by his perceptual system, also at a subawareness level. In particular, this holds true for the processes of noticing, stimulus encoding, and the setting up of specific frames of mind for problem solving. The noticing capability, which is of special interest to us here, is rooted in man's sensory memory, which is to be distinguished from the short-term and long-term memories already mentioned.

The sensory memory functions as a temporary storage for stimuli of very short duration (about fifty milliseconds). It can be shown experimentally that visual or auditory signals emitted for shorter orders of magnitude of time are not perceived. Above this threshold, on the other hand, they are noticed and can be remembered. Moreover, the signals need not be discrete; they can be of up to about five bits of information in length. Thus, one is led to the conclusion that at the perceptual level man can process about one hundred bits of information per second. This fact has two implications.

The first is that human information processing must be selective, because the other memories have much longer access and fixation times, and sensory memory decays very rapidly (at most within one-two seconds). In particular, from the parameters of fixation, decay, and retrieval time in the various memories, one obtains the estimate that the sequence: sensory memory, short-term memory, and long-term memory, ends up producing a real-time selection ratio of the order of 1:500 (see Table 7.1). It should be noted, however, that in nonreal time (i.e., on a time scale not related to the immediate demands of the environment) the order of magnitude of this ratio may be different. This follows from the "deferred updating" theory of the mind/brain information-processing system. In the light of this theory, aimed at explaining the purpose of sleep (see Potzl, 1960; Ben Aaron, 1975), sensory memory—called circadian memory—is conceived as being constantly scanned in real time for incoming inputs. The information which cannot be immediately used or transferred to a higher order memory, is not lost, however. At least part of it is retained, and accumulated during the day for delayed ("off-line") interpretation and organization during the night. This off-line process taxes the undivided attention and information-processing capability of the mind/brain system and is necessitated by the very fact that this monopolization cannot take place during waking hours. Accordingly:

> During all of this processing, short-term memory is incommunicado, but this need not be construed as inactivity. . . . Normal sensory input is inhibited, producing the state of oblivion which characterizes sleep.
>
> In many cases, it seems possible for short-term memory to "wake up" before circadian memory has been fully erased. Should this happen, that portion of circadian memory under the scrutiny of short-term memory might still contain the residuum of the sorting operations. The

constitution of this residuum is dependent on the needs of the sorting process—it will most likely not be formatted in the way expected from normal sensory input.

Since the format is different, the contents of circadian memory, at this time, might appear, to short-term memory, to be incoherent. Short-term memory, accustomed as it is to interpreting well-formed information in circadian memory, will try, as best as it can, to interpret the ill-formed information.

The process of interpreting the incoherent residuum in circadian memory is taken to be the process of "dreaming" (Ben Aaron, 1975, p. 249).

TABLE 7.1: Orders of Magnitude of Some Parameters of Human Information-Processing*

Memory Type	Write Time in Seconds	Read Time in Seconds	Capacity in Chunks	Decay Time
Long-term memory	5	0.5	quasi-unlimited**	quasi-permanent-memory
Short-term memory	0.5	milliseconds	7± 2	after several seconds
Iconic (visual) memory	milliseconds	milliseconds	4 ± 1	less than 1 second
Echoic (auditory) memory	milliseconds	milliseconds	6	after 1-2 seconds

*The experimental paradigm which allows one to estimate the value of these parameters and to differentiate between fixation and retrieval time (write and read time) in various memories, is as follows: Write time is experimentally determined by the length of time that a stimulus must last to be recorded in the appropriate memory; for shorter time exposures there is no stimulus recall. Read time, on the other hand, is estimated by the time required for previously memorized information to be recalled upon the presentation of a predetermined cue. Memory capacity is measured by the number of meaningful and discriminable stimuli (chunks), which can be recalled out of strings of such stimuli to which the subject has been exposed on the appropriate time scale. Finally, decay is assessed by the time lapse, after which information previously recorded in the particular memory cannot be recollected. (With regard to the short-term memory, it has been argued that it can hold information for more than just a few seconds; however, this turns out to involve internal rehearsals.) It bears stressing again that the values indicated are mere (and very rough) orders of magnitude. For a discussion of the research difficulties, and a review of the range of findings from which the data in this table are abstracted, the reader is referred to Neisser (1967, pp. 15-22; 199-208; 219-242); and Newell and Simon (1972, pp. 792-795).

**The hardware (i.e., physical) capability of the human brain which underlies this statement has the following parameters: 10E+10 to 10E+11 neurons (i.e., 10 to 100 billion memory cells), each one having 10,000, perhaps 100,000 linkages. The number of relationships available to store information is therefore staggering, in the order of 10E+14 to 10E+15. By comparison, there are less than 10E+10 seconds in a hundred years.

The point of interest to us is, of course, that we should expect social information processors to face the same kind of structural constraints. In particular, we should expect to find off-line information processing in bureaucracies, and should anticipate the study of the principles which govern the postponement and performance of operations until after offices are closed to the public, to be a topic of theoretical and substantive interest.

In any case, the second implication mentioned earlier is that in terms of hardware capability, man is endowed with a rather sensitive interrupt capability. Indeed, the ability to process one hundred bits of information per second makes for an alert noticing system, by any real time standard.

Let us now consider the interrupt system presumably serviced by the noticing capability just discussed. The first point to be noted is that we actually know very little about this system. At the same time, however, the existence of such a system cannot be doubted and is easy to establish. Thus, it is a commonplace of daily experience that environmental stimuli can catch our attention and cause task interruptions. Furthermore, "Sudden intense stimuli have easily observable effects on behavior. They also have well-substantiated effects on the CNS [Central Nervous System]. . . . These effects produce substantial disruption of the electroencephalogram pattern. . . . A plausible, and not novel, interpretation of these CNS effects is that they amount to an interruption of the interpreter that manages the goal hierarchy; that is, they supplant the present goals with a new hierarchy[3] (Simon, 1969b, p. 109).

A concomitant of these effects is a subjective feeling in the subject, as well as various physiological symptoms, which typically accompany emotional reactions. This suggests that there is probably a close connection between what is generally called emotional behavior, and the interrupt system. If one adopts this perspective, then:

> The emotional stimulus is to be regarded as more often *interrupting* than *disrupting* behavior; [it is only] when the emotion-producing stimuli are persistent as well as intense, [that] they sometimes become disruptive and produce nonadaptive behavior. This occurs if the stimuli continue to interrupt, repeatedly, the evoked response program and hence to prevent an organized behavioral response to the original interrupting stimulus (Simon, 1969b, p. 110).

There are interesting consequences of the identification of emotions with the operation of the interrupt system. Thus, Simon notes that social situations tend to be more emotional in character than many other situations. In terms of the theoretical view under discussion, this would mean that the interrupt system operates more frequently in social situations than in others. Simon argues that this is likely to be the case because in order to be adaptive, the selective use that the interrupt system makes of the noticing mechanism should vary with the nature of the environment. In particular, in rapidly changing and unpredictable environments, heavier use should be made of the noticing system. Although physical environments sometimes have these characteristics, as a rule these should be found in social situations to a much greater extent; the reason is that "the most active part of the environment of man, and the part most consequential to him, consists of living organisms, particularly other men" (Simon, 1969b, p. 111). Thus, according to this argument, a task performed in a social situation can be expected to be accompanied by a constant monitoring of the reactions of others, leading to the relative frequency of interrupts and to the concomitant observation that social situations tend to be laden with emotion. It is interesting to note that this interpretation is in agreement with Bales' body of experimental findings, which clearly shows that group problem solving takes place at two levels, the task level and the social level (Bales, 1958).

In short, it is clear that human information processing is extraordinarily complex and at the same time paradoxical. On the one hand there is a body of research which suggests that people rely generally on few cues for decision-making. Some studies even suggest that, as a rule, no more than two cues are actually used; moreover, should these cues be inconsistent, one is often discarded: "It is typical for one or two attributes to be used as a focus and small corrections made by reference to other attributes. . . . Even with only two cues, Slovic (1966) found a strong tendency to focus on one, with the second used to make small corrections" (Posner, 1973, p. 80). That is to say, there are good reasons to believe that in everyday life the experimental results that we have discussed may, if anything, turn out to be overestimates, rather than underestimates.

At the same time, however, it should be emphasized that this need not be the case for creative thinking or unique decisions. These processes are not sufficiently understood to be currently modelable to any significant extent, let alone with the degree of accuracy that we have documented. The evidence that we have reviewed is therefore strictly about what constitutes conceptually and experimentally *repetitive* and *routinized* decision-making.

The point to keep in mind is that amazing feats of information processing, in the form of perception, interpretation, priority ordering, organization, and internal bookkeeping must be assumed to be a characteristic of every waking instant. If one adds to these functions the ability to think creatively, and to engage at times in rather involved logical analyses,[4] the conclusion which emerges is clearly not that human information processing is simple. Rather, it would appear that as part of its extraordinary capabilities, the human brain is *also* capable of setting up programs for routinized decision-making. For motoric skills this capability has long been common knowledge; for cognitive decisions, however, it would seem that the very same ability is less generally recognized.

These considerations suggest that it would be misleading indeed to infer from the demonstrable functional simplicity of human routines for recurrent decision-making that human information processing is simple. Rather, the paramorphic simplicity of such routines is likely to bear witness to the fact that recurrent decision-making is but one information-processing activity among the myriads which are constantly carried out. At best, one could hypothesize that, perhaps for reasons of economy, the human equivalent of the supervisor sets limits on the size and complexity that consciously or unconsciously created routines for recurrent decision-making may have. One could speculate that the constraint has the function of avoiding a careless waste of information-processing resources; in particular, it could be a safe-guard against unchecked decision-making overspecialization at the expense of future adaptability. Indeed, for an information processor which has the ability to improve and override many of its learned programs, the adaptive gain in flexibility obtained by preserving resources for creating additional routines whenever the need arises—as it does constantly—may be greater than the cost of having to use stringently limited procedures for any one single recurrent decision-making situation.

In conclusion, and returning to our concern, the important consideration is that from an empirical point of view if decisions can be assumed to be made recurrently, we will expect them to be functionally simple, as well as accurately modelable, although this need not be taken in any way as reflect-ing on the thought process itself. With this qualification in mind, the findings discussed obviously have far-reaching implications for the notion of discretion in role decision-making. In particular, they imply that the term may be a misnomer.

NOTES

1. For additional reasons, related to the properties of linear models and of the characteristics of the environments in which decisions are made, see Dawes and Corrigan (1974), and for a mathematical development of their argument, Wainer (1976). These findings are discussed in Chapter 11.

2. This can be demonstrated with a simple experiment suggested by Newell and Simon. Consider the task of having to divide a number by an integer, for instance 35642 by 7, the answer being yes if the number is exactly divisible by 7, and no otherwise. The crucial test of the proposition is the time required for performing this task with several numbers, for instance:

35642
49416

.
.

As Newell and Simon (1972, p. 797) put it, "In terms of this test, the human is a completely serial information-processing system, for almost all information processing operations." [The possible exceptions being some highly automated and motor activities, e.g., patting one's head with one's hand, and rubbing circularly one's stomach with the other.]

3. A goal hierarchy is synonymous with a program. In a serial information-processor, the instructions and the routines (or subroutines) constituting a program must be explicitly ordered to form an unambiguous hierarchy. The instructions and routines are then processed and executed according to this order. When the execution of a program requires it to branch off to a subroutine, or to execute a compounded instruction, a goal hierarchy is automatically created. The computational purpose of the subroutine or instruction is in this case the top goal of the hierarchy, while the intermediary steps are subgoals. Because instructions can be complex and routines can themselves involve calls to other subroutines, very complex goal hierarchies can occur during the execution of a program.

4. Although this capability too is limited, naturally, as mathematicians begin to realize. The point is well made in the following editorial of *The New York Times:*

Crisis in Mathematics. Mathematics, school children are taught, is the most exact of sciences. An answer to a mathematical problem is either right or wrong; maybe is excluded. The proof of a mathematical theorem is either correct or incorrect, and a good enough mathematician can always come to a firm conclusion. But now, according to Science magazine, such ideas may be obsolete. Mathematics, too, is in a state of crisis in which the old verities are at least suspect, if not actually destroyed.

Take the case of a certain statement in a branch of advanced mathematics called "homotopy theory," a subject we won't even try to pretend we know anything about. Anyway, one mathematician produced a long and complex proof that the statement was correct. About the same time another mathematician came up with a similarly complex and long proof that the statement was incorrect. The two investigators exchanged proofs and each sought to find an error in his rival's work. Neither succeeded.

Then there is the shattering discovery that some mathematical theorems require proofs that are so long that even computers can't work the proofs out in any acceptable period of time. An Israeli mathematician has suggested a possible way out. The trouble, he believes, is that mathematicians are too demanding; they won't accept the idea that a proof may be wrong once in a while. If mathematicians will just accept proofs which have even a slight probability—say, one in a billion—of being wrong, then, he thinks, a lot of impossible proofs can become possible.

At the root of this crisis, some mathematicians hold, is the fact that some of the long proofs now being published are pressing the limits of the amount of information a single human mind can handle. That may be, but we know a lot of people who thought mathematicians had approached that limit a long time ago—about the time of Euclid, in fact (New York *Times,* June 2, 1976, p. 36).

PART THREE

THE ROUTINIZED IMPLEMENTATION OF POLICIES

Chapter 8

THE PREMISES REVISITED

At the end of Part I it was noted that the purely artificial and instrumental logic and raison d'être of bureaucracies indicate that their decisions should be modelable with as data their rules, procedures, and criteria. On theoretical grounds, whenever this is not the case, there is room for either social control or improved efficiency.

The variety of conditions of willful misrepresentation and misuses which necessitate social control are rather obvious and need not be elaborated here. The problem of improved rationality and efficiency, on the other hand, should benefit from our discussion of the characteristics of repetitive human decision-making. As will be recalled, two major problems were noted. The first was related to the notion of discretionary decisions; the second had to do with the validity of some of the assumptions underlying the cybernetic view of decision-making. At a more fundamental level there was also an implicit proposition, which must now be made explicit, that the present situation not only could be improved upon, but *needed* to be improved upon.

In the light of the evidence presented in Part II, these questions can now be fruitfully discussed. The issue of the prima facie validity of a cybernetic view of routinized decision-making will require relatively little elaboration, as this discussion follows rather directly from some of the points made in Part II. The discussion of the problems presented by discretionary role decision-making also builds on this evidence. This question, however, requires further elaboration. Making explicit the rationale on which the need for—as distinct from the feasibility of—a largely automated bureaucracy rests, similarly requires a somewhat extended treatment; so does the question of the potential dangers of the kind of modeling discussed. These are therefore the topics to which most of the present chapter is devoted. The underlying theme is an attempt to clarify the nature, extent, and usefulness of discretionary role decision-making, which, too, are often misperceived. Altogether, the discussion yields a set of reassessed premises for understanding the need for improvement and for guiding the analysis of the discretionary bureaucratic operations which should be modeled, and possibly automated.

Discretionary Decisions

To begin the present discussion with its major theme, then, one important conclusion to which one is led by the evidence presented in Part II is that there appears to be a basic misconception about both the nature and quality of repetitive decision-making. The overwhelming evidence is that man develops stable rules which are relatively easy to model. That is to say, while decisions may be discretionary in terms of role prerogatives, the fact is that they become rapidly stereotyped. As a consequence, and within the limits of human reliability—and at times of explorative behavior—such decisions are far from being indeterminate. Rather, they are very predictable, and can be modeled with a surprising degree of accuracy—whether the decision-makers themselves, or the people who are in complementary role sets, are aware of the fact or not. In short, while nondiscretionary decisions must be, by definition, modelable, it has been shown that discretionary decisions *may* be.

This fact raises the possibility that many decision-making operations of clerical bureaucracies could be readily automated. It has also two implications of importance. One is that in automated bureaucracies the role of many employees can be anticipated to shift from the responsibility of having to carry out routine decisions to that of having to design strategies by actual behavior (in a manner reminiscent of Dudycha and Naylor's anticipation, see Chapter 6), so that the best strategies can be retrieved and formalized. This should be primarily useful for those decision-making positions in the organization where formalizing a priori rules, procedures, and criteria appears to be a difficult or impossible undertaking on grounds other than the fact that the cases referred to the decision-makers are exceptions calling for policy-making.

The second implication is that even without replacing the clerical operations which can be programmed, such an endeavor may provide a base rate model against which present operations could be gauged and problems located, and with the help of which contemplated solutions could be scrutinized in advance.

To give substance to this point, consider such repetitive tasks as determining the eligibility of clients for a service or the process of hiring and promoting under some system such as the civil service. In all such cases where political or particularistic considerations are illegitimate, comparing the output of the model for a sample of actual cases with the corresponding real-life decisions generates possibilities of mismatches which are of interest. Such mismatches will be traceable to oversights in either the model or the referent system, and to the degree to which the latter lacks reliability. A useful process of understanding, monitoring, pretesting, and testing, can therefore take place. In this connection, it is noteworthy that an important reason why this kind of modeling is useful is that both in form and logic the referent structure and the type of simulation considered are similar in ways which are not matched by probabilistic flow models. In particular, the extent and detail of the parallels between an information-processing simulation of a bureaucracy and the organization (itself conceived as a programmed information processor) can be expected to help locating and interpreting both the sources and levels of mismatches in ways in which a collapsed probabilistic conceptualization obviously cannot.

In terms of premises, then, the important point is that repetitive bureaucratic decisions can be modeled whether they are discretionary or not. Moreover, as will be discussed more fully in the next chapter, it can be noted that in nondiscretionary decision-making the endeavor has a clear methodological advantage over some of the work reported in the psychological literature. The reason is that in the laboratory, the retrieval of the subjects' decision-making rules usually requires the use of a rather artificial procedure— the generation of a protocol. On the other hand, the requirements of orderly social intercourse and the logic of bureaucratic decision-making imply that the data required to model the process of nondiscretionary bureaucratic decision-making are exactly those which are *naturally* generated and available in the form of rules, directives, procedures, forms, and criteria. At the impersonal level, therefore, a model and its referent structure can theoretically be designed with any degree of desired isomorphism. For discretionary decision-making, precision is also attainable (see Chapter 6). Moreover, in this case an additional consideration deserves attention. As Weber has noted, purposeful systems of rules, and bureaucracies in particular, express a social trend toward the rationalization of social action; in systems of this kind, discretion is an incongruence. Modeling these decisions is therefore not only a necessity for capturing the whole of routinized decision-making, but the endeavor in itself has the advantage of being able to contribute to the unfolding of this ongoing sociological process, at least as far as the operation and social functions of bureaucracies are concerned. In short, discretionary decisions are empirically modelable, and theoretically there are reasons to believe that the endeavor should prove useful.

The Cybernetic View

A second premise whose assessment is of importance is whether or not a cybernetic view of human and organizational decision-making has some prima facie validity and the extent to which this view may hold promises of usefulness. The problem of assessment arises from the fact that, within the constraints of his information-processing capabilities, man has the ability (however limited) to be analytical, to order unambiguously preferences, and to choose among them logically. At the same time, however, in all but exceptional cases, he tends not to do so. In terms of expectations, one can therefore choose to work with the underlying assumption of an analytical model and treat discrepancies with empirical observations as errors. Conversely, one can adopt a purely cybernetic view and expect man and organizations never to be analytical and qualify this view whenever the need arises.

The relevant consideration is that strictly speaking neither view is correct, or more accurately, both are. As we have seen, there is a theoretical rationale and a large body of evidence to suggest that although man can devise and use algorithms, he can also program himself—consciously or without awareness—to operate cybernetically. The evidence furthermore suggests that man naturally operates under this latter mode for most recurrent tasks of decision-making. Ontologically, therefore, one is led to the assumption that human repetitive decision-making may very well be governed by the principle known in programming as *default*. This concept refers to the procedure whereby an operation is carried out in a privileged mode—the "normal" mode—unless this mode is actively overridden. During a computer run, for instance, a number is generally treated as an integer, unless there is a specific instruction to the contrary; by default of such an instruction, the normal and automatic mode of operation remains, or reverts, to what it is "naturally," i.e., fractions are disregarded. Incidentally, in computers (as probably in men), the rationale for the default principle is information-processing efficiency, especially of memory and utilization of registers.

Quite clearly, the default principle makes possible a nondogmatic choice of the basic model with which one prefers to work. That is, the adoption of one model does not require or amount to the exclusion of the other. Rather, it simply expresses an assumption about what is normal and frequent as opposed to what is exceptional and rare. On the strength of the evidence presented in Part II, I shall adopt the position that the normal mode of human and organizational repetitive decision-making is cybernetic. That is, whenever there is no clear evidence that heuristic decision-making is overridden by personal motivation or organizational arrangements and procedures (as, for instance, the logic of science requires), the expectation will be that recurrent decisions are made cybernetically by default. Normally, therefore, the anticipation is that decisions are based on very few variables and follow heuristic rather than analytic principles.

This axiomatic choice of primacy between the two models yields a perspective which is in many ways a reversal of the view that pervades the literature (cf., Steinbruner, 1974). Not surprisingly, therefore, the choice has several important implications. One of them is related to the definition and the study of what is conceived as errors. Another is that it focuses one's attention on the question of the structural conditions and mechanisms which support and reinforce the predominant mode of decision-making, or conversely, effectively override it—either by design or by accident.

To summarize, neither the analytic nor the cybernetic model are held to always be appropriate. But because of the fact that, as a rule, man can only satisfice and not maximize, attends to a few cues at one time, cannot order preferences well, and engages in analytical problem solving only as a last resort, and even then reverts to his habitual mode of decision-making at the first opportunity (cf., Perrow, 1974a, p. 14; Simon, 1957, pp. 196-206), the cybernetic and heuristic perspective (which assumes these very properties) appears to be a far better choice for a base rate model than is the analytical view. To put it differently, there are sound theoretical and empirical reasons for wanting to examine departures from *this* model, rather than the other way around. This is essentially the rationale for the choice of perspective.

The Need to Model Recurrent Decisions

The third general premise which deserves attention, and which is of particular interest in this chapter, is related to the image we hold about the potential usefulness of automating the processes of bureaucratic decision-making, which, in the light of the present discussion, can be so handled without impropriety. As we have seen, in terms of feasibility, a major potential stumbling block—discretionary role decision-making—has, for all practical purposes and intents, turned out to be empirically a nonproblem. Conceptually also, a model whose assumptions may have struck one as disqualifying it for serious consideration has been shown to be less of a heresy than might have been anticipated. Assuming, therefore, that routinized decision-making—whether discretionary or not—can be modeled, the question of usefulness becomes especially topical. I have previously alluded to this question. However, now that the problem of feasibility begins to appear less insuperable than it was at the outset, it is useful to consider this issue somewhat more systematically.

The first relevant consideration stems from the fact that human information-processing capabilities are both limited and misperceived. It stands to reason, therefore, that complex systems involving thousands of delegated tasks might also be misperceived by their participants and clients, and above all by those persons who are responsible for the systems' proper operation. Capturing the workings of a system in a methodic manner might therefore constitute a nontrivial contribution to knowledge and understanding, independently of any attempt to gain more reliability, a task which properly requires the additional step of replacing part of the system by its model.

Consider the possibility of increasing knowledge and understanding, leaving aside for the time being the question of gains in reliability. The question which has to be confronted is the following: is the present state of affairs such that it justifies the costly and time-consuming kind of modeling envisioned? Or, because the retrieval and modeling of the nondiscretionary routine component of decisions are trivial, the question can be rephrased and operationalized as follows: how satisfactory or imperfect is the present state of affairs regarding repetitive discretionary role decision-making?

From an information-processing point of view, it can be argued that nothing short of a radical improvement is necessary. If this statement appears extreme, it is for the most part only because the image that most of us hold of the present situation acts as an unchecked, and as we shall immediately see, largely unwarranted premise.

Consider the need to capture and monitor repetitive role decisions which are discretionary, for instance, in the case of medical care. One might say (see Hoos, 1974; and Chapter 2 in this book) that automating the files of doctors will not necessarily contribute to the improvement of diagnoses or of public health. From the present point of view, however, the danger with this view is that by some non sequitur it can implicitly be taken as suggesting that the present situation calls for less than a dramatic improvement; indeed, to many, common wisdom suggests that the way things are is more or less satisfactory. How wrong such an assumption is and how dangerous it can be, are easy to illustrate. I shall do so with a study carried out on a medical topic.

The study (see Hoffman, 1968; and Hoffman, Slovic, and Rorer, 1968) was about the medical diagnosis of benign versus malignant gastric ulcers. Such diagnoses are generally arrived at with the help of a radiological examination, a task which rests primarily on the analysis of seven signs or cues. These cues are (cf., Hoffman, 1968):

(1) presence or absence of an extraluminal ulcer;
(2) presence or absence of associated filling defect;
(3) regularity or irregularity of ulcer contour;
(4) preservation of rugal pattern around the ulcer;
(5) evidence of associated duodenal ulcer;
(6) location of the ulcer in the greater curvature;
(7) smallness of the ulcer crater.

Theoretically, therefore, and as far as these cues are concerned, there are 2^7 or 128 possible configurations of X-rays. Medical expertise, however, holds that 32 of the possible patterns are empirically implausible. Accordingly, only the remaining 96 patterns were used in the study. A typical case, and the seven-point scale on which the judges were asked to express their professional opinion, is shown in Figure 8.1.

Hoffman et al. performed their study with six practicing radiologists, and three radiologists-in-training at the University of Oregon Medical School. Each subject was asked to judge twice the 96 cases, i.e., made 192 judgments in all. The aim of the researchers was to investigate the configurality of human decision-making. For our purpose this aspect of the study need not concern us. The findings themselves, however, are of considerable interest. They are easy to summarize (cf., Hoffman, 1968, pp. 70-72):

(1) The judges were found to be consistent with themselves, i.e., the intrajudge reliability upon reexamining the same case was generally high.

(2) At the same time the degree of interjudge agreement was surprisingly (and chillingly) low: "Intercorrelations among the ratings of judges make this point clear. Twenty-one of the 36 interjudge coefficients are .40 or lower, and 15 of them are .25 or less. Even if corrected for attenuation due to unreliability, these coefficients are closer to .0 than to 1.0" (Hoffman, 1968, p. 70).

(3) The conclusion, therefore, is that such analyses are probably necessary if decision-making of this kind is to be improved at a faster rate than unsystematic confrontations of diagnoses allow. In particular, it appears urgent to clarify which symptoms are regarded as positive indicators of malignancy by some clinicians while others disregard them, or even relate to them as contra-indicators (cf., Hoffman, 1968, p. 71).

Case #037		
	Yes	*No*
(1) Extraluminal	x	
(2) Filling Defect		x
(3) Regular Contour	x	
(4) Rugal Pattern		x
(5) Duodenal Symptoms	x	
(6) On Greater Curvature		x
(7) Small Crater	x	

Benign   Malignant

1 2 3 4 5 6 7

Figure 8.1: SAMPLE PROFILE OF THE X-RAY RESULTS OF A HYPOTHETICAL ULCER PATIENT (SOURCE: Hoffman, 1968, Figure 3.6, p. 69)

The results of this study are anything but exceptional. They are compatible with other findings which indicate that medical systems are ridden with errors; for instance, if time inaccuracies of over ten minutes in the administration of medication to the patients are included in the count of errors, hospitals may make as much as 60% errors in the daily care of patients. This situation should not surprise us, if we recall the nature of heuristic decision-making. Moreover, it is not surprising to find that research on labeling recurrently demonstrates how easily human and organizational decision-making can be led astray when the structure of their underlying heuristics is taken advantage of. For instance, in one study, sane pseudo-patients gained admission to hospitals on the East and West Coast by complaining of hearing voices. After gaining admission, they ceased all simulation; in particular, they behaved naturally and answered honestly to all questions. Nonetheless, none of the pseudo-patients were detected, and except for one, were all diagnosed as being schizophrenic. In a follow-up to this experiment, the staff of one hospital was informed of the possibility that pseudo-patients might seek admission. About ten to twenty percent of the incoming patients were thereafter judged to be pseudo-patients, although actually none were (Rosenhan, 1973). It should be noted that in this tradition of research the cause of such mistakes is attributed to the operation of inappropriate expectations. But semantics are, of course, immaterial; by whatever name one chooses to call the phenomenon, the fundamental process of interest, i.e., the operation of heuristic decision-making and the monitoring of a few selected variables, is unmistakable.

Needless to say, these examples do not bear directly on the issue of the value of computerizing the medical files of patients. The point is that no matter how unjustified or unsuccessful some attempts at rationalizing role and institutional decision-making may have been in the past, the need to do so is great; that is, the extent of past failures must not be construed as meaning that the present situation is even remotely satisfactory. Conversely, of course, one should avoid devising remedies which may be even worse than the malady. But for this to happen, the remedy would have to be very ineffective indeed.

To further illustrate the need for improvement, consider another standard finding, widely documented in industrial relations and management research. This kind of finding is usually discussed in the context of the study of communication. It has to do with the extent to which misconceptions are prevalent in organizations. Such misconceptions become of interest to us when they affect views and perceptions which in a given organizational setting fulfill the role of what Simon (1976) has called "decision premises." A set of representative findings of this kind is presented in Table 8.1. The data are from answers to the question: "Different people want different things out of their jobs. What are the things you yourself feel are *most important* in a job?" Workers were asked this question about themselves; foremen were asked to answer the question about themselves and about what they believed their subordinates felt; general foremen were similarly asked the question about themselves and about their foremen. The tabulation is of the three first choices out of a list of ten items. These items are grouped under three headings, rather than in the order in which they were asked.

The most important findings which emerge from Table 8.1 can be summarized in one sentence (cf., Likert, 1961, p. 49): superiors consistently overestimate the importance that their subordinates attach to economic variables, and underestimate the importance attached to other variables:

Thus, with regard to "high wages," 61 per cent of the foremen estimate that their subordinates will rate it of great importance but only 28 per cent of the men actually do so. Similarly, 58 per cent of the general foremen expect their foremen to attach great importance to this item but only 17 per cent of the foremen conform to these expectations.

It is likely that, for a variety of reasons, these data [Table 8.1] understate the importance of economic motivation. . . . The important point for this discussion of the data in Table 8.1, however, is the extent to which the foreman and the general foreman are in error in estimating how their subordinates see a situation.

In contrast to their estimates on the economic items, the superiors consistently underestimate the importance to their subordinates of those dimensions of the job which deal with such human factors as "getting along well with the people I work with," "getting along well with my supervisor," and "good chance to turn out good-quality work." Among workers, for example, 36 percent rated "getting along well with the people I work with" of great importance, but only 17 per cent of the foremen estimated that their subordinates would consider this item one of the three most important. The general foremen displayed similar errors in estimating the importance of these items to foremen.

Further appreciation of the magnitude of the error in the superiors' estimates is obtained from another kind of analysis. If the items are ranked in the order of importance as viewed by the men (column 1 in Table 8.1) and if the same is done for the foremen's rating of the items *for themselves* (column 3 in Table 8.1), the correspondence in the rankings is fairly marked ($r = +0.76$). But if the items as ranked by the men's responses are compared with the items as ranked by the foremen's estimates of the men's responses, there is virtually no relationship between the rankings. The general foremen and the foremen are seriously misinformed as to the motivations of their subordinates (Likert, 1961, pp. 49-51).

These findings, it should be stressed, are about people who are in daily contact, and about topics which are rather central to their role relationships.

TABLE 8.1: What Subordinates Want in a Job Compared with Their Superiors' Estimates

	As Men	As Foremen		As General Foremen	
	Rated the Variables for Themselves	Estimated Men Would Rate the Variables	Rated the Variables for Themselves	Estimated Foremen Would Rate the Variables	Rated the Variables for Themselves
Economic variables:					
Steady work and steady wages	61%	79%	62%	86%	52%
High wages	28	61	17	58	11
Pensions and other old-age security benefits	13	17	12	29	15
Not having to work too hard	13	30	4	25	2
Human satisfaction variables:					
Getting along well with the people I work with	36%	17%	39%	22%	43%
Getting along well with my supervisor	28	14	28	15	24
Good chance to turn out good-quality work	16	11	18	13	27
Good chance to do interesting work	22	12	38	14	43
Other variables:					
Good chance for promotion	25%	23%	42%	24%	47%
Good physical working conditions	21	19	18	4	11
Total	*	*	*	*	*
Number of cases	2,499	196	196	45	45

Source: Likert, 1961, Table 4.2, p. 50. (Originally from Robert L. Kahn, *Human Relations on the Shop Floor*. In E. M. Hugh-Jones (ed.), *Human Relations and Modern Management*. Amsterdam: North-Holland, 1958.)

*Percentages total over 100 because they include three rankings for each person.

If under such conditions decision premises can be unwittingly but systematically distorted in this manner, one cannot but wonder about what happens
when relationships are less sustained, as for instance when role judgments are
made on the basis of only one or two interactions. In bureaucracies this
situation is a frequent occurrence, in particular when the completely formalized aspect of decision-making (i.e., the processing of forms) is supplemented·
with interviews by role incumbents with discretionary privileges.

There is a whole literature on this topic, and the findings are very much
what we would expect them to be. Indeed, decision-making based on interviews is notoriously unsatisfactory. The problems range from mistakes in
information gathering all the way to wrong decision-making properly speaking (Smith and Wakeley, 1972, pp. 165-171). To illustrate, in an investigation
of information gathering by means of interviews of the data required for
establishing the eligibility of clients for benefits, it was found that except for
the sex of the applicants, all the information included a number of errors.
The percentage of some of the actual errors was as follows (cf., Weiss and
Davis, 1960; Smith and Wakeley, 1972, p. 165):

Item	*Percentage of errors*
Nature of disability	10%
Education	15%
Length of previous employment	29%
Rehabilitation assistance received	55%

Of course, it could be that these mistakes were in part due to the fact that
some of the social workers had been misled or were trying to affect positively
or negatively the chances of their clients to qualify for benefits. In such case
the problem was above all one of social control. But whether this was so or
not, the point is that "it is indefensible to assume the validity of purportedly
factual information obtained by interviews" (Weiss and Davis, 1960). That is,
while the danger of computerized files based on mistakenly filled or filed
forms is a genuine one (cf., Hoos, 1974), we must not loose sight of the
degree to which the present situation may be similar or even worse and
therefore require improvements.

An even more dramatic example of the inherent weakness of discretionary
role decision-making for the kinds of evaluative and judgmental tasks which
are usually performed in face to face interactions or in interviews, is provided
by the following study which deals with decision-making proper.

The study (Kelly and Fiske, 1951; Smith and Wakeley, 1972, pp. 166-167)
was carried out three decades ago at the University of Michigan and remains
to this date one of the most ambitious of its kind. Its major aim was to
determine what are the best means to evaluate professional aptitudes. The

specific population consisted of hundreds of psychology students already admitted to graduate school in various universities throughout the United States. The students were brought into Ann Arbor for a full week of intensive testing and credential evaluation followed by personal interviews with dozens of professional psychologists. That is, in this case the interviewers were all specialists and more highly trained than most role incumbents performing similar tasks usually are. A three year follow-up to this study was carried out with the aim of attempting to validate the evaluations and predictions made at assessment time. For the purpose of this validation various indices of professional aptitude and success obtained in the follow-up were used. The results of one of these analyses are presented in Table 8.2.

The most striking finding is, of course, that if anything, the evaluation based on the interviews, *detracts* from the other—less, or nondiscretionary— modes of evaluation; other findings were more neutral, and at times even mildly positive—the multiple correlation with the addition of the interview rising in one case from .29 to .31. A conservative conclusion is therefore that at best a long interview (two hours) performed by specialists adds practically nothing to the validity of evaluations achieved by more standardized means; and clearly, under less optimal conditions the interview may be assumed to be useless or even counterproductive (cf., Smith and Wakeley, 1972, pp. 166-167).

There are various explanations which attempt to account for the poor showing of face to face interactions and of interviews, as settings for engaging in evaluative decision-making. For instance, part of the problem might be structural. Thus, in one study of eight firms whose hiring practices were based in part on interviews, the investigators found that the average interview lasted only ten minutes. Perhaps even more revealing was the finding about time utilization: on the average one minute was spent in silence; during actual exchanges, however, the interviewees spoke only for about three minutes, while the interviewers did so for about six (Daniels and Otis, 1950; Smith and Wakeley, 1972, p. 163).

Table 8.2: The Validity of Interviews

Basis for Estimating Probable Academic Performance	Correlation with Actual Academic Performance (three year follow-up)
Credentials alone	.26
Credentials and objective test scores	.36
Credentials, test scores, and two hour interview	.32

Source: Kelly and Fiske (1951, p. 168), quoted by Smith and Wakeley (1972, p. 167)

Of course, from a heuristic point of view, the bulk of the problem is expected to arise, and should stem from a very different source. Under task conditions where the correctness of one's decisions is not readily assessable, the normal expectation is that decisions will have low validity due to both systematic errors and the lack of human reliability (see Chapters 5 and 6).

In any event, the discrepancy between the recurrently documented shortcomings of interviews, and their continued use, gives rise to a question: why in the light of the evidence, should they still be so widely used?

One explanation is that interviews may well fulfill latent functions (cf., Smith and Wakeley, 1972, pp. 170-171). Thus, an applicant is likely to feel more deprived if he is rejected without, rather than after an interview. Similarly, an applicant who is accepted or hired without an interview may well develop the impression that the organization is impersonal. These undesirable outcomes are not unlikely to be taken into consideration by the decision-makers who determine whether or not an organization will institutionalize interviews. Additionally, the same decision-makers may well be more willing to recognize the shortcomings of interviews in general, than to accept the fact that they themselves, or their specific organization, make poor decisions or judgments in such situations. Lastly, and more fundamentally, face to face interactions may fulfill an important information-processing function, bearing on the confidence in the decisions. In this respect, we all share the intuitive feeling that seeing or talking to a person adds valuable input to whatever decision has to be made. In the light of the clear evidence to the contrary, one might speculate that while the data and our intuition might both be valid, what really happens is a confusion of the rationale for confidence reminiscent of the finding documented by Oskamp (see Chapter 5)—although not necessarily identical. In the present case it might be that, in a manner resembling peripheral vision, face to face interactions give the opportunity for a kind of "peripheral checking" process to operate. Such a process might be conceptualized as a higher-order heuristic with interrupt capability. If activated by mismatches between the environmental cues—constantly monitored at subawareness levels—and the template of complex characteristics implicitly assumed to be normally part of the task situation, the role of such a meta-heuristic would be to change the definition of the situation, and concomitantly to switch the focus of problem solving. At the same time, should the "peripheral checking" mechanism have been given an opportunity to operate in an actual interaction with the object of the decision (rather than with an abstract description), and yet not have been activated, subjective confidence in the decision might conceivably be greatly increased. That is, it might be that direct contacts increase our confidence in having used the proper problem-solving heuristic (i.e., in not having overlooked implicitly assumed characteristics, which would call for an override of the heuristic), and that this, in turn, contributes to an inappropriate increase in the confidence that we have in the value of the heuristic *itself.*

In any case, it is probably fair to say that social myths to the contrary, discretionary role decision-making in its various forms—diagnoses, interviews, daily interactions—is anything but satisfactory, and needs being improved upon as a matter of some urgency.

From the information-processing point of view adopted in this book, the major problem which characterizes the present situation is that the perception of discretionary role decision-making rests on ambiguities regarding three related processes. The processes are problem solving, production enactment, and evaluation. Let us consider each in turn and attempt to clarify the nature of the difficulty.

Problem solving can refer to the creative process whereby a solution is invented in order to solve a problem. It can also mean, however, that a known solution has to be chosen among those which are in the repertoire of a decision-maker. In practice, there is a continuum between these two poles, and solutions are predominantly either invented or retrieved. Conceptually, nonetheless, in one case the process which is involved is essentially creative, while in the other it amounts above all to a retrieval and matching procedure. Herein lies one problem. This follows from the fact that subjectively as well as in terms of social definition, a task which from an information-processing standpoint is of one type can be misperceived or improperly defined by either or both individuals or the social environment. When such a confusion does occur, the inevitable result is that inappropriate expectations and criteria are applied to the assessment of decisions. In all probability, this is fundamentally what happens in the case of most instances of discretionary role decision-making; they continue to be perceived as being creative long after they have become stereotyped by either individual routinization (through habit) or organizationally induced conformity (through the rewards and punishments mediated by the process of accountability; see for instance Thompson, 1967, Chapter 9). Conversely, of course, solutions which are genuinely routine (or even discretionary, for that matter) may very well become relaxed, in the sense of becoming unsystematic or even arbitrary (through practice or otherwise) and thus invalidate the central expectation of standardization that wide-scale bureaucratization necessarily implies. I shall return to these problems in the context of the discussion of the routinization of policies (see Chapter 10).

Presently, the distinction of importance is that the bureaucratized process of decision-making is logically primarily a process where predetermined solutions are matched to problems. In that the process differs from what happens in the political realm, in part of the judiciary, or at the upper levels of bureaucracies, where decisions and conflic resolutions are often unique and are primarily constrained by the condition of being legitimate. This distinction is also a major characteristic which differentiates operations (systems) mainly controlled by outcomes from systems (operations) primarily controlled by procedures and, at the most elementary level, concept formation from concept attainment (cf., Bruner, Goodnow, and Austin, 1957, especially pp. 21-22 and 30-32).

This consideration leads to the second and related source of confusion. Indeed, not distinguishing between problem solving in the sense of creative thinking, and in the sense of matching appropriate procedures to problems, blurs the necessity—and the feasibility—of gearing our expectations to an appropriate model of what routinized decision-making is—in theory at least.

In terms of information-processing, the search and matching processes which are at the heart of routinized decision-making (whether discretionary or not) are amenable to a *production system* conceptualization. In order to understand the clarification of expectations that this notion conveys, it is useful to examine the concept in its programming context.

In this context, a production system refers to a list. Such a list consists of "a set of pairs of conditions and actions to be performed when conditions are met" (Brooks, 1975, p. 33). Each condition, and the associated action to be taken if the condition is met, is a *production*. A production has the form of an all or nothing statement: if the condition is not met, no action takes place; if it is, the appropriate action is carried out. Each production, it should be noted, is independent of the others, i.e., there is no explicit branching between actions. At the same time, actions modify the entities to which they are applied, and this in turn affects the conditions that these can meet. In other words, the state of the task world changes constantly, and "all control is accomplished through differences in the meeting of conditions and the execution of associated actions" (Brooks, 1975, p. 34). The following is a notional example of a production:

Basket not empty → process content of basket.[1]

There is a number of advantages to conceptualize the control structure of an information processor engaged in task performance as a production system. For one thing, this is demonstrably effective (Newell and Simon, 1972; Brooks, 1975). Perhaps even more importantly, this conceptualization has a powerful theoretical rationale. To quote from Newell and Simon (1972, p. 804), the following are some noteworthy arguments:

(1) A production system is capable of expressing arbitrary calculations. Thus it allows the human Information Processing System (IPS) the information processing capabilities we know he has.

(2) A production system encodes homogeneously the information that instructs the IPS how to behave. In contrast, the standard control-

flow system divides program information into the content of the boxes, on the one hand, and the structure of the flow diagram on the other. In a production system this division does not exist, except to the extent that the ordering of productions carries additional information. Production systems are the most homogenous form of programming organization known.

(3) In a production system, each production is independent of the others—a fragment of potential behavior. Thus the law of composition of production systems is very simple: manufacture a new production and add it to the set. This arrangement provides simple ways for a production system to grow naturally from incremental experience.

(4) The production itself has a strong stimulus-response flavor. It is overly simple to identify the two constructs, since productions also have additional properties of matching, operand identification, and subroutine calling that are not apparent in any of the usual formulation of S-R theory. . . . Nevertheless, productions might well express the kernel of truth that exists in the S-R position.

(5) The productions themselves seem to represent meaningful components of the total problem-solving process and not just odd fragments. This is true in part because we, the scientists, sought to define them that way. Nonetheless, it remains true that such an organization of meaningful pieces describes the data.

In order to operationalize a production system, the most important task is to specify the conditions of matching, the subroutinizing, and the sequential flow of control on the action side of the productions. But conceptually, the important point is that the notion of a production system clarifies the fundamental nature and structure of what a bureaucratized task theoretically is. Specifically, the procedural relationship between conditions and actions implies that in a well-defined bureaucratic task, the major problem-solving function is that of condition recognition. This activity translates into the problem of pattern recognition which, incidentally, sets a lower boundary to what mechanized information processing can do, in the same way—although not in the same sense—that invention sets an upper one to this same activity.

In any event, because the central element in a production is the link which relates the condition side to the action side, control of operations in a bureaucracy (especially of lower and middle echelons) tends overwhelmingly to be of the procedural rather than of the outcome type. Indeed, after a procedure has been routinized, the proper effect is assumed to be achieved if actions are performed according to their associated conditions (determined—presumably for good reasons—by the policy-makers of the bureaucracy). But this, of course, need not be the case. The public is generally more (painfully) aware of this fact than are some clerks. However, because the routinized aspect of discretionary role decision-making is often overlooked, it would appear that the myth that such decisions tend to be controlled (and validated) by outcomes rather than procedures is more widely shared.

Whatever the case may be, and whether the existing misconceptions stem partly from ambiguities in, and misunderstandings of, problem solving, production enactment, and/or adequate evaluation (by outcomes versus by procedure), it must be recognized that the present situation is also anchored in a very different rationale. Indeed, in many quarters the perpetuation of the present situation is defended not because of lack of awareness or understanding of its shortcomings, or of the feasibility of significant improvement, but because remedies are held to involve dangers which might be worse than the malady. This question of potential dangers must therefore be examined.

Possible Dysfunctions

As the reader may recall, some of the dangers feared to be inherent in the process of computerizing bureaucratic tasks have already been discussed in Chapter 2. Thus, on the basic of selected examples examined by Hoos (1974), it was noted that these dangers include, among others, the perpetuation of mistakes in files, the development of impersonal patterns (especially questionable in educational settings), and more generally the waste of resources—above all through the creation of indigested data banks. These shortcomings will now be briefly reexamined.

Quite clearly, the question of erroneously stored information and of the tendency to implicitly trust the validity of computerized files, constitutes a very serious problem. In this respect, however, two things should be pointed out. First, it is not at all certain that this potential danger is any worse than is the present situation with noncomputerized files—as some evidence presented earlier in this chapter suggests. Second, precisely because mistakes made by the computer can be so dramatic, it is not at all inconceivable that, on the average, errors made by computers are more quickly and more thoroughly corrected than are clerical mistakes. Of course, this is primarily an empirical question. But to the same extent that there are grounds to justify a speculatively based pessimism, there are also reasons to justify a more optimistic outlook. Specifically, the conjunction of the strong normative expectation that mistakes and debugging are unavoidable, together with the fact that there is likely to be less ego involvement to cover up mistakes (except, perhaps, on the part of the programmers—but then the objective nature of the programming tasks makes misrepresentations among specialists very difficult), suggests the likely hypothesis that a computerized bureaucratic process may involve less mistakes per unit of time/consumer, than does the equivalent process in a clerical bureaucracy. This hypothesis—should it be validated—would parallel what is observed in air travel: accidents involving aircraft are much more likely to be dramatic and to make (good) headlines than are car accidents. As is well known, however, airplanes are a much safer means of transportation (per mile/passenger traveled) than are cars.

The development of impersonal patterns and their potential dysfunctionality in education, as well as in general, is a second possible danger of importance. However, as in the previous case, there is also another side to the coin. Considering first the case of education, it is also true that on the basis of the phenomenon known as *social facilitation,* studying and drilling alone (rather than in a social setting), can be expected to *enhance* learning rather than to inhibit it. Indeed, in man—as in all the animals studied—it appears that the mere presence of conspecifics raises the level of activity. As a consequence, when the activity is a well-learned response, the rate of emission of this activity increases. Conversely, however, when the activity is in the process of being learned, it is the rate of emission of errors which grows: learning itself, therefore, is *impaired* (Zajonc, 1965; Zajonc and Sales, 1966; Zajonc, Heingartner, and Herman, 1969; Henchy and Glass, 1968; and for a summary of this research: Freedman, Carlsmith, and Sears, 1974, pp. 171-175).

Not surprisingly, therefore, actual studies of the effect of computerized teaching and drilling do not necessarily bear out all the fears that the notion of impersonal teaching raises. More research (by substantive topics and type of students being taught) than is presently available is needed before a final evaluation can be made. Nonetheless, a study which deals with the teaching of diagnostic skills to medical students might already have uncovered trends which stand as good a chance as alternative hypotheses of being confirmed by future research. In this study, the author concludes:[2]

> The comparison between human and machine teaching can be summarized as follows: The Professor gives more additional information, and the dialogue is faster. The computer, however, has two advantages: its teaching is more rigorous than that of the usual teacher; even more importantly, it forces individual work and efforts that one can avoid in a group situation. For this reason all the students are agreed that machine teaching is more efficient   (Varet, 1974/1975, p. 430).

The effects of mechanization are not only feared in education. More generally, mechanization, in particular the "ideal type" found in industry, is held to be the model of the problem; this problem is viewed as centering around the feelings of alienation fostered by the associated process of dehumanization. This development has been described by Marx in the following terms:

> In handicrafts and manufacture, the workman makes use of a tool, in the factory, the machine makes use of him. There the movements of

the instrument of labour proceed from him, here it is the movements of the machine that he must follow. In manufacture the workmen are parts of a living mechanism. In the factory we have a lifeless mechanism independent of the workman, who becomes its mere living appendage (Marx, 1906, pp. 461-462).

As this quotation clearly shows, however, the problem originally raised by Marx is not one of impersonality in the sense of anonymity (let alone in the sense of universalism), but in the sense of a means-end relationship between man and machine, and ultimately among men themselves. Whatever the value for modern factory workers of the Marxist analysis may be, it is quite clear that views directly or indirectly derived from this perspective can teach us very little about white-collar mechanization, when the master-servant situation described by Marx does not hold. Indeed, an accountant who is given a desk calculator is unlikely to experience any of the ills of mechanization implied in the above quotation.

In a similar manner, the reaction of the clients of a bureaucracy to an automated service may have little to do with what a careless derivation from Marx's observation, or from common wisdom, would lead us to expect.

Consider, for instance, the case of the Automatic Teller Machines (Electronic Funds Transfer System). According to the New York *Times,* in 1976 there were about 4,000 such machines in use in the United States. In terms of function, most of the operations performed by the automatic tellers are rather standard. This includes "police" functions which, however, are not without a humor of their own. Thus:

> The more sophisticated machines allow withdrawals, generally up to $100 a day, in increments of $25, from checking or savings accounts or as loans against a credit card; deposits in any amount to checking or savings; transfers from checking to savings, credit card to checking, savings to checking; and payments for mortgages, loans and the like in cash, or as a deduction from checking or savings.
>
> To perform any of these operations, the user inserts a plastic card or credit card, punches in a code number of four to six digits, selects the type of transaction, punches in the amount and waits a few seconds while the machine whirs, types, sticks the card back out and pops open a small drawer containing money, a receipt or a notification that something was punched wrong.
>
> Some machines are so programmed that if you try to swindle them, make the same mistake three times running or overdraw, your card is 'eaten'—swallowed up and not returned. That is called being "hot carded," and requires a trip to the bank and an explanation of what you tried to do to the Tillie (King, 1976).

The important point is that, despite the fact that the machines were originally intended to offer extended service after normal banking hours, their popularity with customers exceeds this limited use. Moreover, there are grounds to believe that among the reasons which make these automatic tellers popular, is precisely the fact that they are impersonal. Thus, Wayne King reports in the same article in the New York *Times:*

> A young women who also uses the machines often during banking hours said: "Why not? They're fun, and I'm tired of being hassled by some snotty clerk who asks for an I.D. and does everything but fingerprint me when I want to cash a $20 check."
>
> Others appear to use the machines to preserve some kind of anonymity. "No right, no wrong, just bread," said a young Atlanta woman.
>
> A spokesman for Chase Manhattan in New York, which has only five machines, three of them in Grand Central Terminal, has found that besides cash withdrawals, a major machine item is "small loans" of $25 to $50 from the Bank Americard.
>
> "Apparently," said the spokesman, "people are loath to use the tellers for these small advances; they don't want to look the teller in the eye and admit they must have some cash to tide them over" (King, 1976).

Of course, a reportage does not purport to be a rigorous study and the issue should be methodically investigated before any firm conclusion can be reached. But at this point it is probably safe to say that there is as much ground to justify investigating the actual impact of "impersonal" information processing as to support speculations of one kind or another.

Another potential danger is more related to monetary cost than to social harm. This is the problem of sterile data banks where "useless information is efficiently stored" (Hoos, 1974; Laudon, 1974, p. 303). It has been suggested that the roots of this problem lie above all in "the absence of a theory of information capable of suggesting what kinds of information are required by the nonroutine decisions typically made by political executives" (Laudon, 1974, p. 302). This, of course, may very well be the case (in part at least). But whether or not it is so, the important consideration is that we should expect the problem to be significantly different when decisions are made repetitively—rather than nonroutinely—as indeed we shall later see is the case.

Although waste and irrelevance, as well as the other issues discussed earlier, constitute salient dangers, the most fundamental objection that the notion of a computerized bureaucracy evokes, is probably related to the belief that this inexorably starts a process of centralization. Such a development—if it were unavoidable—would obviously constitute a danger of exceptional gravity.

The notion that the computerization of bureaucratic tasks necessarily leads to a process of centralization, appears to have two major sources. These are related to the image that we have of the impact of technology on organizations, and to assumptions about the power drive of management, i.e., the problem of the "power pie."

There is little doubt that, in general, much of the literature generates the impression that mechanization, formalization, and standardization, are conducive to centralization in the sense of transforming a man into a cog, which is reminiscent of Marx's description. In part, this follows from the fact that there is good evidence in support of the proposition that technology and organizational structure are related and that alienation is in turn affected by changes in technology and structures (Woodward, 1965; Blauner, 1964; and for a summary of the literature, Laudon, 1974 [Chapter 3], and Becker and Neuhauser, 1975 [Chapter 2]. In part, the compelling imagery of huge corporations and vast assembly lines together with actual examples of misuses of authority, are probably also responsible for this widely shared belief.

But empirically it turns out that the situation is quite different. Indeed, even for blue-collar work, standardization and automation are not necessarily conducive to centralization. Thus, as Laudon notes, a variety of studies "support the notion that the introduction of more sophisticated technological devices in blue-collar jobs result in more autonomous and smaller work groups, greater required skills, and less personal supervision" (Laudon, 1974, p. 25; see also Blau et al., 1976). But for our purpose, the question of real interest is of course whether or not the automation of white-collar tasks is accompanied by a process of centralization, in particular of control and decision-making. The answer, as it turns out, is most surprising: there is a body of evidence to suggest that, on the whole, it is the *converse* which occurs.

This is unexpected because the view that formalization and standardization, which are the hallmarks of bureaucratization, are associated with centralization of authority in organizations goes back to Weber and is also expressed in the writings of a number of other thinkers, e.g., Merton (cf., Blau and Schoenherr, 1971, pp. 113-115). This notion, however—perhaps because it sounds so reasonable—turns out to have been accepted for years without any empirical tests. When such tests were finally performed, in particular by Blau and his associates (in the United States—see Blau, Hydebran, and Stauffer, 1966; Blau, 1968) and by the Aston Group (in Great Britain—see Child, 1973), the striking result was, as Perrow summarizes it, "that the more structured the activities of an organization (that is, the greater the degree of bureaucracy), the greater the degree of decentralization of decision making or authority" (Perrow, 1974b, p. 39).

This inverse relationship between bureaucratic formalization and standardization, on the one hand, and centralization of authority and decision-making, on the other, suggests that fears that the latter development is inevitable when a bureaucracy undergoes a process of automation, may very well be groundless. In point of fact, the study of a police regional information system

(PRIS) led its author to precisely this conclusion. Specifically, he stated in the summary of his research: "One of the principal findings of our study [is that] a centralized information system is fully compatible with a highly decentralized administrative structure" (Laudon, 1974, p. 214). More generally, the conclusion which currently best summarizes the available data is that "Whatever the implications for centralized management of the extensive use of computers in arriving at managerial decisions may be in the future, the little systematic evidence that exists on the subject indicates that automation does not foster centralization at present" (Blau and Schoenherr, 1971, p. 125).[3]

Of course, the intriguing question that these findings raise is one of interpretation. Why should *more* bureaucratic formalization and standardization be found to be associated with *less* centralization?

At least two possible explanations have been advanced. The first was given by Blau and Schoenherr (1971, p. 118; see also Blau et al., 1976, p. 32), and is summarized in the proposition that "conditions that make operations more reliable also foster decentralization." More specifically, and taking the existence of an extensive body of personnel regulations as an example, Blau and Schoenherr argue that

> both strict conformity with personnel standards and the elaboration of these formalized standards encourage decentralization of responsibilities. Standardized personnel procedures are not so much a source of centralized authority as an alternative to it.
>
> The interpretation . . . assumes that standardization actually improves the reliability of operations, thus furnishing objective grounds for delegating resonsibilities. The reduction of objective risks resulting from reliable operations . . . is the mechanism through which standardization promotes decentralization in organizations (Blau and Schoenherr, 1971, p. 120).

Although this interpretation is relatively novel in the sociological literature, there are reasons to believe that some management specialists may have known intuitively the kernel of truth that it contains for quite some time.[4] Nevertheless, there are obviously limits to the extent to which formalization and decentralization can coexist unless, as has been noted with tongue in cheek by Perrow, one is willing to follow in the footsteps of one thinker, "who quoted with approval an army officer in World War I who remarked that the army is the greatest of all democracies, because when the order to move forward is given, each man decides on his own whether to obey or not" (Perrow, 1974b, p. 36). The question arises what exactly is meant by such terms as "democracy" or in our case, "decentralization."

This question of meaning leads to the second interpretation mentioned above. In essence, this second view holds that the paradoxical relationship under discussion can to a large extent be explained by the manner in which decentralization and the notions of power and control are defined. Brzezinsky (1967, p. 20, quoted by Perrow, 1974b, p. 39), gives a striking example of this when he observes that "It is noteworthy that the U.S. Army has so developed its control systems that it is not uncommon for sergeants to call in and coordinate meassive air strikes and artillery fire—a responsibility of colonels during World War II." While this example is obviously a case of decentralization, the point, as Perrow notes, is that "the ability of the U.S. Army to destroy more living things today than in World War II has increased. There are more decisions to make. The sergeant of today makes more decisions than the colonel of World War II because the lethal output of the system is so much higher"; at the same time, however, it is very doubtful that the colonel feels robbed of authority, or that he has lost any in the process (cf., Perrow, 1974b, p. 39). The reason is, of course, that relating to power and control as a zero-sum game may be quite misleading. This has been shown by Tannenbaum (1968), who has documented in a number of studies that when the amount of power exercised by various echelons in an organization is measured, the steepness of the slope of the curve need not be related to the magnitude of the area under it. That is to say, centralization and *absolute* amount of power can be largely unrelated. One result of this empirical finding is that the present interpretation does not contradict the proposition derived from the previous explanation that tight control over the premises of decisions facilitates the decentralization of actual decisions. On the other hand, the findings reported by Blau and his collaborators, together with Tannenbaum's results, suggest that while formalization and standardization do not necessarily lead to centralization in the mechanical sense which is usually feared, they are likely to create a problem for the bureaucratic aspect of policy-making concerned with the generation and maintenance of working premises; this problem is, in effect, the one raised by Wieck (1969). We shall see in Chapter 10 that it need not be without a solution.

The foregoing discussion has shown that in terms of our immediate concern some widely shared beliefs about the potential dangers of automated bureaucracies are less than well-supported by available evidence. At the same time, and to avoid any misunderstanding, it should be stressed that the discussion was not meant to imply that these dangers are illusory. The point that I have endeavored to make is merely that these dangers are neither necessary nor unique to the process of increased computerization (this is particularly true for the problem of potential misuses, which will be discussed in Chapter 11). In line with this remark it should be noted that while some widely shared fears may be currently unwarranted, there are other pitfalls which, although less generally recognized, should nonetheless also be given some attention. I shall briefly mention a few of them.

Other Potential Dangers

To avoid an insidious pitfall, it is important not to be misled by the sense in which the automation of some functions of bureaucracies may contribute to the rationalization of their modus operandi. For a number of reasons—one of them being to avoid redundancy—I shall not engage in a detailed discussion of the possible definitions of the concept of rationality; such discussions can be found in a number of books on policy-making or large-scale organizations (e.g., Dror, 1968; Simon, 1976). It is important to stress, however, that in the following pages there is one sense that the term is *not* meant to have, i.e., that a certain solution or procedure, at whatever level of application, is the "best" in some sense.

This exclusion follows from the logic of the heuristic perspective adopted in this volume. It also highlights a fallacy not always recognized, which has been lucidly pointed out by Dror in the context of the prisoner's dilemma. Specifically, he notes that the obvious is often disregarded:

> As a result [of the dominant strategy] both rational prisoners will talk, and will spend fifteen years in prison thinking about the limitations of pure rationality. If, on the other hand, each of the two prisoners follows a hunch that he should keep quiet, they will each spend only five years in prison, saving ten years each. . . .
>
> Here we have mathematical proof that pure rationality is inferior to extra-rationality as a decision-making method for persons in certain situations. This should inspire either attempts to break up the game (which have not worked) or attempts to draw conclusions within the decision sciences themselves as to where pure rationality ceases to be the ideal mode for decision making and policy making (almost none of which have so far appeared) [Dror, 1968, p. 152].

Although no attempt is made in this volume to draw the boundary to which Dror refers, it is clear that the heuristic approach cannot make any claim to rationality in the sense of comprehensive problem solving and "best" solutions (cf., Chapters 2 and 4). Spelling out and objectivizing routinized processes of organizational decision-making must therefore be seen for what it is: a means which helps understanding the need for, and which facilitates the systematic introduction of redundancy—not a technique for furthering the cause of rationality in any other sense.

Another pitfall is not related to improper expectations. Rather, it results occasionally from the reliance on a concrete procedure. The problem consists of the (sometimes unwarranted) use of group settings for institutional decision-making.

To understand the nature of the problem it is necessary to distinguish between what is called in the literature "Eureka" and "non-Eureka" types of problems.[5] The former have unique and unambiguous solutions. A mathematical problem versus the task of drawing a man, or having to solve a crossword puzzle versus having to devise one, would be examples of Eureka and non-Eureka-type problems, respectively.

The point of this distinction is that while group decision-making generally enhances the quality of problem solving for Eureka-type problems, this is not true for non-Eureka problems, which tend to be adversely affected by group settings including "brain storming" (Kelly and Thibaut, 1954; 1969; Taylor et al., 1966). One important reason for this is that group members appear to have a natural tendency to be somewhat critical of their peers and, as a result, excel at catching each other's mistakes (Shaw, 1958). Specifically, when the problem is of the Eureka type (and is not too complex), the very fact that the problem has a unique and unambiguous solution also implies that mistakes are readily demonstrable. Under such conditions, group problem solving turns out to be more efficient because (1) mutual criticism rapidly uncovers errors, and this reduces the time spent on mistaken paths, and (2) this same process decreases the likelihood that a mistaken solution will be misconstrued by the group as being correct. Conversely, problems which are creative in the sense of accepting a variety of solutions (e.g., devising a crossword puzzle), tend to have ambiguous cues for gauging the quality of efforts; moreover, this ambiguity is greater the further away one is from a solution—a fact which makes it difficult to evaluate the contribution that intermediate steps make to problem solving. As a consequence, the very same tendency to engage in mutual criticism noted above is instrumental for open-ended problems in breaking up trains of thought, more than it is in correcting "mistakes"; the result, not surprisingly, is a degradation of the quality of problem solving due to mutual interference by the participants. In other words, the nature of the problem, together with some aspects of group dynamics and of social situations per se (cf., Chapter 7 and the social facilitation phenomenon in this chapter) interact in complex ways to determine the relative advantage that group decision-making has over individual decision-making. It should be noted that the situation is further complicated by the effect that group problem solving has on motivation (French and Coch, 1958), risk-taking (Brown, 1965, Chapter 13; Secord and Backman, 1974, pp. 379-383), and also on reliability, if not on validity (Goldberg, 1970; Smith and Wakeley, 1972). Although these considerations are of course of interest in themselves, their primary importance lies in their relevance for the task of interfacing computerized decision-making with the function of devising decision-making strategies and heuristics in the manner envisioned by Dudycha and Naylor (see Chapter 6). They should be kept in mind for this purpose.

A third pitfall that is often overlooked has already been noted in Chapter 5—we encountered it while discussing Parkinson's "law of triviality." It was noted that given the nature of human information-processing limitations, dysfunctional decision-making behavior may reflect more on the ignorance or unrealism of the expectations of the social environment than on the irresponsibility of the participants. Conversely, and to the same extent that contempt may be misguided, de Groot's (1966) and Chase and Simon's (1973) experiments have shown that there is little room for mythical beliefs about inordinate mental powers. It should never be forgotten that decision-making is neither worse nor better than the *heuristics* which are used, and that *both* man and machine are always fallible. A complementary relationship between human and mechanical information processors is useful for organizational decision-making only to the extent that trade-offs are possible between such characteristics as speed and reliability, on the one hand, and flexibility and inventiveness, on the other. But as every experienced artillery man knows, while radar-aided heavy guns are more accurate than are traditional guns, the very best use of even modern guns is achieved when an observer completes the system. In other words, the fallacy which should be avoided is to believe that eliminating one of the components of man-machine systems is a goal in itself, or that this could propel us magically into some perfect world outside the domain of heuristics. Rather, it must be kept in mind that relying more heavily (or exclusively) on either man or machine for decision-making merely represents a different choice of trade-offs, and a different partition of possible pay-offs; *in either case a continuous process of review and monitoring is an unavoidable necessity.*

Because this chapter has discussed issues which are central to the perspective adopted in the last part of the book, it is useful to conclude the discussion with a summary of the points which have been made.

Synopsis

Due to existential requirements and to the characteristics of man's limited information-processing capability, the (quasi) totality of human and organizational problem solving and decision-making is per force heuristic; also, cognitive maps of the environment and of cause-and-effect relationships are at best truncated, and at worst a misleading imagery. Moreover, reliability, validity, and above all self-insight into the nature and quality of one's information processing (e.g., predictability of decisions, confidence in their accuracy, value of interviews, etc.), are clearly limited. Together these considerations suggest that objectivizing in an articulated whole whatever formalized chain or process of complex organizational decision-making can be effectively modeled is in itself an important contribution. For one thing, this step is a necessary strategy for overcoming the truncated grasp that each and every actor must have in a sizable organization of any chain of delegated tasks of nontrivial length, let alone possible discontinuities among tasks. For another, introducing changes in a system, as opposed to simply following its operation, can only benefit from the existence of a working model of the system. In short, for any given problem, man needs help to unfold, follow, and check his own thought process.

In combination, man's information-processing limitations, on the one hand, and the growing importance of organizational bureaucratic decision-making, on the other, make the modeling of such systems increasingly useful and perhaps even unavoidable if understanding, monitoring, and steering such systems are to remain manageable.

The modeling effort per se is in any event feasible. This follows from the logic of the formalized mode of operation of bureaucracies and from the fact that discretionary role decision-making of the repetitive kind is rather easy to model. This task, moreover, finds a natural theoretical framework in the concept of a cybernetic system. The basic reason for the compatibility lies above all in the fact that routinized decisions depend on very few variables and on simple heuristics, which is precisely what the notion of a servo-mechanism requires.

These considerations apply to the case of routinized decision-making, to which the present discussion is explicitly confined. However, this restriction is not without advantages. In particular, it allows one to deal with the problem of discretion and to be in a position of applying with some power the cybernetic paradigm to the problem at hand; additionally, it avoides a number of pitfalls which have generally plagued the systems approach until now. Foremost among these is the mistake of substituting an arbitrary program for man's creativity and the disregard of the fact that problems of individual intransitivities—let alone Condorcet's and Arrow's paradoxes—are still without satisfactory solution. At the same time, the strategy of limiting the focus of attention to repetitive decision-making forces the realization that by the very fact that bureaucratic procedures are routinized, they proclaim—at least implicitly—that they are tested and validated solutions to whatever problem is deemed to fit the conditions of their application. In this connection, Coleman (1972) and Campbell (1975) have argued that, as a general trend, such a development is unavoidable in policy-related matters. The reason is that in modern societies social decision-making and action can seldom await the results of disciplinary research; as a result, policies, programs, reforms and, in our case, procedures, tend increasingly to be implemented and to become routinized without adequate evaluation. To combat this trend, both Coleman and Campbell have suggested that social scientists should consider shifting their research focus and adapt their methodologies to the real-time dimension of policy-related problems rather than to keep trying to force new policies or procedures into the mold of rigorous experiments. The idea of modeling routinized bureaucratic decision-making partakes in this philosophical approach. Specifically, it aims at transforming the monitoring of the effectiveness of policies and procedures into an ongoing activity carried out by means of a built-in relationship between normal operations and cumulative research. The focus in the present case is, however, on existing and implemented policies rather than on impending ones, and on rationalization (in the weak sense discussed earlier) rather than on creative problem solving.

The feasibility of the task has been considered at some length. The purpose of the discussion, however, was only illustrative—as it could well afford to be—inasmuch as in the literature, the feasibility issue is rather noncontroversial. Chapter 6 has shown this to be the case in terms of the measurement and retrieval of decision rules. More generally, Dreyfus (1972) argues that from an artificial intelligence perspective, the kind of computerized decision-making envisioned is nonproblematic; indeed, this task is trivial, and consequently, "The challenge for artificial intelligence does not lie in such *ex post facto* formalizations of specific tasks" (Dreyfus, 1972, p. 250). This may be true (although the documentation of social and organizational heuristics may well turn out to contribute valuable insights to the field of artificial intelligence). But, even if in the final analysis the topic must be regarded as being pedestrian—so be it. The important point is that routinized decision making *can* be modeled, that there is a clear need for doing so, and that some dangers—in particular alienation and centralization—are not inherently related to the endeavor. Additionally, routinized decision-making involves only the application of available procedures—a fact which makes the use of a closed-system viewpoint legitimate (at least so long as the rate of retention of existing procedures is high). This, in turn, allows the use of a programming paradigm, which is itself embedded in a cybernetic framework (operatively centered around the notion of decision-making servomechanisms, i.e., the heuristics of the role incumbents).

On the assumption that the reader is comfortable with these premises, we can now proceed to the next task and the following chapters, where the foregoing rationale is taken for granted. In this connection, I should mention that spelling out and clarifying the premises is an important aim of this essay. Indeed, I feel much less committed to the procedures and solutions which will be discussed later than to the diagnosis of the problem. The latter, and the underlying needs, are very real; the solutions, on the other hand, are much more debatable.

As the reader has noted, establishing the nature of some current inadequacies has required a psychological discussion which was much longer than the sociological one. This emphasis was necessitated by the state of the art in the relevant subdisciplines of psychology and sociology. This emphasis, however, should not be taken as reflecting on the contribution that the latter literature makes to our knowledge and understanding of bureaucracies or bureaucratic decision-making. On the contrary, it is precisely because the

purely information-processing aspect of bureaucracies has been less emphasized in the (extensive) literature on formal organizations (with a few exceptions—notably Simon's work), that the psychological discussion has been
expanded in an effort to balance the picture. In other words, the foregoing is
not intended as a representative review of the literature pertaining to
bureaucracies. It is an addendum to the topics usually discussed in this
literature, and at the same time an attempt at making an argument. As such,
the major aim of the discussion was to emphasize that routine decision-
making and information processing per se are research topics and constitute
theoretical vantage points whose importance has tended to be overlooked or
at least underrated in the investigation of bureaucracies.

NOTES

1. For additional and more detailed examples, see Newell and Simon (1972).

2. The quotation is a free translation from the original in French.

3. For a further confirmation of this conclusion, and a documentation of the
interactions which may generate exceptions, see Blau (1973, pp. 184-188; 279-280); and
Blau et al. (1976).

4. Cf. the following principle of Federal reorganization quoted by Hoos (1974, p.
65): "A President whose programs are carefully coordinated, whose information system
keeps him adequately informed, and whose organizational assignments are plainly set
out, can delegate authority with security and confidence."

5. This distinction is not without some relationship to the discussion of the two
meanings of problem solving, see pp. 91-92.

Chapter 9

REPETITIVE BUREAUCRATIC
DECISION-MAKING IN OPERATION

After the extensive background discussion in Part II and the reassessment of some relevant premises related to the feasibility and desirability of modeling repetitive bureaucratic decision-making, which was the topic of the last chapter, the reader may be willing to grant that the endeavor might be theoretically desirable and perhaps feasible. The actual feasibility and usefulness of carrying out such a task remain, however, to be documented. This is the task of this chapter. In the next, the viewpoint which emerges from the discussion as a whole will be elaborated.

The chapter is divided into five sections. The first introduces an additional concept—that of multiple goals—whose treatment in terms of the information-processing paradigm discussed in Part II helps to relate the individual and organizational levels of analysis. The second section reviews findings of studies which have approached the study of organizational and bureaucratic decision-making from the heuristic perspective. The third touches on the relationship of these studies to the theoretical perspective adopted in this book. The fourth presents additional findings directly related to this perspective. The fifth is a brief conclusion.

A Note on Multiple Goals and Criteria

As an introduction to the discussion, it is useful to consider the notion of multiple goals in individual and organization problem solving. Consider first individuals. They often pursue several goals simultaneously. These can be as diverse as power, wealth, esthetic fulfillment, personal happiness, etc. For any given action, these goals can, in turn, serve as criteria of evaluation. In some cases only one goal is relevant, in others any combination of them may be. For instance, when one decides on what time of the day to climb a mountain, the esthetic value of the view at sunrise may be the only important factor. Conversely, when a young lady has to make a choice between two suitors, most or all factors may be relevant.

When analyzing organizations, we face the same problem, only more so. In fact, any social system can be viewed as a collection of individual and collective goals. These can be clear and concrete, or ambiguous and nonoperative; not less importantly, they may be shared and activated to various degrees at different times.

This characteristic of goals raises an important problem, because on the basis of the discussion in Part II we saw that on theoretical grounds we cannot expect more than *sequential* problem solving. At least all the evidence points to the fact that this is the manner in which man processes information. And except for the illusion created by time sharing, the computer as an information processor is completely isomorphic with man in this respect. Understanding how simultaneous multiple goal problem solving is nonetheless possible at the individual level—as opposed to being paramorphically retrievable by multiple regression techniques (see Chapter 6)—is therefore of great importance. As we shall see, this will provide us with a conceptual framework for moving to the organizational level of analysis.

The fundamental difficulty with which we are confronted stems from the inadequacy of the solution to the problem of multiple goals which is used in the normative approaches to decision-making. In fact, the individual and economic theory of decision-making always deals with *one* goal. When a multiple goals situation arises, the theory assumes that the goals can be made to be commensurate on some scale (money, utilities) and be arranged in a joint preference ordering. Trade-offs can then be computed, and goal or preference-order achievement can be maximized. Yet for descriptive purposes, many goals are incommensurable, and the probabilistic omniscience and the computational performance assumed by the normative theories are not only questionable but demonstrably inadequate.

The scientists working on problems of artificial intelligence face the same difficulty, in particular when they attempt to program computers to play complex games—a case in point being chess. As in the instance of heuristic itself, it may be instructive to consider how in the case of chess, the seemingly intractable problem of multiple and incommensurable goals is amenable to a heuristic solution.

Basically, the solution consists in finding a way to avoid having to compute trade-offs between objectives. In their *Human Problem Solving,* Newell and Simon (1972) present a theory in the context of which this is shown to be feasible. In the general case, the solution amounts to creating a list of goals. Operatively, and in order to avoid both having to engage in trade-offs and cases of indetermination, the goals have a minimum satisficing value and are arranged in hierarchical order. If the satisficing value of all goals can be achieved, an attempt is also made to improve the outcome by means of a search for a Pareto optimal solution. If, on the contrary, a satisficing value for all goals is unachievable, the predetermined hierarchy of goals sets a priority ordering among them in the same way that the ordering of the instructions of the tick-tack-toe heuristic (see Chapter 4) determines in which order they are to be disregarded when the need arises.

To give substance to these remarks, consider the following concrete example from chess given by Newell, Shaw, and Simon (1958) and summarized by Miller et al.:

> [T]he traditional chess heuristic [has been analyzed] into six independent "goals": (1) King safety, (2) material balance, (3) center control, (4) development, (5) King-side attack, and (6) promotion of Pawns. This ordering of the goals is significant, because the machine always tries to achieve them in that same order. That is to say, first the machine will look to see if its King is safe. If not, it will try to defend it; if so, it will go on to the next goals. The next thing the machine will do is to check up on the possible exchanges, to make sure that its pieces are adequately protected. If not, the machine will protect them; if so, the machine will turn next to center control. Can it move its Pawns into the center? If so, it is done; if not, the machine turns to development, then to attacking the King, and finally, if none of those goals leads to a good move, the machine will consider the Pawn structure.
>
> When the move generator has proposed something to do, the machine does not automatically accept it, of course. The proposal must be evaluated to see if it really achieves the desired results. The evaluation cannot be limited to a single goal, however, for a move that would look very good to the center-control Plan might utterly destroy the King's position, or lose a piece, etc. The proposed move must be analysed in terms of all six goals. The value of a move is a vector. . . .
>
> Now, when the machine has found a move *that all the different heuristic goals approve* [emphasis added] the move may still not be made. There may be an even better move possible. Thus, the machine has the problem of making a choice among the moves after they have

been evaluated. There are several different ways it could proceed, but there is one thing it cannot do: It cannot wait until all the possible proposals have been made and evaluated in order to select the one with highest value. There are far too many proposals possible. Newell, Shaw, and Simon suggest that the simplest choice procedure is to set an acceptance level arbitrarily (a mechanical "level of aspiration") and simply to take the first acceptable move. In order to avoid the possibility that no conceivable move would meet the criterion, a stop-order can also be imposed; save the best move discovered up to this point and, if the time-limit expires before an acceptable move has been found, make the best one that was found (Miller, Galanter, and Pribram, 1960, pp. 185-186).

As this description indicates, trade-offs between goals are avoided; the procedure rests instead on the multiple cut-off principle. Under normal circumstances this procedure amounts to a multivariate method of stepwise selection, with each goal acting as a constraint. That is, comparisons—let alone compensations—between traits are, as a rule, not made. In the simplest case of one satisficing level per goal, a Pareto optimal solution is sequentially sought with the constraint that no goal value will fall below this satisficing level as a result of the optimization; when no action (move) can guarantee that all aims will achieve their minimum satisficing value, the side conditions of the goal heuristic (cf., Chapter 4) attempt to ensure at least that this will be the case for selected objectives, according to a predetermined priority ordering. Such a procedure obviously does not guarantee a unique, let alone an optimum solution. It is, however, a procedure that any sequential information processor which is existentially constrained by the necessity to rely on heuristics can apply. Furthermore, it suggests a possible cue both to individual multiple goal problem solving and to the principle of composition of goals in complex systems of decision-making. We shall immediately see that this is a valuable clue indeed.

Modeling Organizational Decision-Making

We are now in a position to turn to the first study to be considered. It was carried out by Cyert and March (1963) and is reported in their *A Behavioral Theory of the Firm.*

The rationale for Cyert and March's endeavor was their dissatisfaction with the economic model of decision-making of the firm (a dissatisfaction which parallels in time that of the psychologists discussed in Chapter 5). This model, as already noted, implies that organizations (business or otherwise) are omnisciently rational systems of decision-making. For normative purposes, at the aggregate level of analysis, or for long-term trends, such a view— unrealistic as it may be—has demonstrable usefulness. For the analysis of concrete individual firms and daily operations, however, it is very inadequate, and the authors consequently chose to adopt the heuristic viewpoint. Because firms are instances of organizations that engage in repetitive decision-making, and because in this case quantification is easily achieved, the usefulness of the heuristic approach for the organizational level of analysis is well introduced by this first class of applications.

In brief, the findings of Cyert and March can be summarized as follows:

First, the authors discovered four general organizational decision-making heuristics (or short-cuts, rules of thumbs, and relational concepts, as the authors refer to them). These are the *quasi-resolution of conflict, uncertainty avoidance, problemistic search,* and *organizational learning.*

QUASI-RESOLUTION OF CONFLICT

This principle describes the manner in which organizational goals are actually implemented. As noted above, according to the normative theory of decision-making, a single goal is maximized, or a set of goals are made commensurate (in terms of money or utilities) and then optimized. As opposed to this idealized view, Cyert and March found that even in economic organizations where the usefulness of this theoretical view could be expected to be the greatest, actual practice is utterly different. In particular, the various goals (for instance the profit goal, the market share goal, the inventory goal, etc.) are not reduced to a common denominator, and neither is there any significant attempt to compute trade-offs. Rather, each of these (and other) goals act as *independent constraints* which have *all* to be met for a solution to be satisfactory (Cyert and March, 1963, p. 41). These goals are rank ordered for search and emergency purposes. They have critical values—at times an acceptable range bounded by lower and upper critical values. The disruption of these values evokes corrective standard operating procedures (Cyert and March, pp. 113; 123; 150-161).

The process by which goals are made salient rests on the action or reaction of the members of the organization (e.g., heads of various departments—sales, production, advertisement, accountancy, etc.) who are responsible for, or especially affected by, the manner in which a particular goal is achieved. Because in such a process all the organizational goals are never simultaneously evoked, and because the subset of those that are evoked in any particular instance act only as constraints, the procedure does not yield optimum solutions, nor does it necessarily remove all or most inconsistencies among conflicting goals—hence the name of the principle. In Cyert and March's words:

> We have argued that the goals of a business firm are a series of more or less independent constraints. . . . Goals arise in such a form because the firm is, in fact, a coalition of participants with disparate demands,

changing foci of attention, and limited ability to attend to all organizational problems simultaneously.

... because of the form of the goals and the way in which they are established conflict is never fully resolved within an organization. Rather, the decentralization of decision making (and goal attention), the sequential attention to goals, and the adjustment in organizational slack permit the business firm to make decisions with inconsistent goals under many (and perhaps most) conditions (Cyert and March, 1963, p. 43).

As the case of chess has demonstrated, such a goal structure and its related decision-making procedure can be rigorously formalized. The empirical feasibility and power of doing so in the case of organizations will be illustrated shortly.

UNCERTAINTY AVOIDANCE

Just as the firm bypasses the need to establish a well-defined preference order for outcomes, so it does not attempt to compute probabilities. Rather, it avoids the need to estimate risks by replacing computations with feedbacks, and by endeavoring to arrange for itself a *negotiated environment.* Thus:

[O]ur studies indicate [that] ... organizations avoid uncertainty: (1) They avoid the requirement that they correctly anticipate events in the distant future by using decision rules emphasizing short-run reaction to short-run feedback rather than anticipation of long-run uncertain events. They solve pressing problems rather than develop long-run strategies. (2) They avoid the requirement that they anticipate future reactions of other parts of their environment by arranging a negotiated environment. They impose plans, standard operating procedures, industry tradition, and uncertainty-absorbing contracts on that environment. In short, they achieve a reasonably manageable decision situation by avoiding planning where plans depend on predictions of uncertain future events and by emphasizing planning where the plans can be made self-confirming through some control device (Cyert and March, 1963, p. 119).

In order to avoid a possible misunderstanding about the role of feedback, it should be noted that long-term strategies, plans, and expectations are present in almost all firms. The point made by Cyert and March, however, is that actual production decisions come to be made on the basis of ongoing (i.e., daily or weekly) feedback reports. Thus:

Consider, for example, the production-level decision. In most models of output determination, we introduce expectations with respect to future sales and relate output to such predictions. Our studies indicate, to the contrary, that organizations use only gross expectations about future sales in the output decision. They may, and frequently do, forecast sales and develop some long-run production plans on paper, but the actual production decisions are more frequently dominated by day-to-day and week-to-week feedback data from inventory, recent sales, and salesmen.

This assumption of a "fire department" organization is one of the most conspicuous features of our models. Under a rather broad class of situations, such behavior is rational for an organization having the goal structure we have postulated. Under an even broader set of situations, it is likely to be the pattern of behavior that is learned by an organization dealing with an uncertain world and quasi-resolved goals. It will be learned because by and large it will permit the organization to meet the demands of the members of the coalition [i.e., the collection of goals] (Cyert and March, 1963, p. 119).

Quite clearly, this mode of operation brings to mind the cybernetic model of decision-making. The similarity becomes even more pronounced when the two other general heuristics are considered. This can now be done very concisely.

PROBLEMISTIC SEARCH

This is the principle according to which search is originated by a problem and depressed by a solution. The major characteristic of problemistic search is that it is simple-minded, i.e., in general the search is in the vicinity of both the problem symptom and available alternatives. Evaluations are in terms of the notion of "feasibility" rather than elaborate computations or forecasts. The predominant form of a problem symptom is a failure or anticipated failure on some goal indicator. This triggers the "simple-minded" problemistic search until lack of success necessitates a more complex search (Cf., Cyert and March, 1963, p. 121).

ORGANIZATIONAL LEARNING

This principle is especially important for understanding the nature of organizational problem solving. For the purpose at hand its essential characteristics are as follows: Organizations accumulate experience. This experience takes selectively the form of positive and negative precedents, which are often idiosyncratic to the organization. These precedents, in turn, are relied upon and used as analogies; the point is that in most cases these constitute the device by which organizations can, and in fact do, avoid engaging in the kind of decision-making that the analytical paradigm assumes.

THE HEURISTICS IN OPERATION

In short then, the behavioral image of the firm which emerges is that of an organization having, among others, the following characteristics:

(1) It monitors and solves problems in terms of one or few goals (at any one time).
(2) The goals are evoked by failure or anticipated failure of their critical values.
(3) This evocation rests on the monitoring of (short-run) feedback.
(4) Problem solving, should it be required, then takes the form of a simple-minded search for solutions. In particular, remedies are looked for in the vicinity of the problem symptoms and among available alternatives; past experiences are relied upon as precedents to provide solutions by analogy; the acceptability of the solutions—predominantly standard operating procedures—is determined by the degree to which they meet the critical values of the relevant goals conceived as constraints, i.e., by the extent to which they are "feasible" rather than by how they fit with an optimum solution.

It should be emphasized that these characteristics are held to hold true "as a rule," that is, in the sense of being the privileged mode of operation as discussed in Chapter 8.

After abstracting this general model from their studies, Cyert and March proceeded to test it. The operationalization carried out for this purpose (for a department in a large retail department store) involves numerous steps, among them the following:

(1) identification of goals and of their critical values;
(2) identification of feed-back loops, in particular their time-lag;
(3) retrieval of standard operation procedures;
(4) formalization of the general heuristics;
(5) investigation and formalization of individual heuristics.

This operationalization is reported in great detail in Cyert and March (1963, Chapter 7) and the reader is invited to consult this work for specifics. To illustrate the nature of the empirical task performed, the following example will suffice as the previous discussions make it a simple matter to generalize from it.

Thus, one decision-making procedure involved the task of estimating (conservatively) future sales, the result being used to place advance orders. The heuristic was inferred from observation, although there was no evidence that the head of the department was aware of the rule of thumb that he was actually using (he did not describe his behavior in such terms). The procedure had the following form: "The estimate for the next six months is equal to the total of the corresponding six months of the previous year minus one-half of the sales achieved during the last month of the previous six-month period" (Cyert and March, 1963, p. 134).

After retrieving in such fashion the needed heuristics and estimating the parameters required for completing the model, the authors proceeded to embed it in a program. Indeed, "the natural theoretical language for describing a process involving these phenomena is the language of a computer program." The reason, already noted, is that while the heuristic and cybernetic conceptualization of the decision-making process is amenable, in part at least, to a representation and a solution by other means, it is most conveniently and naturally represented as a flow chart (cf., Cyert and March, 1963, p. 125). In particular, such a chart fulfills in the actual decision-making process a function which is similar to that fulfilled by the organizational chart in representing lines of authority. In the case of information-processing and decision-making tasks, however, the chart has the advantage of being easily made not only as detailed, but also as operative as one wishes it and its computer program equivalent to be.

Turning now to the findings themselves, Cyert and March used one set of data to develop their model (made of submodels) and another to test it; the model attempted to follow and capture the decision-making process that lead to output and price determination. The following results pertaining to the submodels of price determination illustrate the general nature of the findings:

Mark-up. . . .
    The definition of a correct prediction was made as stringent as possible. Unless the predicted price matched the actual price to the exact penny, the prediction was classified as incorrect. The results of the test were encouraging; of the 197 predicted prices, 188 were correct and 9 were incorrect. Thus 95 per cent of the predictions were correct. An investigation of the incorrect predictions showed that with minor modifications the model could be made to handle the deviant cases. However, at this point it was felt that the predictive power was good enough so that a further expenditure of resources in this direction was not justified.
    Sale pricing. In order to test the model, a random sample of 58 sales items was selected from the available records. For each item the appropriate information as determined by the model was used as an input to the computer. The output was in the form of a price that was a prediction of the price that would be set by the buyer. Again we used the criterion that to be correct the predicted price must match the actual price to the penny. Out of the 58 predictions made by the model, 56 (or 96 per cent) were correct.
    Mark-downs. . . .

The test for a correct prediction was as before—correspondence to the penny of the predicted and the actual price. A total sample of 159 items was selected and predictions made of the mark-down price for each item. Of the 159 prices predicted, 140 were correct predictions by our criterion and 19 were wrong. This gives a record of 88 per cent correct—the poorest of the three models. Though this model doesn't do as well as the other two, its record is, in our view, adequate (Cyert and March, 1963, p. 147).

Quite clearly, these results bear out the expectations that the theoretical discussion has raised. But whereas the findings have little surprise value in themselves, a few remarks are nonetheless in order.

First, it should be noted that Cyert and March's models are much more complex than those pertaining to the individual level of analysis which were discussed in Part II. This introduces a potential element of imprecision in the sense of the possible diffusion of modeling errors among the various elements and levels of the model. On the other hand, the fact that we are dealing with social (organizational) decision-making rather than with an individual process should be expected to increase the reliability of the retrieved components of the model. Indeed, because of the need for orderly and predictable working relationships, the norms and sanctions of an institution always attempt to foster consistency through conformity. In terms of their reliable assessment and retrieval, the institutional and institutionalized heuristics (i.e., standard operating procedures, and role-implemented heuristics) can therefore be expected to stand to personal heuristics in the same relationship (function-ally, rather than statistically) as the latter stand to statistical averages in a noninstitutionalized setting. Because of the accuracy with which repetitive individual heuristics can be estimated, there is clearly a ceiling to this advan-tage. The results are consequently a rather strong test of the feasibility and robustness of the generalization of the approach to organizational decision-making, despite the often feared pitfall of diffusion of errors due to model-ing. The reason for this robustness is rather straightforward and is directly related to the usefulness of the heuristic viewpoint as a theoretical rationale for merging the modeling methodology with the substantive process under discussion. Let us briefly examine why this is the case.

Consider the two following experiments carried out by Cyert and March to justify one aspect of their theory of the firm. The first was addressed to the question of the generation of errors in the sense of possible systematic biases in decision-making. In addition to unreliability, it is not unlikely that local-ized interests (e.g., those of a particular department) might influence how assessments and decisions are made and transmitted to other parts of the organization. Not surprisingly, this was found to be the case (Cyert and March, 1963, pp. 67-71). Building on this rather obvious finding, Cyert and

March then proceeded in their second experiment to attempt to study the law of composition of these errors, i.e., the process of diffusion of errors in complex human systems of decision-making. To their great surprise, they found that there was no such diffusion. Indeed, under a variety of arrangements of conflicting interests, the finding was that there was no persistent difference in final output among the different groups; after the participants had become socialized to their respective decision-making system, the systems themselves looked alike in terms of performance. The explanation of the phenomenon ex post facto strikes one as being rather obvious:

> [A]fter the fact . . . it seems clear that in an organization of individuals having about the same intelligence, adaptation to the falsification of data occurs fast enough to maintain a more or less stable organizational performance. For the bulk of our subjects in both experiments, the idea that estimates communicated from other individuals should be taken at face value (or that their own estimates would be so taken) was not really viewed as reasonable. *For every bias, there was a bias discount* (Cyert and March, 1963, p. 77; emphasis added).

This counterbiasing corrective mechanism led Cyert and March to disregard the communication variable in their theory of the firm. For the present purpose this same mechanism has another theoretical interest. By modeling the actual heuristic process of organizational decision-making, rather than a superimposed normative abstraction of it, it is worth bearing in mind that *this self-correcting process is itself modeled.* Theoretically, therefore, diffusion of errors in a large model can be limited to measurement errors rather than being compounded by the far greater danger of the composition of errors due to an artificial conceptualization of the referent process. It could be of course, and the discussion in Chapter 8 gives grounds to expect that this self-correcting process might at times be found wanting. But as noted in Chapter 2, in such a case the problem lies in the referent system itself, and the theoretically quasi-isomorphic approach to modeling decision-making that we are discussing is precisely a means to uncover and help correct this kind of shortcoming.

Another problem can be stated as follows: because the heuristics and feedbacks in the model deal exclusively with short-run daily decision-making, the question arises as to how valid and useful the kind of modeling effort discussed may be over time; the effort might indeed amount to creating a time-bound photograph and nothing more. The problem of the time scale which makes modeling useful is an important one, and will be dealt with later. As we shall see, it can be reduced to the question of the rate of procedural changes in an organization, and of their significance for output determination (as measured by sensitivity analysis). In the present case some important anchoring procedures (for model output determination) have been found to have remained unchanged for periods of over 40 years (cf., Cyert and March, 1963, p. 138). A moment of reflection shows that this should not be unexpected, especially if one takes into consideration the complex interdependences which exist in large organizations. As a consequence of the cost, the complexity, and the ramifications of genuine transformations, important changes are likely to be made on rare occasions, and then only as a last resort. Under such circumstances, routinized procedures may have both a degree and a rate of inertia which can easily be overlooked. The next study to be considered will illustrate and document the extent to which this is the case.

AN AGGREGATE STUDY

This study by Davis, Dempster, and Wildavsky (1966) is important on several counts.

The first is substantive. The research deals with the process of budgeting in governmental bureaucracies. As such it provides a first conceptual generalization toward processes of decision-making which are not readily quantifiable, at least as far as the independent variables are concerned. At the same time, the fact that the dependent variable is numeric in natural form permits a strong test of the modeling effort.

The second is that the study is longitudinal; it covers a fifteen year period (1948-1962), and therefore allows one to test the usefulness of model building for more than short-term purposes.

The third is that the process of budgeting involves a strategic encounter (in the game theory sense) between the units which make a given request (e.g., agencies), and the authority which must approve it (e.g., Congress). The feasibility of retrieving the heuristics of the parties to an institutionalized relationship involving strategies can therefore be examined.

The study itself can be concisely described as follows: It is based on sixty-four federal agencies and subagencies—over half of all the nondefense federal agencies at that time. Its theoretical approach is derived from Wildavsky (1964), who had documented that the officials and role-incumbents who are faced by a deadline and by a quantity and complexity of information which is humanly unmanageable respond in a predictable manner—they simplify the decision-making task by using rules of thumb. As Parkinson's example in Chapter 5 has illustrated, the more complex and the less manageable a task, the simpler we can expect the heuristic decision-making principle to be. Not surprisingly, therefore, Wildavsky found that in the case at hand only two important heuristic principles appeared to be operative. These were the *base*—the last appropriation as a base for computing the new request in terms of a relatively fixed percentage of this base—and the principle of *fair share*—the notion that variations in this percentage should be related to the overall size of the federal budget. In general—although with different views about the proper size of the percentage that should result from these considerations—both sides of the budgeting encounter were found by Wildavsky to rely on them for decision-making.

With regard to the strategies, two are of special importance; they can be described as follows: An agency can choose whether or not to "pad" its budget, and similarly Congress can relate to a request with or without the suspicion that this was the case. Additional strategies are of course possible, and Davis, Dempster, and Wildavsky (1966, pp. 63-132) investigated others as well. The interested reader is referred to this paper for further details about them and about the study as a whole.

The analyses were carried out by means of multiple regressions, much as in the case of the MMPI task discussed in Chapter 6. What had to be empirically estimated for curve-fitting was the size and sign of the b coefficients of such variables as the base. The multiple correlations between the appropriations predicted on the basis of the linear regression models and the actual appropriations are a measure of the predictability of the decision-making process—in this case conceptualizing it in terms of its dependence on the notions (cues) of base, fair share, and on the strategies of "padding" and "discounting."

The results of the study—the size of the multiple correlations—are summarized in Table 9.1. These findings deserve a few comments.

In the first place, it is evident that the magnitude of the correlations confirms what is now a standard expectation. Specifically, the last column of Table 9.1 indicates that over 90 percent of the correlations have a value of .85 or more, the worst fit occurring in the case of the agencies, with only slightly more than five-sixths having a value of .85 or more (see column 2). The reader interested in an analysis of the deviant cases is referred to Wildavsky (1975).

TABLE 9.1: Degree of Predictability of Budget Requests and Appropriations

| R Values | Frequency of Correlation Coefficients | | | | | |
| | Agency-Bureau Requests | | Congressional Appropriations | | Total | |
	N	(%)	N	(%)	N	(%)
.95-1.00	28	(.46)	55	(.82)	83	(.65)
.90-.94	12	(.20)	8	(.12)	20	(.16)
.85-.89	11	(.18)	2	(.03)	13	(.10)
Less than .85	10	(.16)	2	(.03)	12	(.09)
	61	(1.00)	67	(1.00)	128	(1.00)

Source: After Davis, Dempster, and Wildavsky (1966, Table 2, p. 83).

Secondly, it should be noted that these results are based on only one of the two heuristics discussed earlier. The notion of fair share appears to play little or no role when the budgeting process is studied at the aggregate level as it is in this study (cf., Davis, Dempster, and Wildavsky, 1966, p. 87). While this level of analysis is likely to conceal subprocesses, it also shows how robust and powerful the heuristic approach is across levels of analysis, especially for complex phenomena of repetitive institutionalized decision-making. As elaborated in Part II, this is to be expected because the heuristic perspective is likely to be the more fruitful the more complex and institution-alized a decision-making process is. Indeed, while individual rules of thumb tend to be simple and few in number, institutional rules of thumb to be widely shared—as they have to be for a routinized process of hierarchical bargaining to be predictable—are likely to require a further simplification, and the data are consistent with the assumption that they do undergo such a simplification.

Thirdly, it should be noted that these correlations are those that obtain after the best specification of the strategies which characterize the mutual relation-ship between each agency and Congress has been empirically determined (cf. Davis, Dempster, and Wildavsky, p. 82, Table 1). As it turns out, however, in the majority of the cases (over 60%) there is no strategy in either case. Perhaps because most agencies have learned that strategies are useless, they do not engage in "gaming behavior," and Congress responds in kind. In an additional 35 percent of the cases the authors found that "padding" and "discounting" are part of the agency-Congress relationship. It is noteworthy, however, that in this occurrence the relationship appears to be asymmetrical. In none of the instances where Congress seems to have suspected "padding" was there, in fact, any such detectable attempt, and conversely, in all the cases where such an attempt was made, the agency appears to have gotten away with it—perhaps because of a particularly propitious political constellation for specific new programs. The point of special importance is, of course, that the iron law of simple and predictable organizational heuristics is once more in evidence, this time in the presumably much more complex case of strategic encounters.

Lastly, the authors further analyzed the data to search for possible underlying shifts in the decision rules over time. They found that over a fifteen year period such shifts do occur. On conceptual grounds, the shifts may stem from slow and incremental changes or from an abrupt change in policy at a certain point. The authors did not attempt to distinguish through analytical procedures which of these processes accounted for most changes. However, by examining the points in time at which a shift became noticeable, they found that: (1) in most cases, there was only one shift during the fifteen years; and (2) the bulk of these changes occurred in the years 1954 and 1955, that is, during the first two budgets of the Eisenhower administration. Specifically, 46 percent and 70 percent of the shifts for the agencies and Congress, respectively, were concentrated in these two years (Davis, Dempster, and Wildavsky, 1966, Table 5, p. 84). In short, decision rules appear to have a fair degree of stability, especially if one takes into consideration the fact that genuine policy changes do not bear on the issue of whether or not the kind of modeling discussed is useful. To put it differently, while incremental and policy shifts do occur, the fact that only one modal shift was detectable in a relatively large sample and over a 15 year period lends strong empirical support to the proposition that institutionalized decision-making rules are rather stable.

Transitional Remarks

The aim of the preceding section was to illustrate the robustness, feasibility, time-scale relevance, and usefulness of applying the heuristic approach to the organizational level of repetitive decision-making. In particular, Cyert and March's work has shown the usefulness of the application of the information-processing approach for modeling the behavior of the firm. In the process they have developed a theory of heuristic organizational decision-making which is very broad, and their book can consequently be regarded as required reading for the reader interested in deepening and operationalizing his understanding of the approach discussed here. At the same time, their specific aim was to apply the approach to the short-run behavior of firms, and their methodology was essentially that of case-studies. Davis, Dempster, and Wildavsky, on the other hand, showed that governmental bureaucracies demonstrably handle budgeting decisions according to simple heuristic principles. In the process they generalized the approach to a domain of decision-making where the quantification of the independent variables is not generally viewed as naturally numeric, and beyond the level of case-studies. As a means of investigation, they chose the aggregate level of analysis. They did so because, although their approach was heuristic, they elected to use econometrics as their methodology (and pursuing this method, their later work on the federal budgeting process branches off from the heuristic conceptualization and takes the form of a full-fledged econometric model; see Wildavsky, 1975). But the aim of these studies was illustrative, and their similarity and relevance to the theme of this book are more important than are some differences.

In the research we shall consider next, the strengths of both studies are to some degree merged. Specifically, the study to be discussed is again longitudinal and about the process of governmental budgeting, in this case in three cities. At the same time, the approach is not aggregative but genuinely heuristic, as is that of Cyert and March. More important, the study goes beyond the point of demonstrating that bureaucratized organizations are systems of decision-making which are modelable. In so doing, the study raises issues and provides findings which are central to some of the topics of this essay.

Bureaucratized Decision-Making: A Programmed View

The study to be considered is that of Crecine (1969). Its explicit purpose was to generalize the approach of Cyert and March and the work of Davis, Dempster, and Wildavsky to the case of lower-echelon governmental decision-making. The study involves three municipalities, Cleveland, Detroit, and Pittsburgh. Each municipality was modeled in detail in terms of its hierarchy (council, mayor, and departments), its subdivisions (forty-four to sixty-four departments and administrative units in each case), and its budgeting decisions (for instance, in the case of Detroit, for each of the decision-making units, the model generates specific decisions about administrative and non-administrative salaries, materials, supplies and expenses, and equipment and repairs, which can then be aggregated). The model takes the form of a flow chart and a computer program, and, as in the case of Cyert and March's study, describes the short-run decision-making process. Crecine's research covers a time span which ranges from one to ten years according to the cities and subunits considered; its modal time span is about seven years (Crecine, 1969, pp. 44 and 114). It should be noted, however, that the model was developed and then tested on the same set of data. This procedure was adopted in part to avoid the otherwise inescapable problem of underidentification due to insufficient data (for instance, for the Detroit municipality alone, 913 parameters had to be estimated) and in part because the purpose of the study was to demonstrate that the heuristic approach in combination with the computer simulation methodology is adequate to capture and regenerate in great detail the bureaucratic decision-making process. In this connection, should the task of modeling the *process*—which is primarily what Crecine's study is about—be inaccurately carried out (taking into account both the fact that the simulation runs over several simulated years and that the subprocesses in each decision period are short-run and very detailed), a given set of input data might be expected to generate a longitudinal diffusion of errors and end up producing a very poor fit with the actual data (Crecine, 1969, p. 138). This becomes even more evident if one takes into consideration that, in addition to being very detailed, the heuristic model was identical (for theoretical reasons) in the case of all three municipalities, with only parameter changes.

With this background in mind, Crecine's overall findings about the adequacy of his detailed modeling effort are summarized in Table 9.2. This table presents the correlations between the output generated by the process model after several simulated years and the corresponding actual appropriations.

These findings, impressive as they are, are by now of little informative value. It is worth noting, however, that according to the principle that the more careful and precise the observation and measurement of a phenomenon, the more strongly observable it should be in a study, the results of Crecine's research (which is the most detailed of those reviewed) are what one would expect them to be. Additionally, they are also compatible with what follows from the observation that, for the reasons discussed earlier in this chapter, what is lost in measurement simplicity by moving from the individual level of analysis to the more complex social one appears to be offset by the greater regularity generated by the conformity imposed by an institutional setting and by the specific bureaucratic requirement to adhere carefully to standard operating procedures.

The point of importance, however, is that on the basis of our previous discussion, there is a theoretical quasi-isomorphism between the heuristic conceptualization of repetitive bureaucratic decision-making as a clerically implemented program, on the one hand, and its flow chart formalization on the other. This consideration, together with the recurrently demonstrable empirical efficiency of the modeling efforts, lead to a conclusion of great importance: the kind of modeling discussed appears to fall conceptually in the category of *computing simulations* (in the sense discussed in Chapter 2), *and could therefore be used as such.*

This is precisely what Crecine did next. First he considered the residual variance, a task which is commonly engaged in. But as a rule, including the case of Cyert and March, and Davis, Dempster, and Wildavsky, this residual variance is examined primarily for the purpose of discovering inaccuracies in the model.

Because in the present instance the model is conceptually (both with a high degree of accuracy, and down to some reasonable level of detail) a computer program about a clerically implemented one, Crecine went one step further. He conceptualized the residuals not as (or rather, not only as) statistical errors, but primarily as the *nonprogrammed* residuals of the municipalities' process of decision-making. In this light, the deviations are conceived

TABLE 9.2: Fit Between Modeled and Actual Budgeting Decisions

	Cleveland	Detroit (with welfare)	Detroit (without welfare)	Pittsburgh
Correlation (R)	.9933	.9329	.9754	.9955

Source: After Crecine (1969, p. 117, Table VIII-1).

as giving a measure of the mismatches due both to unusual decisions and to the slow incremental change of rules over time noted by Davis, Dempster, and Wildavsky. The intriguing question which arises is what part of the small residual variance we have to consider (which perforce includes also some unavoidable modeling limitations and measurement errors) is due to genuinely nonprogrammed decisions, and what part stems from an over-time drift; the latter is what can be expected to differentiate a social organization from a machine, and it sets the theoretical limit to the quasi-isomorphism which is achievable. On the other hand, the greater the number of nonprogrammed decisions which contribute to the small residual variance that obtains, the more useful and valid is the social computer conceptualization. Indeed, as Newell and Simon (1959, quoted by Crecine, 1969, p. 112) have noted for the individual level of analysis, "If the program makes the same analysis as the humans, notices the same traps, then we will infer, and properly, that down to some level of detail, the program provides an explanation of the human process."

Applying the same reasoning to the organizational level of analysis, Crecine found exactly this kind of additional supportive evidence. Thus:

> If we make the reasonable assumption that the decisions people talk about are those that run counter to expectations, those that need justifying, the explicit analysis of model residuals can contribute to our knowledge of the model's goodness-of-fit and, more importantly, validity. Quite by accident, while trying to attach reasons to particular model deviations, it was discovered that the mayor's budget messages were the best sources of information, by a wide margin. Observing that the text of these budget messages refers only to a small percentage of the budgetary decisions, it became apparent that the actual decision system (mayor) was identifying nearly the same set of decisions as being "different," as was our formal model (by generating large errors or residuals). This observation is submitted as additional evidence that the computer model adequately describes the budgetary decision process. The large deviations that are sometimes found are not "random" in the usual sense; they bear a strong correlation with the "deviant cases" identified by mayors (Crecine, 1969, p. 165).

In other words, as was anticipated on theoretical grounds and on the basis of recurrent empirical tests, conceptualizing bureaucratic decision-making as a clerically implemented program appears to be a fundamentally sound proposition. In this connection it may be noted that there seems to be a parallel between the nature and form of the misperception concerning individual repetitive decision-making, on the one hand, and the one which appears to exist for the same process at the organizational level, on the other. As the reader may recall, we have noted in Chapter 6 one likely explanation for the fact that, intuition to the contrary, individual repetitive decision-making is very efficiently modelable (paramorphically) with few cues. To repeat this explanation: "Possibly our feeling that we can take into account a host of different factors comes about because, although we remember that at some time or other we have attended to each of the different factors, we fail to notice that it is seldom more than one or two that we consider at any one time" (Shepard, 1964, p. 266).

In a similar vein, it would appear that unusual events and the dynamics of coalitions and power structures may divert our attention from the stuff that bureaucracies are really made of, i.e., their every-day operations or, to rephrase what has been said in Chapter 1, the ongoing routine process which unfolds "in between" crises of one kind or another and really turns out to control output. To illustrate concretely the manner in which the misperception I am alluding to can easily come about in the case of bureaucratic decision-making, consider a hypothetical example. Imagine, for instance, a secretary of H.E.W. who elects to initiate or reorganize a number of programs of his choice and to reallocate for this purpose several billions of dollars during one single year—a feat that might well represent the limit of a secretary's power. Such behavior is likely to give rise in the eyes of the public and the members of the department to an image of a high degree of organizational freedom, great personal power, and perhaps also of unpredictability. But although such changes may affect most significantly the lives of thousands of people, as well as the future course of the bureaucracy, and therefore command great attention, the consideration of primary importance is that in a system whose annual budget is on the order of 100 billions, this degree of choice is merely incremental; indeed, for yearly output determination, it verges on the irrelevant, and would only yield a residual from the programmed and predetermined output of the system which would be of an order of magnitude comparable to the size of the residuals that we have discussed. Put differently, the point is that while a theory of the behavior of the policy-making level of bureaucratic organizations is obviously important, the kind of theory under discussion emerges as one whose importance rests on the fact that it deals with processes which appear to control upward of 90 percent of the output of decision-making bureaucracies—whether we are generally aware of it or not.

Having shown by the analysis of residuals just discussed that his model falls conceptually and empirically in the category of what we have called computing simulations, Crecine proceeded next to perform a series of theoretical runs (sensitivity analyses). This produced a series of results which may justifiably be regarded as the first elements of a genuine theory of routinized bureaucratic decision-making. The major findings can be briefly summarized in two points:

(1) It appears that the bureaucratic decision-making system is extremely insensitive to internal changes of parameters (cf., Crecine, 1969, p. 176). This result is unlikely to be idiosyncratic—it has been replicated in a model of the process of municipal zoning decisions in Pittsburgh (cf., Davis and Rueter, 1970, pp. 41-57. This heuristic model yields incidentally the same kind of fit with the process modeled—above 90 percent—as do the examples that we have discussed).

This surprising finding naturally raises important issues. In particular, it suggests that for output determination the bureaucratic decision-making rules and procedures are very redundant and/or robust to the level of the constraints imposed on decisions by the standard operating procedures. It is the *nature* and *substance* of the decision-making procedures and criteria, rather than their coefficients, which appear to be of primary importance. We find here an intriguing similarity between what is found at the individual level of analysis when decisions are paramorphically modeled (see Dawes and Corrigan, 1974; Wainer, 1976; see also the discussion in Chapter 11) and bureaucratic organizations. The implications of this finding and the issue it raises for the problem of organizational inertia obviously deserve further investigations. But as it stands, the result invites a related question which leads to the second of Crecine's major findings:

(2) If the bureaucratized process of decision-making is largely insensitive to the internal changes which would be expected to affect its output significantly, the question arises whether it is responsive to its external environment.

   As it turns out, the answer is simple: yes—but basically through *one* major mechanism: the size of the revenue at the disposal of the bureaucracy. In Crecine's words: *"The primacy of the revenue constraint in the reallocation of resources is the major finding of this chapter* [on sensitivity analysis]" (Crecine, 1969, p. 185; the emphasis is retained from the original).

In other words, the image of the bureaucratized process of decision-making which emerges is that of a program in action whose clerical implementation—perhaps through processes similar in their consequences to the bias-bias discount mechanism discussed earlier—makes its output essentially dependent on the *extent* to which it can run, that is, on the extent to which it can carry out certain activities (through revenue dependence), rather than on the *level* at which it can run (as operationalized by the insensitivity to internal parameters changes).

It is noteworthy that contrary to the prevalent image about decision-making bureaucracies—that the policy-making level makes many attempts to influence the organization of which it is in charge—the preceding findings suggest that to a large extent these attempts are either futile or not enacted. From a different perspective, one could justifiably hold that while bureaucracies are commonly perceived as being resistant to change, and at times machine-like, the *extent* to which this appears to be the case, and especially the degree to which they appear to be unresponsive to pressures from their internal and external environments, reaches almost unintelligible proportions. In this respect, Crecine notes several processes which explain the inertia observed, and which at the same time cast light on some reasons that may account for the prevalent misperception. Three of these processes are worth mentioning:

(1) *The complexity of changes.* This fact explains the insensitivity to external pressures just noted (except through the revenue constraint or in cases of genuine crises). The underlying explanatory mechanism is that the process of public allocation of resources is such that satisfying one demand would almost always imply that all similar demands would also have to be satisfied. This, in turn, would make necessary either a change in the decision-making rules or a complete revision of the yearly budget or both. The magnitude of such a task creates resistance to direct influences which, except for marginal cases (for output determination), yields the kind of results that we have discussed.

(2) *Ordering of servicing-queues.* The image of influentials exerting political or social pressures may nonetheless contain an element of truth. Indeed, while absolute levels and kinds of expenditures (and the underlying decision-rules) have a program-like quality of reproducibility, the bureaucracy has nonetheless a large degree of freedom which, although of limited importance for output determination, may explain the feeling that it is responsive to power pressures. Specifically, a bureaucracy can modify the quantity and quality of its services; more important, it can modify its attention rules, in the sense of *priority orderings.* That is, within stable decision rules concerning, for instance, what streets will be repaired, a question about which department heads usually have a large degree of freedom and might therefore be responsive to pressure is: which street will be repaired *first*? Hence the principle: "*Response to political pressures and elite influences takes the form of a change in departmental attention rules rather than a change in budget level*" (Crecine, 1969, p. 189; the emphasis is retained from the original). Put differently, one important source of the prevailing misperception is that what is *commonly* influenceable in bureaucracies is *which request* will be processed first—not *what* kind of request will be granted.

(3) *The consequences of the quasi-resolution of conflicts.* As we have seen, within the constraints set by the revenue, the process of decision-making and resource allocation is basically (and under normal

circumstances, almost exclusively) controlled from within. Under conditions of quasi-resolution of conflict, and in times of affluence, this internal control appears to take a form that reminds one of the trading of votes in Congress. Thus, it could be held that "the budget is really a set of transactions between departments where attention to one department's goals in one period is traded for attention to another department's goals in a preceding period" (Crecine, 1969, p. 198). This process, of which Crecine found some evidence, is also, of course, compatible with the underlying theoretical concept of a sequential—attention—to—goals, and empirically with the slow over-time drift recurrently observed in the studies we have discussed.

Furthermore, a moment of thought shows that under conditions of scarcity, the same process yields a principle which can be stated as follows: *under conditions of revenue stability, the greater the conflict within a bureaucracy, the greater the inertia, provided the strength of the partners remains roughly equal.* This would seem to account for what Crecine notes about the behavior of the internal shares of the defense department (Crecine, 1969, p. 227, footnote 10), and perhaps more generally about what is sometimes found in political systems. It is in any event a process that Cyert and March have anticipated, and to which Crecine subscribes: "Where resource rationing is necessary, we expect ... a tendency to use arbitrary allocation rules that maintain the relative positions of the members of the coalition" (Cyert and March, 1963, p. 270, quoted by Crecine, 1969, p. 198).

In other words, given these external and internal dynamics, the bureaucracy emerges as an organization which normally behaves in computer-like fashion, and which, to the extent that it responds to political pressures, does so very slowly and incrementally. Furthermore, it follows from the logic of these dynamics that the major pressure group which might be in a position to significantly affect the workings and output of a bureaucracy—to the limited extent to which it can be systematically affected—is its own membership. Under such an assumption, one major concern of this group—salary increases—is directly predictable. This is precisely what Crecine found:

The analysis of unprogrammed budgetary changes ... demonstrated that most changes represented responses, not necessarily to demands of the general public but to other, more limited "publics" in the government's environment ... [within this environment] all municipalities in our sample seemed to be continuously responsive to the needs of their employees through periodic salary increases. . . . [As for the other demands:] Either the decision system is not responsive to general citizenry demands, needs, or problems, or the response is systematic, programmed, and periodic (and "explained" in our formal model) [Crecine, 1969, p. 234].

This then, is the image of the process of repetitive bureaucratic decision-making which obtains when it is comprehensively observed in action. A few general comments and some conclusions about this process are now in order.

Concluding Remarks

As might have been anticipated from the theoretical and empirical discussion, moving from the individual level of information-processing analysis to the organizational one has proved to be not only feasible but enlightening. In the process we have gained a useful complementary perspective on organizational decision-making. A few of the points made during the discussion and some of their implications deserve special emphasis.

In the first place, we have come full circle. What may have appeared at first sight an unlikely thesis—namely that theoretically bureaucracies can be looked upon as social computers—has now be shown to be validated to the point where it becomes a serious scientific proposition. One of its major consequences is that we are graphically reminded of the obvious: bureaucracies are, in the final analysis, the envelope and the instrument *within which* and *by means of which* the operations that they are set up to perform are carried out. In this light, the key conceptual element of interest is the set of standard operating procedures which are applied; the social context in which they are embedded may have a great degree of visibility and, especially if we are dealing with crises or deviant cases, may command great attention. But as in the case of a skin disturbance, the effect need not be more than skin-deep as far as the metabolism of the organism or organization is concerned. Whether this is so is obviously an empirical question. The same observation applies to the question of approach; under certain conditions, and for certain purposes, a perspective of management by crises may be the most useful framework of analysis. At the same time there are compelling theoretical reasons, and strong empirical evidence, to support the view that under a wide range of conditions—intuition to the contrary—the quasi-totality of the variance of the decision-making output of bureaucracies may be determined by the nature and structure of their standard operating procedures, rather than by the more visible but less influential (for output determination) power and social dynamics commonly focused on. A moment of thought shows that this should not come as a surprise; the principle of hierarchical accountability is, in fact, precisely aimed at ensuring that this should be the case. Together with the process of public accountability, this mechanism merely turns out to be much more effective *for overall output determination* than is generally expected.

If only on the basis of this result alone, it could justifiably be held that the information-processing approach and its conceptually related methodology put the whole process of bureaucratic decision-making in a new light. In the next chapter we shall consider the social problems that this new perspective raises and the reconceptualized sociological analyses that it makes salient. However, before we turn to this task, an epistemological question is worth raising: Given that the information-processing approach casts light on the quasi-totality of the variance of the decision-making output of bureaucracies, and given that all the findings and theoretical considerations which make up the perspective that we have discussed are well known, why does this viewpoint remain to this data so peripheral to the general consciousness, and in particular to that of the scientific community of sociologists, political scientists, and students of public organizations? Indeed, as an anonymous reviewer of a partial draft of this essay once noted, the "real focus of concern tends to be on refractory areas of decisions that cannot be routinized." Why should this be so?

It is of course impossible to answer this question in a few paragraphs. A few thoughts on the matter might, however, help to start the discussion and perhaps add to the confidence that the reasoning and the findings presented may have begun to inspire.

In the first place, it can be noted that we are faced with a paradox. On the one hand, we all share the feeling that as systems, bureaucracies are impersonal, unresponsive, and soulless—in short, robot-like organizations in many ways. At the same time we all *know,* both as individuals and as scientists, that they *are* influenceable. One major source of misperception has been discussed in the previous section. However, from an epistemological point of view, one might reason that it is not unlikely that this paradox may have led to a psychological fixation which makes it difficult to see the forest for the trees. Indeed, if we are not careful to look at the whole output of the system, our personal experience is likely to make individual instances salient; in similar fashion, our professional interest is likely to be attracted by cases which for one reason or another are *not* (or cannot be) normally processed, and about which there is nonetheless a sense that some degree of control is possible. The point is that under conditions of nearly total dependency on bureaucratic decision-making, it becomes rational for individuals to scrutinize the process and conditions which make it possible for a marginal or deviant case to be accepted and processed by the organization, and for the scientist to study the dynamics and lawfulness of the phenomena related to these peripheral dynamics. However, this focus, if not kept in perspective and checked against total output, under conditions of individual and scientific partial reinforcement by success, can not only divert our attention from the core of the process but, clearly, can also lead to a narrow focus on processes and cases which are marginal to the system's performance—at least on a time-scale graduated in years rather than longer periods of time. Should this be what actually takes place, then there are grounds to believe that we may have ended up developing a sociology of the *manpower* aspect of bureaucracies rather than a sociology of its core decision-making *function*. As it turns out, for society at large, as well as for disciplinary theory building, the latter may well be the more important task of the two. It is, in any case, a complementary effort which stands out as a challenge.

Should these general considerations be felt to have some validity, a few related observations come to mind. These derive from a reasoning *a contrario*. There are reasons which *should not* have kept us from seeing the forest. The lack of obvious explanation for the fact that they nonetheless appear to have played such a role may well constitute additional support for the argument developed to this point. At least these considerations would seem to undermine the confidence that one may justifiably have in the primacy of the current alternative conception. These reasons include Weber's clear theoretical statement about the essence of bureaucracies; the fundamental nature of human repetitive decision-making; and above all the body of empirical findings which have led to the consensual conclusion that organizational decision-making predominantly follows the principle of *incrementalism* (cf., Braybrooke and Lindblom, 1963). The essence of this principle has been well summarized by Dror:

> The basic idea of this model is that the more different an alternative is from past policies, the more difficult it is to predict its consequences. . . . Largely because of this fact, the more different an alternative is from past policies, the more difficult it is to recruit support for it, that is, the smaller its political feasibility is. Since radically innovative policies have a large chance of having unexpected and undesirable consequences and of being infeasible, this model says policymaking should be basically "conservative," and should limit innovations to marginal changes. . . . One point in this model's favor is that it describes actual decisionmaking behavior. . . . Most public policy in modern (but not all contemporary) societies is made by incremental changes in older policies. . . . [W]e can see why this model . . . has become rather popular (Dror, 1968, p. 144).

From the present point of view, this principle is of great importance, not because of what it teaches us (correctly, as the slow over-time drift documented in the previous sections indicates), but because of the light it casts on what its widespread use apparently conceals from our awareness. The converse of incrementalism, or the complement of a slow over-time drift, is obviously inertia. Quite naturally, once this fact is realized, the compelling question (both scope-wise and time-wise) becomes: how much so? For some psychological reason, following to its logical conclusion this tautological implication of the notion of incrementalism appears to be a difficult step to take. Once it is made, however, it does not come as a surprise that with the proper set of theoretical concepts and the appropriate methodology, and when the whole output of decision-making bureaucracies is systematically observed, the process of interest emerges as being exactly what it might have been expected to be on the basis of converging considerations. In fact, upon reflection, it becomes possible to entertain the hypothesis that under the empirical generalization subsumed by the notion of incrementalism, we may currently have a sociology, and a political and management science, concerned with the phenomena that the term exactly connotes—a body of knowledge which is primarily about the residuals of the process under discussion.

In this light, the epistemological question that I have raised in this section appears even more intriguing. One might ask why it is that Cyert and March's and Crecine's landmark studies have not started a disciplinary trend but have remained on the whole isolated efforts. A partial answer may be found in the comment made over ten years ago by the discussant of a paper presented by Crecine about his work:

> In summary, the paper includes a masterful description of the way that I *feel* budgeteers at the municipal level operate. The descriptive sections have a great deal of value to me as an instructor. It is well written and more thoroughly grounded in comparative analysis than a case study. Yet there remain lingering doubts about the meaning of these findings for municipalities generally. And beyond the immediate scope of Mr. Crecine's work, there are doubts about the findings of similar analyses at other levels of American government (Sharkansky, 1968, p. 148).

The discussions leading to this chapter have attempted to allevaite the kind of "lingering doubts" referred to in this quotation, which apparently make the obvious so difficult to see. Specifically, I have tried to show that on the basis of theoretical considerations and empirical findings which are well known but in somewhat compartmentalized disciplines, these doubts may be much less justified than they appear to be. At the same time it must be recognized that while these doubts are probably unjustified, they are nonetheless psychologically predictable, for the alternative perspective which emerges from the discussion may call for no less than a profound reorganization of some of our social perceptions. It is possible that for this purpose four elements may have been missing from the studies that we have reviewed in this chapter: (1) a clarification of the conditions under which systems analysis and model building may be out of step with social science knowledge; this enables one to anticipate a possible type of useful application; (2) a discussion of the fundamental soundness of this kind of application in terms of human information-processing theory; from this it follows that the modeling accuracy typically achieved is not accidental; (3) the theoretical linkage of the approach to its natural methodology through the axiomatic (rather than ad hoc) focus on repetitive decision-making, the required linking pin being provided by individual heuristics and their retrievability; and (4) a reexamination in the light of the approach of some premises and conceptions which might otherwise act as unwarranted cognitive shields.

To the extent that I have been successful in filling these possible gaps, the implications of the studies reviewed in this chapter can no longer be evaded.

PART FOUR

IMPLICATIONS

Chapter 10

ELEMENTS OF A PARADIGM

As we have seen, the conjunction of the information-processing approach, the computer-modeling methodology, and the reference to total output as a criterion of what the analyses explain, lead to empirical findings which put the process of bureaucratic decision-making in a completely new light. The resulting change of perspective has a number of implications. These translate into general considerations, theoretical issues, and research questions. In this chapter we shall consider some of them, and in so doing, add a few elements to the conceptual paradigm which has emerged from the previous discussions.

General Considerations

The reader may recall that I have argued that it may be feasible, useful, and necessary to model, and also perhaps computerize, certain processes of bureaucratic decision-making. Now that the feasibility and usefulness of the modeling endeavor has been documented (see also Cyert and March, 1963, pp. 284-292), a case remains to be made for its necessity. This is what I shall attempt to do in this section. The corresponding discussion about the computerization of part of the process of interest is undertaken in the chapter dealing with the future of bureaucracy.

Consider the studies reviewed in Chapter 9. They are conceptualized along a continuum at one end of which are processes of decision-making that rest on numeric input and output variables, while at the other they involve purely qualitative data. In this light Crecine's study stands midway between the quantitative pole illustrated by the work of Cyert and March, and the qualitative one which remains an unachieved and challenging disciplinary goal (cf., Crecine, 1969, p. viii). There is no doubt that this view is correct. Yet, conceptualizing the studies discussed in such a manner casts past developments, and those which are needed in the future, in a framework which is neither the only one nor necessarily the most fruitful for theoretical purposes. Indeed, the quantitative-qualitative continuum is basically a measurement one. This continuum must be further traveled to make the methodological progress that the approach still requires. At the same time, for purposes of theory development, the processes of bureaucratic decision-making might be more usefully conceptualized in terms of processes which are more directly related to the substance of social phenomena.

One conceptualization of this kind appears to be particularly pertinent for our purpose. It involves the notion of self-correcting processes, and deserves special attention.

From the point of view of self-correcting versus non-self-correcting processes (which as in the previous instance are the polar cases of a continuum), the studies discussed in Chapter 9 turn out to be exemplars of the same category. They all involve the direct effect of the market, or at least a constant and explicit bargaining relationship. As such, the bureaucratic decision-making processes modeled are to a large extent self-correcting, at least in terms of the interests directly or indirectly represented by the sides to the institutionalized encounters which regulate the one focal activity with which all three studies discussed deal, namely, *the process of allocation of resources.*

However, a moment of thought shows that another fundamental bureaucratic activity—*the process of classification*—might not be in so advantageous a structural situation. This process may or may not overlap those which are primarily qualitative in terms of their variables. But independent of whether or not there is such an overlap, it would seem that modeling this set of activities might be a very necessary task.

To see why this might be the case, it is useful to examine briefly the nature of classificatory tasks. This nature is best determined by examining the process of interest in a scientific context, but initially outside the scientific framework which normally applies. The point of this distinction will immediately become evident.

Consider the following hypothetical description of the development of a new scale, say about *anomie.* An investigator reports that he has developed a questionnaire on the basis of which he classifies respondents along this dimension. The questionnaire and the criteria of classification are the product of his experience, and he has discussed them in a number of meetings with experienced assistants. Furthermore, the scale has been used extensively with good results. In particular, the aides find the scale convenient to use, and most respondents accept the classification that results from its application. A few subjects do argue from time to time, but, in the opinion of the investigator, they do so because some people do not understand the scientific process. A mixture of flexibility in exceptional cases, some marginal changes in either the questionnaire or the criteria or both, and an overall policy of firmness has led to the present state of affairs: the coming into existence of a well-tried, workable, and systematic scheme (reliability over .90), by which thousands of people are constantly being classified.

The fruits of the author's labor—the questionnaire and the criteria of classification—are described in a paper which is submitted for publication. Needless to say, the paper is rejected at first sight.

This sketchy example, simplified on purpose, highlights by omission one fundamental property of the genuine scientific process: the need to specify the validity of a procedure by reference to an objective criterion. Once this is done, the mechanism of replications transforms the scientific enterprise into a self-correcting process.

The administrative process of classification, i.e., the structure of the bureaucratic process of development of forms and standard operating procedures, which is basically what has been described above in simplified and exaggerated manner, can easily fall between the self-correcting mechanisms which are built into a bargaining situation or into the scientific process. Specifically, while the level and the broad categories of the process of allocation of resources are ultimately related to, and held in check by, either the market as a criterion, or congressional review, the underlying scheme of classification upon which daily activities are based does not seem to benefit from such a safeguard. The same remark holds true in the case of processes of classification leading to accreditation, determination of elegibility, and selection (in particular of personnel), which do not necessarily impinge directly on the budgetary allocation of resources. In all such cases, unorganized and lagged feedback (through either public opinion causing congressional intervention, or ad hoc direct individual representations) seems to be the only type of weak and diffuse check imposed on this otherwise largely autonomous set of bureaucratic activities. Of course, categorization is at times a kind of decision-making activity which is no less subject to bargaining than the process of allocation of resources itself; and, conversely, below a certain level of generality the latter may be administratively determined in its quasi-totality.

The point, however, is that whether or not a bureaucratic process or subprocess of administrative decision-making is to a significant extent self-correcting (in the sense just discussed) is an empirical question. When it is, as for size and broad categories of budgeting it might be, modeling is feasible and useful. When it is not, as for numerous classificatory processes it might not be, modeling would appear to be necessary also. Stated differently, when some of the legitimate interests and parties affected by bureaucratic operations are devoid of systematic and effective means which enable them to check and review the administratively determined allocation of resources, or when an objective standard is unavailable (or is not used) to validate nonnegotiated classifications, the danger is great that a scholastic type of situation might develop. As the case of medieval science makes abundantly clear, should such a situation develop in a bureaucracy, it is likely to remain in effect for an indefinite period of time and to be characterized by a subculture of dogmas and accumulated experience. The derivations based on such premises are most likely to be validated by shared beliefs and consensual common sense, rather than by systematic observations or experimentation. Under such circumstances, a self-sustaining (and even expanding) body of "knowledge" can come to serve as an unquestioned, if ineffective, foundation for principles of action. Obviously, as long as the possible existence of such a situation is not investigated, there is no way to tell to what extent this may or may not be what actually happens in the case of non-self-corrective processes of bureaucratic decision-making. It seems clear, however, that in bureaucracies a scholastic type of situation runs the risk of rapidly degenerating into ritualism, with convenience of implementation acting as a major criterion for gauging the adequacy of many standard operating procedures. Under the minimal assumption that such a danger exists, modeling these formal and informal procedures—which, as a whole, appear to control the bulk of the output of decision-making bureaucracies—would appear to be a long overdue and very necessary task indeed.

Still another consideration suggests that the systematic kind of modeling under discussion should not be delayed too long. In particular, in addition to the probable need to break into otherwise inaccessible pockets of inbred and self-perpetuating processes whose objective justification is as likely as not to be anything *but* their output validity, the great explaining power of this kind of modeling may in itself make the endeavor necessary. It can be argued that this follows from the logic of the converse perspective which puts a disciplinary and substantive premium on upper-echelon policy-making rather than on repetitive decisions. Indeed, the rationale for this focus is to further our understanding of the mechanisms and dynamics which explain the manner in which social policies are made and implemented. But although intuitively it is generally realized that in social action, as in physical action, the notion of inertia is important, to date this observation has tended to take the form of a qualitative disclaimer, and consequently to remain somewhat peripheral to the core of the analyses themselves. However, given the magnitude of this property of decision-making in bureaucracies, and our ability to model this kind of activity, it would seem that keeping apart the complementary processes of policy-making and routine decision-making is no longer a useful approach, *especially from the point of view of policy-making*. Unless the study of policy-making is regarded as largely a gratuitous activity, it appears difficult to avoid the conclusion that organizational policy-making may in the future have to explicitly take into account the quantitative (in the sense of rigorously modeled) notion of inertia. Relevance and genuine disciplinary progress may depend on this articulation of perspectives.

This argument can be rephrased in the following manner. From the point of view of policy-making, the kind of modeling under discussion, i.e., the description of the programmed part of the activities of decision-making bureaucracies, amounts to what may also be regarded as a theory of organizational inertia. When the theory and its inherent methodology are applied to a particular case, it becomes possible to describe systematically and in some detail the morphology and dynamics of a bureaucracy's mode of *constant* operation. Because organizational policy-making deals in the final analysis with social and political variables which maintain, steer, or modify this mode of operation, conceptualizing and measuring this central datum would seem to be an inescapable necessity.

In rebuttal, it might be argued that the cost and time required are so great that the effort is likely to be of questionable value. This may well be the case; in fact, in many instances this is very likely to be so. However, if organizational decision-making is viewed as a disciplinary and social topic of importance, it may well turn out that there is simply no other choice. To use an analogy, for centuries men have dreamed about flying, an activity that can be held to be unnecessary. However, should one hold that this activity *is* of value, then the history of the enterprise teaches us that the choice is between Icarus types of grandiose but useless attempts or endless but basically fruitless little jumps, on the one hand, and, on the other, the painstaking resolution to build the necessary means—aircraft with hundreds of thousands of components. Along similar lines, I would argue that if bureaucratically implemented social policies are viewed as an important topic, our choice may be rather limited—at least for the important processes and bureaucratic organizations worth investigating in the first place. Given the apparent redundancy (in the sense of change-neutralizing capacity), and program-like nature of most bureaucratic processes of decision-making, the task and challenge of furthering our understanding of the conditions of effective policy-making by beginning to relate this activity systematically to output—through the conceptual datum mentioned—may well have become not only necessary but, in the long run, inevitable.

Lastly, it can be noted that the necessity to model bureaucratic decision-making may have a more general justification, if a less directly deducible one. A recurrent theme in the discussion of social problems is that the source of many difficulties lies in the contemporary erosion of social legitimacy. Some causes, or concomitants, of this erosion are felt to be a general weakening of social norm and a growing sense of powerlessness and alienation. This explanation might well be accurate, although in social matters causality is often difficult to establish, which means that alternative explanations are always possible. To take just one example, it was long held that the primacy of religion in the Western world was undermined by the emergence of science after the Renaissance. Scholars today tend to believe that it is the prior weakening of religion which made the emergence of science possible. In a somewhat similar vein, it is possible to entertain the hypothesis that alienation and various attempts "to beat the system" may not be due to a weakening of social norms. Rather, as we have seen in Chapter 4, the most rational problem-solving behavior of an intelligent being confronted by a heuristic organism or organization is to attempt to find the weak spots of its heuristic, and defeat it. In this light, some of the growing social malaise may stem from the fact that men are increasingly groping to assert the uniqueness of their intelligence. Faced with a spreading number of organizations which are functionally almost pure and machine-like heuristic decision-making systems, they may intuitively have begun to react in a profoundly rational manner, rather than in an amoral one. The problem may indeed lie with what the social system has become, rather than with man's disinclination to uphold its norms.

The foregoing discussion has tried to show that there are considerations which suggest that in the long run it might be necessary to model certain processes of bureaucratic decision-making. But whether or not this will turn out to be the case, this kind of effort has been shown in Chapter 9 to be at least useful. To a large extent this usefulness stems from the fact that by means of modeling, bureaucratic decision-making could be viewed in a new light, as quite different from what it is usually perceived to be. The resulting change in perspective, in turn, makes salient theoretical issues and research problems heretofore largely unattended to. We shall now be concerned with some of them, in particular as they relate to the pivotal process of routinization of policies.

The Routinization of Policies

As already noted, the current focus of interest in bureaucratic organizations tends to be on the socio-political dynamics of the systems rather than on their information-processing function. As a result, one dominant concern— although by no means the only one—is the problem of authority, its emergence, maintenance, and delegation. In a quasi-stable environment, and stretching somewhat the original meaning of the term in Weber's writings, this general problem can be viewed as dealing with the question of the routinization (and maintenance) of authority.

The parallel problem in an information-processing framework of analysis translates into the question of the routinization of policies. The content of this question can be given a beginning of substance if we consider the following truism. In a very broad sense, the term policy refers to the notion of a guideline or a blueprint which gives direction to activities. While a policy can have various levels of abstraction, its effects are, of course, determined by the specific mode of implementation. As we have seen, in bureaucracies the overwhelming controlling factor of output are the routine decisions. Whatever it was in intention (explicitly or implicitly), a bureaucratic policy is therefore for all practical purposes coextensive with the set of standard operating procedures which presumably implement it. Retrieving this set of procedures, it will be recalled, may regenerate as much as eighty to ninety percent of what the policy actually is; it does not regenerate, however, the original ideas behind it. This obvious consideration leads to the central theoretical and research problem mentioned above. It can be stated operatively in the following manner: *how does a specific policy become the set of standard operating procedures which embodies it?* The aim of this section is to raise this very general question, and to begin to put it into focus by outlining some of its dimensions as well as a possible research strategy. The brevity of the discussion reflects on what I feel can be usefully said in a preliminary discussion, but emphatically not on the importance of the problem.

Consider the following characterization of clerical bureaucracies by Campbell (1971, pp. 31-32):

> The natural inclination of the staff in any public office is to adjust to the demands of their fellow staff members. Clients, customers, the public, interfere as strangers with the ingroup social system that develops among the staff. There arises an unconscious tendency to define the agency's mission narrowly so that there are as few clients as possible. In case of doubt, an applicant is sent to some other agency, or is told there is no agency for his needs. The customers accepted are given the type of service most convenient for the staff member, not most needed. . . .
>
> These same pressures exist in business enterprises. Many of us have felt like unwanted intruders in some fancy department stores. But in the business world there is a powerful feed-back system from us customers. Stores that have no customers go out of business. No such feed-back exists at the present time in most government service agencies.

This characterization, even if only partially accurate, captures in a nutshell the two major sets of (interrelated) issues which give to the process of routinization of policies its great importance.

DISTORTIONS

The first class of issues is substantive and is related to the possibility that, owing to social dynamics, policies might undergo systematic modifications or distortions in the process of their routinization or of their repetitive implementation. In particular, policies and procedures are likely to be subject to fluctuations in the reliability of their application. More important, they are also likely to undergo a process which adapts them to the *internal* needs and constraints of the organization. It is for probing this kind of modifications that the paradigm and the programming conceptual framework may find one of their most practical applications to the analysis of clerical bureaucracies. The reason is that all modes of implementation introduce specific distortions related to the characteristics of the procedures used for this purpose. To paraphrase what Breznitz and Lieblich have said of simulations in general, the very nature of operationalizations implies that there is no logically necessary correspondence between policies and a particular system that is devised or used to implement it. Such a system is but a sample from a large population of possible means for solving the same. problem. A structure of this kind, however, is a coherent system in its own right, and is at least partially independent of its subject matter and of the uses to which it is put (cf., Breznitz and Lieblich, 1972, p. 72). In this light programming is no exception to the rule, and it imposes specific distortions of its own, a point to which we shall return later. Conceptually, however, this mode of implementation clarifies the organizational modifications inserted in the process by the *social* nature of bureaucracies. It does so by providing a yardstick to compare and contrast the processes of routinization and of repetitive implementation of policies in clerical bureaucracies, with the pure information-processing equivalent of these functions—the programming task and a program run.

A RESEARCH STRATEGY

Consider the process of routinization of policies and, to take full advantage of the perspective adopted in this work, a policy which has already been routinized. Under normal conditions such policies are embedded in the forms, standard operating procedures, and criteria, by means of which relevant information is used for decision-making; it is because such data are relatively easy to retrieve from official (normative or written) "code books," and from the repetitive behavior of role incumbents (through observation, interviews, or multiple regressions, see Chapter 6) that modeling bureaucratic decision-making can be so efficient; it is because these procedures turn out to have a surprising degree of stability that they have the functional status of a program instruction or routine. The general sociological question that these characteristics raise has been stated at the outset of t^{b} $_{?}$ section. But additionally, because the end product of the process of routinization of policies is well defined and accurately measurable, a research strategy which takes advantage of these facts suggests itself. Its essence is to take a set of forms, standard operating procedures, and criteria as the focal point of investigation. Working backwards, the relevant questions then become the causes and frequency of changes, and their relationship to both policies and outcomes.

To focus the discussion, Figure 10.1 presents in schematic form a bureaucratic decision-making process. In this figure the solid lines and boxes stand for the results which were anticipated or believed to obtain, and the dotted ones for actual occurrences. Because the type of retrieved model discussed in Chapter 9 is about actual outputs and processes of implementation, its counterpart in Figure 10.1 are the boxes related by arrow B; the functional equivalent to an instruction or routine on which we are currently concentrating is therefore part of the dotted box from which this arrow emerges.

The point of figure 10.1 is that it highlights some important reasons that may account for mismatches between policies and the objectives actually achieved. In particular, the output may be unable to generate the desired effect. More importantly, the intended mode of implementation may overlap only partially with the actual one, a fact which is liable to distort the output

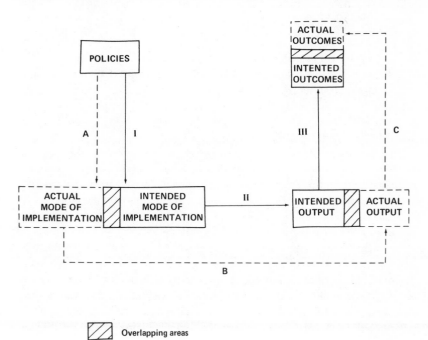

Figure 10.1

and the impact of policies. We can now return to the strategy of research mentioned above—a backward search for explanations.

The crux of the matter is that when the logic of Figure 10.1 is merged with this strategy of investigation, three categories of questions emerge. These are:

(1) The question of stability and its maintenance, an issue which translates into questions of parameters and classes of causes; for instance, how long has a particular set of forms, standard operating procedures, and criteria been in operation? when were these elements changed last? why?

(2) The second class of questions is related to the demonstrable effect— through a trial run—of these changes on actual output.

(3) The last category of questions is at the heart of the problem of routinization of policies. Building on the clarifications provided by the answers to the two first sets of queries, it now becomes possible to investigate potential distortions in the process of routinization of policies by comparing both the intentions and the anticipations, on the one hand, and the current beliefs, on the other, with actual practices and outcomes.

Substantively, the essence of the first class of questions can be captured by the title that the appropriate type of research could be given, namely, *the story of a form* (or of criteria, and/or standard operating procedures).

The second set of issues centers around the problem of the evaluation of the changes documented by this type of investigation. Operatively, this largely amounts to a sensitivity analysis, with the discarded procedures and/or parameters replacing the current ones, the purpose being to establish the actual impact of the modifications on output.

The last category of questions is aimed at documenting the potential existence of problems during the routinization of policies in a particular organization and for specific processes. It largely amounts to retrieving (by analysis of memos, minutes, and interviews) and comparing the intentions of, and the beliefs about, the effects of changes with those which are actually demonstrable by means of the sensitivity analyses.

At this point, two things are noteworthy. The first is that the availability of a powerful and objective model is what gives to this kind of research design much of its usefulness. Indeed, it is through sensitivity analyses that the actual effects of the changes in procedures can be related to their intentions. Moreover, as a result of the objective and reenactable manner in which potential discrepancies between beliefs and actual occurrences are established, a nonnegligible side advantage is that the common problem of facing policy-makers or high-echelon executives who discard findings about actual practices as atypical, or as of little importance for overall output determination, can be greatly minimized.

The second point is that the kind of research design just discussed merely leads to the documentation of the information-processing problems which may distort the routinization of policies in a particular organization. For the analysis of the roots of the problem, the demonstration of possible discrepancies in a clerical bureaucracy can only act as a stimulus for the sociological analysis which is then called for. This task requires in part that the same variables that we have discussed be reconsidered, but this time in relation to the social structure and dynamics of the organization, i.e., as dependent rather than independent variables. The reason is that the logic of the information-processing approach developed in this book rests on a conceptualization whereby procedures and criteria mediate between role-incumbents and decisions (see box A in Figure 10.2). Once decisions have been regenerated by means of the accurate formalization of these all-important mediating variables, they, and the model in which they are embedded, become a topical datum for sociological analysis.

For this level of analysis, the social characteristics of organizations which may account for particular modes of creation, maintenance, and application of the standard operating procedures are of primary importance. The relevant sociological questions that these problems raise include: how are the stability and the changes in procedures related to the authority characteristics and structure of the bureaucracy? to turn-over of personnel? how are the role-incumbents' values and S.E.S. background characteristics related to reliability? are changes primarily attempts at modifying output (i.e., policy-oriented), or responses to internal needs? how is the process of routinization of policies affected by the committee structure of the organization (it will be recalled that Chapter 8 noted that individual versus group settings affect problem solving in significant ways, including creativity, reliability, and risk-taking)? how is this process affected by the nature and extent of

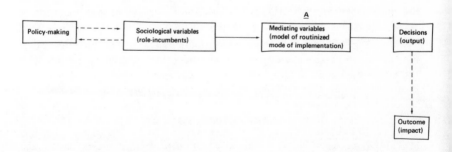

Figure 10.2: LOGIC OF THE RELATIONSHIP BETWEEN INFORMATION-PROCESSING AND SOCIOLOGICAL VARIABLES

discretion? by the degree of centralization of authority? by the type of control—by procedures versus by outcome—which is prevalent? by the criteria and frequency of control? how and by whom are arbitrary or accidental modes of routinization detected and corrected?

As the reader will have recognized, many of these questions, and the variables which operationalize them, are regularly discussed in the sociological, management, and political sciences literature. The point is, however, that they should also be considered in relation to the bench-mark provided by the kind of explicit model under discussion. A compelling reason is that the importance of these variables clearly lies as much in their relationship to the process of routinization of policies, and through it to the all-important mode of routine operation of bureaucracies, as to their direct effect on policy-making. The needed integration between the study of policy-making and of policy implementation may indeed ultimately depend on our willingness to engage in some such articulation of research. It should be pointed out in this connection that given that the standard operating procedures explain for all practical purposes all the variance of the output of decision-making bureaucracies, this kind of sociological analysis is likely to be especially useful in explaining variations between, rather than within, departments or organizations—at least for policy implementation and output.

The Problem of Validity

Turning now to the second aspect of Campbell's remarks, they call attention to a set of issues that are directly related to the problem of self-corrective versus non-self-corrective processes raised in the opening section of the chapter. This class of questions is primarily methodological and revolves around the issue of validation, a condition without which no corrective process can take place and no policy—whether routinized or not—can be gauged. The issue of validation is complex and the problems that it raises have at best partial solutions. Some of the difficulties are at the heart of the current efforts to develop new research designs and a new methodological philosophy to make validating studies and scientific research compatible with the requirements of the time-constrained environment in which policy-makers must act (Campbell, 1971, 1975; Coleman, 1972, 1976).

THE DIFFICULTIES

Typically, the problems of validation that the decision-maker or scientist confront include the necessity to act with partial knowledge of consequences; the lack of resources to design follow-up evaluation studies both synchronized and comprehensive enough for the task of assessing the impact of all policies; the absence of control over (and at times knowledge about) important variables affecting the impact of policies, a fact which limits the feasibility of conceptualizing policies as quasi-experiments; the lack of consensual criteria of validation (e.g., major interests satisfied, short-term versus long-term consequences); the shortcomings of existing statistical indicators (Bauer, 1966; Shonfield and Shaw, 1972; Land and Spilerman, 1975); and, as a result of all these, the questionable reliability of whatever evaluations are nonetheless feasible. The best illustration of the dangers that these difficulties create for tasks of assessment can perhaps be found in Morgenstern's *The Accuracy of Economic Observations* (1963; see also Biderman, 1966, p. 82, and Gross, 1966, pp. 165-166). In this work the author documents the fact that inadequately validated data can, at times, lead to important conclusions and policies which may turn out to be responses to nonproblems. This stems from the fact that in most economic time-series, the margin of error ranges from 10 to 20 percent. For long-term trends and long-term policy-making, this level of precision is generally acceptable; for short-term assessments, however, it is often insufficient. Moreover, the problem is compounded by many of the difficulties just mentioned. In the present example they include in particular the fact that

> economic statistics are not, as a rule, the result of designed experi-
> ments. . . . In general, economic statistics are merely by-products or
> results of business and government activities and have to be taken as
> such, even though they may not have been selected and designed for
> the analyst's purpose. Therefore, they often measure, describe, or
> simply record something that is not exactly the phenomenon in which
> the economist would be interested. They are often dependent on legal
> rather than economic definitions of processes (Morgenstern, 1963, pp.
> 13-14; quoted by Gross, 1966, p. 166).

If one takes into account the fact that in the social sciences knowledge and experience about ongoing assessments is probably at its highest in economics, the problem of obtaining valid feedback for assessing and guiding the implementation of social policies in general takes on its true proportions; this problem is what makes the process of routinization of policies a matter of guesswork, at least in part, a fact which facilitates the occurrence and routinization of distortions caused by the source of feedback which *is* available—internal needs and demands.

A CONVERGING STRATEGY OF RESEARCH

It is clear that problems of outcome validation of this magnitude are unlikely to be solved by any single procedure or approach. The perspective developed in the preceding chapters is no exception to this. This perspective, however, may nonetheless contribute something to the current research and conceptualization efforts, in that for bureaucratically implemented policies it recasts the problem in a somewhat different mold. Consider the two research strategies that Coleman distinguishes by the names of input-output analysis versus social audit designs. Input-output analysis has the following logic:

> The essential characteristic of this research design is that the policy inputs are measured, policy outcomes are measured, and the two are related (with, of course, the use of experimental or statistical controls to neutralize the effect of situational variables). Whatever institutional structure intervenes is taken in effect as a black box into which the input resources go and out of which the desired outcomes and side effects come (Coleman, 1972, p. 18).

This kind of analysis, which characterizes most evaluation studies, is typically carried out by means of multiple regression techniques, i.e., a selected outcome—the dependent variable—is regressed on a set of inputs and situational characteristics—the independent variables. The logic of this type of design is diagrammed in Figure 10.3A.

As opposed to this class of designs, Coleman (1972, p. 19) suggests that the audit approach, which derives its name by analogy from the financial audit, might be a valuable additional means to document and improve the

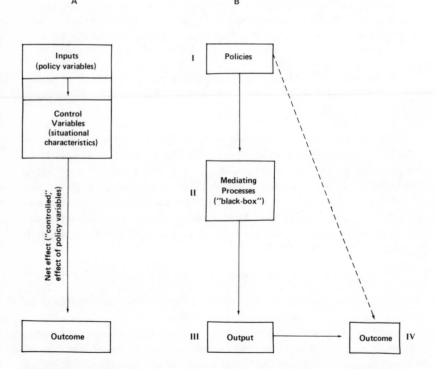

Figure 10.3: TWO TYPES OF RESEARCH CONCEPTUALIZATION

outcome validity of policies. The essence of this approach is that it attempts to go into the black box which mediates between inputs and outcomes. In particular, it aims at following a particular process through its major paths, and in so doing to probe the extent to which systematic transformations or distortions of the inputs or the policies affect the latters' intended consequences; (strictly speaking, it can be noted that Coleman advocates this kind of study for processes of allocation of resources; however, he does so on grounds which, from the present point of view, apply *mutatis mutandis* to processes of classification as well; cf., Coleman, 1972, pp. 18-19). The structure of this type of design is summarized in Figure 10.3B.

Two things are noteworthy in connection with this figure. The first is that for studies of validity an audit type of research is not a substitute for input-output studies:

> Just as with a financial audit, the flows of resources are examined to discover the paths that resources take and the possible loss of these resources through diversion. As in a financial audit, proper use of resources does not insure the ultimate effectiveness of the resources, but it does tell whether the resources are available at point of use, and if they are not, where and how they got lost. A social audit is not a substitute for a study of the effectiveness of resources which have reached their destination. It should be accompanied by such an examination (i.e., by an input-output study) [Coleman, 1972, p. 19].

When modifications or distortions are suspected to occur, however, the great virtue of audit studies is that they can cast light on whatever degree of inefficiency or invalidity input-output studies document. This is especially true if systematic modifications or distortions intervene between policy-making and outcomes, an occurrence that the very existence of standard operating procedures makes likely. In short, the claim is that studies of validity call for a two-stage type of research; that is, they should begin with a documentation and verification of outputs, and only then be followed by an assessment of outcomes.

Secondly, if the "black box" (box II in Figure 10.3B) is relabeled routinized policies, or standard operating procedures, the logic of audit studies for validity research becomes isomorphic with the backward and sociological types of research that the present approach calls for on substantive grounds; a glance at Figures 10.1 and 10.2 will convince the reader that this is indeed the case. This is not surprising if we take into consideration the fact that, in Moore's words, the substantive aim of the kind of heuristic analysis discussed in the previous chapters is also basically aimed at "opening up the black box that intervenes in certain types of decision-making activities and of making explicit a large part of its contents" (Moore, 1968, pp. 204-205).

By its very logic then, the approach developed in this book meets some of the prerequisites felt to be necessary for advancing our understanding of the problems of validity of social policies—at least those which are bureaucratically implemented. Moreover, as will be recalled from Chapters 4 and 6 (see also Chapter 12), the readily achievable formalization of heuristics in terms of multiple regressions provides a convenient mode of operationalization for taking direct advantage of the contribution that modeling can make to carefully designed studies of validity of the type advocated by Coleman.

A Note on Systems Analysis

In order to guide the process of date gathering necessary to build decision-making models, it is necessary to rely on a conceptual framework. As noted in Chapter 2, and as many of the previous discussions have illustrated, the underlying framework is that of systems analysis. The programming and cybernetic aspects of this framework are well spelled out in the works of Cyert and March (1963), Crecine (1969), and Steinbruner (1974). The heuristic use of the systems viewpoint in raising sociological questions of the kind discussed in the last part of Chapter 8, or in the second section of this chapter (see also the next chapter), are cogently described in Merton (1959, pp. 50-84), and Blau (1963). All these operationalizations of the systems viewpoint share abstract characteristics, which are discussed in most texts on systems analysis (e.g., Kirk, 1973; Fitzgerald and Fitzgerald, 1973; Shannon, 1975). In the foregoing discussions, these operationalizations have been illustrated with attention to specific details. This characteristic of the discussion has forced us to disregard a few general principles shared by most endeavors which fall under the heading of systems analysis. In this section we shall briefly examine a couple of them. The purpose is to give substance to two abstract issues, and to note how they are related to the specific reliance on the notion of systems which characterizes the type of modeling that we have considered.

The first of the general issues of interest is that of the objectives of the modeling endeavor. As always when a systems analysis is involved, this is the first question that should be considered. Two classes of objectives can be distinguished: those of the system, and those sought by the builder of the model. The objectives of the system are a matter of empirical investigation of the kind described in detail by Cyert and March (1963) and Crecine (1969). The objectives of the model builder, on the other hand, are exogenously determined. However, they bear directly on the form that the former investigation takes; in particular, they determine to a large extent the endogenous goals of the system which will be selected for inclusion in the model.

Because of the importance of the exogenous aims in model building, it is useful to clarify as much as possible what their nature is in the present case.

In summary form, much of the approach described in the preceding chapters can be stated in the form of the following objectives:

(1) to provide an objective model with which to come to grips with a process whose size and complexity overloads the information-processing capability of the human mind, and therefore the ability of administrators and interested parties to genuinely control and/or modify the system;

(2) to improve the efficiency of the system by clarifying the source of inadequacies (see below), and the extent of unnecessary lack of reliability in both discretionary and nondiscretionary decision-making;

(3) to create a framework for the continuous evaluation and monitoring of the validity of procedures which, because they are routinized, presume to be means of proven effectiveness.

These aims are the criteria against which the understanding or improvement of an existing level of bureaucratized decision-making has to be evaluated.

Within the framework of these objectives, the second general issue of interest is that of the description of the empirical structure in terms of a system. This task is guided by the exogenous objectives of model building, by the particular processes which are focused on, and by the theoretical and conceptual approach used for model-building—in our case the information-processing approach and its inherent notion of heuristics.

On an abstract level, the steps involved in this task are discussed at length in the systems analysis literature, in particular in the works cited at the beginning of this section (e.g., Kirk, 1973) and in Chapter 2. The following brief discussion will help concretize the form that some of these steps take in the case of the present application.

Concisely, then, the process of identification of a system's morphology (as well as its objectives) rests above all on three sources of information: written material, the persons in charge of—and legally responsible for—the performance of the system or subsystem, and key operators in the system. The ultimate aim of the analysis is to yield a decision-making flow chart or, more accurately, a set of flow charts, in particular at different levels of abstraction, of the kind illustrated in Figure 10.4 (this specific example is about the procedures and parameters in which the price determination policies of an oligopolistic industry were found to be embedded—see Morgenroth, 1964).

The translation and abstraction of the fact-finding stage of a systems analysis into this kind of information-processing flow chart take place through the identification of the major decision-making functions which are involved in the decision-making process as a whole. It should be noted that in the present context the notion of function simply refers to an observable difference between an input and an output. More specifically, in our case the input is a question, and the output a choice (e.g., box 13 in Figure 10.4).

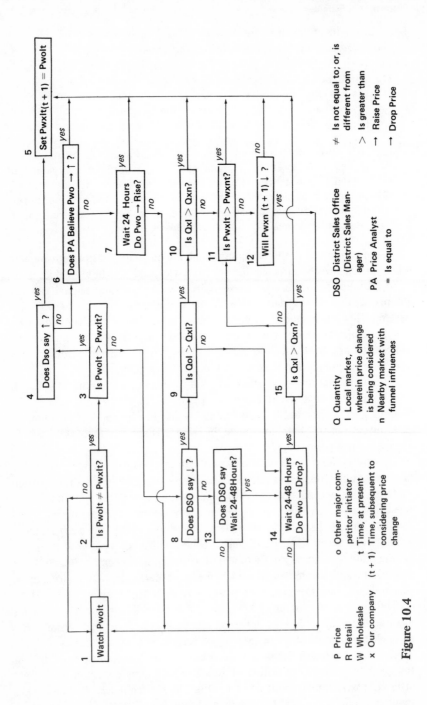

Figure 10.4

1 Watch Pwolt

2 Is Pwolt ≠ Pwxlt?

3 Is Pwolt > Pwxlt?

4 Does Dso say ↑ ?

5 Set Pwxlt(t + 1) = Pwolt

6 Does PA Believe Pwo → ↑ ?

7 Wait 24 Hours Do Pwo → Rise?

8 Does DSO say ↑ ?

9 Is Qol > Qxl?

10 Is Qxl > Qxn?

11 Is Pwxlt > Pwxnt?

12 Will Pwxn (t + 1) ↓ ?

13 Does DSO say Wait 24-48 Hours?

14 Wait 24-48 Hours Do Pwo → Drop?

15 Is Qxl > Qxn?

P Price
R Retail
W Wholesale
x Our company

o Other major competitor initiator
l Local market, wherein price change is being considered
n Nearby market with funnel influences
t Time, at present
(t + 1) Time, subsequent to considering price change

Q Quantity

DSO District Sales Office (District Sales Manager)
PA Price Analyst

≠ Is not equal to; or, is different from
> Is greater than
↑ Raise Price
↑ Drop Price
= Is equal to

188

Documenting the procedures by which this transformation is achieved, as well as the conditions and constraints (e.g., box 9), and the standard operating actions (e.g., box 7) which structure a decision-making process, constitutes the core of the task of identification.

Figure 10.4 is also a convenient example for concretizing a few remarks previously made:

The first remark of interest is that once the procedures which determine the bulk of the decision-making output of a bureaucratic process are summarized in visual form, as they are in Figure 10.4, the question of the relationship between intentions and beliefs and actual practice becomes very salient. Indeed, the illustration makes it very clear that any process of nontrivial complexity immediately falls beyond what the unaided human mind is capable of grasping. In particular, the effect of the procedures and criteria on output and the relationship of these to original intentions and policies are at best conjecturable (cf., the two previous sections).

Additionally, Figure 10.4 illustrates the sense in which an information-processing chart parallels an organizational chart. It also clarifies the fundamental difference between the two types of charts, and the specific contribution that the information-processing representation can make.

The obvious difference between the two kinds of charts is that instead of the traditional lines of authority and communication which relate departments or organizational roles to each other, the information-processing chart describes the decision-making procedures, conditions, and functions (in the sense just discussed) that constitute a decision-making system. It is noteworthy that because of the inherent logic and constraints of a flow chart (and later, of programming), a variety of organizational contingencies, among them role boundaries, are often disregarded (see Figure 10.4); this is one example where the present mode of operationalization, like any other (see the second section of this chapter), introduces its specific kind of modification.

At the same time, and even without proceeding to the programming stage, the flow-chart mode of representation has the advantage of lending itself to use as an important conceptual aid. The reason is that it provides a basis for putting the particular organization of a process of decision-making into perspective. Specifically, by being able to disregard temporarily the actual constraints, role boundaries, and modes of organization within which an existing clerical bureaucracy operates, alternative modes of organization become immediately apparent. In the case of applications to clerical bureaucracies, the stage of systems analysis which determines the decision-making logic of a system is therefore useful for breaking thinking habits.

Lastly, as repeatedly noted, the consideration that in bureaucracies the procedures underlying many decision-making processes are routinized, together with the fact that the basis of a bureaucracy's legitimacy is always instrumental, implies that the procedures must bear a clear and demonstrable relationship to the achievement of the system's instrumental objectives or at least to its internal ones (should these be part of the official policies). It is because this might not be the case, no more than drawing an *empirically* derived organizational chart guarantees that dual or conflicting lines of authority will not emerge, that the feasibility of documenting whether this expected relationship actually holds is a valuable contribution that model building can make to clerical bureaucracies. Indeed, problems of non sequitur of this or other kinds should not be expected to be less frequent in clerical systems than they are in everyday discourse—in any event not without evidence to the contrary.

Chapter 11

THE FUTURE OF BUREAUCRACY

In the preceding chapter we have considered the relevance and some potential implications for clerical bureaucracies of the conceptual scheme which has emerged from the previous discussions. After this exploration of some possible applications and contributions of the approach to present-day bureaucracies, we can now pursue and complete the presentation of one of the underlying arguments of this essay. For this purpose the present chapter is divided into two main sections. The first takes notice of the contemporary state of affairs and examines some dynamics of change inherent in the situation; the second considers possible future developments of bureaucratic decision-making which in the light of the present approach are both likely and practically feasible.

The Problem

It will be recalled that in the opening pages of this book I have argued that it might be both feasible and necessary not only to model, but also to computerize certain processes of bureaucratic decision-making. Paradoxically, after the discussion leading to Chapter 9 the reader might justifiably wonder whether the computerization task is not redundant. Indeed, by the yardstick of the reproducibility of output, it would seem that for all practical purposes, and without our being aware of the fact, bureaucracies may already have undergone such an unlikely transformation—in spirit and behavior, if not in form.

The unexpected nature of bureaucracy as it emerges from the evidence presented in Chapter 9, or its mutation at some point into what this discussion has shown it to be, brings to mind a somewhat related development undergone by an imaginary corporation described by Hacker (1964). Hacker's discussion is about processes which are already completely automated, and about a firm; obviously, therefore, this discussion is only partially relevant to our present concern. However, the question of the essence of a large organization, and the problematic nature of its inner logic under the drive of its members—cf., Campbell's comments in the previous chapter—is remarkably well raised in the intriguing scenario described by the author. The excerpt of Hacker's discussion which follows will therefore provide us with a thought-provoking introduction to our own discussion, and also, as we shall see, with the opportunity to start it by pondering what some large-scale bureaucracies may have already become *without* computerization and automation.

Let us follow the argument developed by Hacker in the context of a fully automated firm. Extrapolating from corporations to large bureaucracies, we note that:

> Unlike the religious and guild structures of earlier centuries, the large firm of today has no theoretical rationale linking power, purpose, and responsibility. Indeed, the dilemma is even more fundamental. For there is no satisfactory answer to the first question of all: what is a corporation?
>
> The problem, which extends beyond the simple one of definition, may be illustrated by an imaginary conversation taking place not too many years from now. The setting and the topic of the discussion happen to be political, but the dialogue would take much the same form were it extended to other spheres where corporate power is exercised:
>
> By 1972 American Electric had completed its last stages of automation: employees were no longer necessary. Raw materials left on the loading platform were automatically transferred from machine to machine, and the finished products were deposited at the other end of the factory ready for shipment. AE's purchasing, marketing, and general management functions could be handled by ten directors with the occasional help of outside consultants and contractors.
>
> Beginning in 1962 AE's employee pension fund had started investing its capital in AE stock. Gradually it bought more and more of the company's shares on the open market, and by 1968 it was the sole owner of AE. As employees became eligible for retirement—some of them prematurely due to the introduction of automation—the fund

naturally liquidated its capital to provide pensions. But instead of reselling its AE shares on the open market, the fund sold the stock to AE itself, which provided the money for pensions out of current income. By 1981 the last AE employee had died, and the pension fund was dissolved. At this time, too, AE became the sole owner of its shares. It had floated no new issues, preferring to engage in self-financing through earnings.

By 1982 the ten directors decided that AE would be well served by the passage of legislation restricting the imports of certain electrical equipment. They therefore secured the services of a public relations firm specializing in political campaigns. The objective was to educate the public and sway grassroots sentiment so that Congress would respond by passing the required bill. The public relations firm was given a retainer of $1 million and told to spend up to $5 million more on advertising and related activities.

Within months the public began to hear about the dire consequences that would follow the importation of alien generators. National security, national prosperity, and the nation's way of life were threatened by a flood of foreign goods. The public relations firm placed several hundred advertisements in newspapers and magazines, and almost a thousand on television. At least fifty citizens' committees "spontaneously" arose to favor the legislation, and over two hundred existing groups passed resolutions in its support. Lectures were given to women's clubs, and films were shown in high schools. By the end of the year—an election year—public sentiment had been aroused and hardly a Congressman was unaware of the popular ferment.

The bill was introduced in both chambers, and a good majority of senators and representatives, abiding by the wishes of their constituents, voted for it. The President signed the bill, and it became law. AE's profits were substantially higher the following year.

A group of senators, however, were curious about what had been going on, and they decided to investigate AE's foray into the political arena. One of the directors was happy to testify, for he knew that no law had been violated. No bribes had been offered, certainly, and no contributions to legislators' campaigns had been made. Toward the end of the enquiry, after all the techniques employed by the company and the public relations firm had been brought out, the following colloquy took place:

Director: ... And if we undertook these educational and political activities, it was our view that they were dictated by the company's best interests.

Senator: Now when you say that these campaigns were on behalf of the "company's" interests, I am not clear what you mean. Were you acting for your stockholders here?

Director: I am afraid, Senator, that I cannot say that we were. You see, American Electric has no stockholders. The company owns all its stock itself. We bought up the last of it several years ago.

Senator: Well, if not stockholders, then were you acting as a spokes-man for American Electric's employees—say, whose jobs might be endangered if foreign competition got too severe?

Director: No, Sir, I cannot say that either. American Electric is a fully automated company, and we have no employees.

Senator: Are you saying that this company of yours is really no more than a gigantic machine? A machine that needs no operators and appears to own itself?

Director: I suppose that is one way of putting it. I've never thought much about it.

Senator: Then so far as I can see, all of this political pressure that you applied was really in the interests of yourself and your nine fellow directors. You spent almost six million dollars of this company's money pursuing your personal political predilections.

Director: I am afraid, Senator, that now I must disagree with you. The ten of us pay ourselves annual salaries of $100,000 year in and year out, and none of us receives any bonuses or raises if profits happen to be higher than usual in a given year. All earnings are ploughed back into the company. We feel very strongly about this. In fact, we look on ourselves as a kind of civil servant. Secondly, I could not say that the decision to get into politics was a personal wish on our part. At least eight of the ten of us, as private citizens that is, did not favor the legislation we were supporting. As individuals most of us thought it was wrong, was not in the national interest. But we were acting in the company's interest and in this case we knew that it was the right thing to do.

Senator: And by the "company" you don't mean stockholders or employees, because you don't have any. And you don't mean the ten directors because you just seem to be salaried managers which the machine hires to run its affairs. In fact, when this machine gets into politics—or indeed any kind of activity—it has interests of its own which can be quite different from the personal interests of its managers. I am afraid I find all this rather confusing.

Director: It may be confusing to you, Senator, but I may say it has been quite straightforward to us at American Electric. We are just doing the job for which we were hired—to look out for the company's interests (Hacker, 1964, pp. 3-5).

As Hacker goes on noting, the difficulty that this example aims to highlight is the problematic and elusive nature of the interests served by a large organization. The case of an automated firm makes this point clear for business corporations. But, in the case of large bureaucracies, especially governmental ones, the fundamental difficulty is that this problem is already acute before any automation takes place. In the absence of a market to calibrate and justify the use and consumption of resources by such organizations, the interests served by their activities is from the start problematic. This is so because bureaucracies are normatively instrumental entities which in principle, even when they are clerically staffed, derive no legitimacy whatsoever from the function that they fulfill for their members. That is, while a business firm is conceived in part as deriving its social justification from the jobs it provides, a bureaucracy has no such recognized role. Rather, its legitimacy rests entirely on some specific social function, and the assumption that it is fulfilled provides the rationale that replaces the market as a decision-making and evaluation mechanism. These specific functions translate operatively into social needs fulfilled, and interests served. As Coleman (1976) has pointed out for policy research, however, there is a major flaw in the manner in which relevant interests are represented. Indeed, as Coleman further notes, much of what can be said about access to research information also applies to the more general question of the ability to affect administrative decision-making. Thus:

> The central defect in policy research as it is presently initiated and designed is the absence of any conception of interested parties, parties who have legitimate interests in different types of information. . . .
> There is no conception that research problems may be initiated by the stockholders, workers, or customers, to provide information that can be of benefit to one of these interests. . . . Nor should it [be] otherwise, because the customer has no legitimate voice in the manufacturer's policy decisions, except as he exercises that voice in the market. The same, however, cannot be said for policy research and government policy, for the citizens who are affected by the policy also have a legitimate voice in that policy (Coleman, 1976, pp. 305-306).

The point, then, is that in the absence of systematic and effective means to review and affect administrative decision-making, the legitimate social interests affected by contemporary large-scale bureaucracies may be in a structural situation not unlike that described by Hacker. Phrased differently, without a market or an adequate articulation and operationalization of relevant interests, a number of bureaucratic processes of decision-making are on fundamental grounds nonvalidated and non-self-corrective. In some cases the interests served by the activities of such organizations may therefore already have become as divorced from the social good as those of Hacker's corporation, and in the light of the discussion in Chapter 9, as mechanical—all this without any automation whatsoever.

This fundamental problem is at the heart of the growing concern voiced about the dangers of unpublicized but systematic distortions which are inherent in the spreading of administrative decision-making. Beutel, for instance, believes that: "[The] perversion of the policies and purposes behind laws by substitution of the administrators' own policies and purposes in its application to the public, completely ignoring the plain provisions of the law, is a common phenomenon" (Beutel, 1975, p. 251).

This characterization echoes the similar conclusions reached by the members of the 1967 President's Commission on Law Enforcement and Administration of Justice. Specifically:

> The decision making process has often become routinized. . . . In effect, much decision making is being done on an administrative rather than on a judicial basis. Thus, an examination of how the criminal justice system works and a consideration of the changes needed to make it more effective and fair must focus on the extent to which invisible, administrative procedures depart from visible, traditional ones, and on the desirability of that departure (Katzenbach et al., 1967, p. 10).

In short, the heart of the matter is that for significant aspects of social life large-scale bureaucratic systems may be already functionally as machine-like and as autonomous as Hacker's corporation became after automation.

This possibility was implicit in the preceding chapter when the issue of rationality versus immorality was raised in connection with the remarks about social alienation. For our present concern this potential state of affairs has two additional implications of importance.

The first is related to a point made by Hoos (1974). It will be recalled (see Chapter 2) that one of this author's criticisms against much of contemporary systems analysis is that the analysts tend to usurp the role of the policy-makers. This takes place during the process of operationalization, and is a consequence of the fact that many of the assumptions required for this purpose can be shown to imply consequential value judgments which are properly the prerogative of elected representatives, not of appointed, or self-appointed, experts.

However, a moment of thought shows that exactly the same thing can be said, *mutatis mutandis,* about bureaucratic officials, and exactly the same criticisms apply point for point to the bureaucratic implementation of policies. Indeed, the administrative routinization of policies does not rest any less on value judgments than does the design of a system. And the bureaucratic norms and criteria of appointment and promotion do not guarantee any more that the administrative career officials will be sensitive to, or representative of, relevant social interests than we have the right to expect appointed analysts to be.

In other words, to the extent that Hoos' critique was perceived as compelling, the routinization and implementation of policies by public bureaucracies is open to most of the same criticisms which apply to some contemporary systems analyses. The operationalization and routinization of policies in clerical bureaucracies is indeed daily carried out by thousands of administrative officials who perform much the same tasks for which analysts are being castigated. The unrepresentativeness and arbitrariness of the latters' choices and decisions merely happen to be much more visible because systems analyses tend to objectivize processes, and because experiments and innovations by outsiders often invite criticisms which are commensurate with the attention that endeavors of this kind command, and with the potential threat to habits that they constitute. But the crux of the matter is that analytically the shortcomings are shared. The weaknesses of systems analysis are merely the disclosed tip of the iceberg.

The second implication is sociological, and it constitutes, in effect, another aspect of the problem just noted. Under structural conditions of unrepresentative expertise, and in the absence of social knowledge or means of validation (cf., Chapter 10) commensurate with the implications of expertise, the various potential malfunctions of clerical bureaucracies depend for their correction on two sources. The first is the political process, which, as noted in the preceding chapter, is at best lagged. The second source is the representations of individuals or groups, who may request either the redress of wrongs or errors or special favors (mostly given in the form of priority of service—see Chapter 9). In either case, however, a safe generalization from the sociological literature is that the lower the socio-economic status of the petitioner, the less the likelihood that a wrong will be rapidly redressed, or that a change in priority ordering will be granted—if it is considered at all. And of course, because of the pyramidal structure of society, only a few, including perhaps some segments of the middle class, have a significant opportunity to influence any given bureaucratic outcome.

The conclusion to which one is drawn is, therefore, that in contemporary industrialized societies, the experience of the majority of the population may be that they are confronted by clerical bureaucracies which are already as impersonal and have as arbitrary interests as did Hacker's hypothetical firm. To the few, such organizations may appear and in fact be very human. But to the many, who by definition cannot all benefit from priority servicing, much less from the prerogatives and exceptions which may account for all or part of the 10 to 20 percent of residual variance typically found in the output of clerical bureaucracies, the situation is likely to appear quite different. The only significant effect that they can have on bureaucracies is having mistakes corrected; this probably contributes to the overall procedural reliability of bureaucracies. But obviously there is little advantage in supporting a clerically staffed organization if the dealings with it are mainly restricted to attempts at having mistakes and misunderstandings corrected by those same actors who were responsible for them in the first place; certainly not if even in such instances the complainant tends to be presumed guilty and is required to bear the burden of the proof. At best, this type of situation can be expected to foster feelings of alienation, which have historically accompanied bureaucracies. Under norms of equality, furthermore, discretionary exceptions become increasingly unacceptable. And under norms of rationality, alternative modes of organization may become not only admissible but, as the example of the Tillie in Chapter 8 has illustrated, even attractive.

In sum, then, because the fundamental function of bureaucracies is to routinize the implementation of policies, their procedures must be standardized. Because this mode of operation conflicts with the individualization of services, they have developed into, and are perceived as, unrepresentative and machine-like organizations. Under such conditions, one fundamental criterion, especially in the case of governmental bureaucracies, must inevitably be universalism—and the dynamics of change just noted may theoretically lead in two major directions. We shall now note one, and discuss the other.

Future Developments

One possible corrective development lies in the direction of attempts to obviate the problem of unrepresentativeness by directly increasing the flexibility and personalization of services. Basically, one guiding aim of this type of improvement is to replace the norm of universalism with individualization, an approach which builds on the present structure of clerical bureaucracies—which is taken for granted. That such a development is possible is demonstrated by the fact that it has occurred in some bureaucratized organizations, notably hospitals, where the logic of in-house task forces allows quasi-routinely individualized decisions to be made and quasi-customized services to be given (cf., Thompson, 1967, pp. 17-18). Whether this mode of organization, or some variation of it, is practical and generalizable to other bureaucratic systems is an open question which falls beyond the scope of this book.

The second type of possible corrective development is the topic to which the remainder of this chapter is devoted.

In a nutshell, the basic assumption underlying the kind of anticipated development on which we shall now focus is that the major shortcomings of the present situation are inherent in much of the bureaucratic function of repetitive decision-making; they are aggravated by the characteristics of the clerical mode of implementation (i.e., errors, idiosyncrasies, and personal needs)—but do not stem from them. Accordingly, in the long run the remedy is likely to lie in a direct confrontation of the problem rather than in incremental attempts to humanize a process which, despite the appearances, is in *essence* largely and fundamentally mechanical. Paradoxically, this strategy is likely both to stimulate and facilitate the emergence of a new breed of clerical bureaucracies, which may well have some of the desirable properties whose very absence today creates the need for the kind of computerization that we shall now examine.

The discussion begins with an outline of the type and modality of computerization which is envisioned; this outline completes the related discussions in the previous chapters. The rationale for believing in the likelihood of this development is then considered together with possible dysfunctions and a structural arrangement for minimizing them.

COMPUTERIZATION: MODALITY AND SCOPE

Both the modality and potential scope of the processes of bureaucratized decision-making which can be computerized have already been discussed in some detail in the preceding chapters, especially in Chapters 9 and 10, but two more points are of importance.

The first is about modality. It will be recalled that Chapter 6 documented the surprising degree to which repetitive processes of decision-making which are normally held to be either discretionary or professional or both, are paramorphically modelable; this led researchers to raise the question of how robust the retrieved models are, a line of investigation which resulted in the conclusion that about three cues are sufficient for capturing the bulk of the repetitive process of individual decision-making. This finding was followed, in turn, by a comparison of the paramorphic models of man with man himself, a comparison which showed that because of the computer's perfect reliability, the decisions of the models are more valid than are those made (presumably with them) by their originators.

These explorations, each punctuated by an unexpected development, have led to one more astounding finding. If decision-making can be accurately modeled, and if in the process most cues turn out to be redundant, the next unlikely question is whether the weights that decision-makers attach to the few cues that they do use are really useful. In terms of the multiple regression operationalization discussed in Chapter 6, this amounts to the question of the contribution that accurately estimated b's or betas make to the validity of the paramorphic models.

This apparently unpromising question is precisely the one that Dawes (1973) set out to investigate in a series of studies. For this purpose he proceeded to replace in a number of models, including the MMPI model discussed in Chapter 6, the multiple regression weights, first by random values (although correctly signed), and then by equal weights. The amazing results of this investigation are reported in detail in Dawes and Corrigan (1974). In an earlier report, Dawes informally summarizes the findings as follows:

The results surprised hell out of me. In the examples discussed in this paper, linear models whose weights were randomly selected in the manner just described *on the average* outperformed the linear models whose weights were selected on the basis of the experts' judgments. That is, the correlations between predicted output and obtained output were on the average higher. In each case, we constructed 10,000 such random models—so the superiority is quite well established. Equal weighting schemes were better yet (Dawes, 1973, p. 14).

The results to which Dawes refers in this passage are summarized in Table 11.1. Column one presents the validity of the judges' decisions, while column two presents the same data for the models (normally estimated). Columns three and four show by comparison the findings of Dawes and Corrigan's investigation. (It can be noted that these results have since been shown to be general and derivable from the mathematical properties of linear models; however, both the extent to which the results are robust and the degree to which the constraints involved in this derivation are restrictive, are debated issues—see Wainer, 1976, 1978; Laughlin, 1978; Pruzek and Frederick, 1978).

The significance of these results is twofold. In the first place they set the limits and clarify the methodological reasons for the extraordinary robustness of the individual models of decision-making that we have discussed. That this is not the whole story, however, is evident from the fact that the limited number of cues which is sufficient for the modeling endeavors is not implied by the remarkable properties of linear models, but is a derivation from the theoretical analysis of the processes of interest. For the purpose at hand, therefore, we find ourselves in a situation where meaningful conceptualiza-

TABLE 11.1: Comparative Validity of Decisions

	Average Validity of Judge	Average Validity of Judge's Model	Average Validity of Random Model	Average Validity of Equal Weighting Model
Prediction of neurosis vs. psychosis (MMPI task)	.28	.31	.30	.34
Illinois students' prediction of GPA	.33	.50	.51	.60
Oregon students' prediction of GPA	.37	.43	.51	.60
Prediction of later faculty ratings at Oregon	.19	.25	.39	.48

Source: After Dawes (1973, Table 2, p. 15).

tion combines with a powerful methodology. Obviously, these characteristics make the task of retrieving the individual models that one may need even easier. Moreover, they suggest that whether or not computerization is contemplated, the answer to the question of the proper use which should be made of a judge should take the form of an operative principle which can be stated as follows:

> Use him only to identify relevant variables. If criterion information exists, do a regression analysis to obtain optimal weights—but these weights may depart from optimality if the ratio of sample size to predictor variables is too small. If there is no criterion information available, use equal weighting—i.e., convert the values on each predictor dimension to standard score form and then add them together (Dawes, 1973, p. 15).

In other words, repetitive discretionary decision-making should in any case be formalized. On both theoretical and methodological grounds, such a step can immediately be expected to yield a significant increase of validity of whatever repetitive process of bureaucratic decision-making is modeled and computerized.

This brings us to the second point—in substance, a warning about the scope of the kind of computerization which is possible. In order to avoid any possible misunderstanding, it is useful to emphasize that the type of computerization just discussed, which in its equal-weights form is the most practical for large-scale computerization of bureaucratic processes of decision-making, implies a purely *paramorphic* type of modeling. This follows from the fact that with it we are now two steps removed from the referent processes of interest. Specifically, in the kind of modeling hitherto discussed, the actual configurative nature of the referent processes was disregarded—although with little loss in accuracy, as we have seen. The models so developed were therefore quasi-isomorphic with the referent processes in a *functional* sense (yet theoretically with as much details as desired), but in the same sense that propellers are functional equivalents to wings. By additionally disregarding weights, however, we now reach a level of artificiality where functional similarities are of a still higher degree of abstraction, e.g., the computerized processes of decision-making now resemble the actual referent process about as much as rockets resemble birds; the trade-off in our case is a gain in simplicity and validity, as it is a gain in speed in the other. But what should be kept in mind is the following: as birds have given to man the idea of flying, so the properties of human repetitive decision-making suggest the use of the computer for the performance of the tasks that this process involves. It should not be forgotten, however, that although flying vertebrates may have been at the origin of aeronautics, in its developed form the latter is not a science of birds, and neither is the information-processing paradigm in its linear and equal-weights form a science of human information processing. This development may be based on sound theoretical grounds and, as the empirical results available would tend to indicate, be very helpful, but the point is that it is an outgrowth whose justification is no longer based on its exact fit with the actual processes *but on its functional equivalence for some purposes, and on its superiority by some criteria.*

Should this type of computerization materialize, one trend started by bureaucracies can be expected to continue. Any new mode of organization must either adapt itself to the environment, or adapt the environment to itself. It is a matter of record that most bureaucracies, like most industries, have expressed their nature and achieved their potential of efficiency by adapting the environment to their (mechanical) mode of operation rather than the other way around. Thus, roads were constructed to provide the kind of constant environment needed by vehicles. The process of classification of clients, and the standardization of services, fulfill a similar role for bureaucracies. More generally, "We see that mechanization has more often proceeded by eliminating the need for human flexibility—replacing rough terrain with smooth environment—than by imitating it" (Simon, 1960, p. 34).

The computerization of bureaucratic processes of decision-making cannot be expected to be an exception to this rule. One should therefore be prepared for the cost, whatever advantages the development may otherwise entail. The question of costs and benefits is one of the topics to which we now turn.

THE DYNAMICS OF CHANGE REVISITED

With the completion of the presentation of the core methodology of the task of computerization, three questions arise. The first is related to the advantages to be gained from this transformation; the second pertains to the possible forms that the interfacing between computerized bureaucracies and their operators, on the one hand, and the public, on the other, might take; the third concerns the costs or dysfunctions which may accompany such a development. The first question is the object of this subsection; the two others, and a few additional points related to the first, are discussed in the subsection which follows.

We have noted that three problematic characteristics of present-day large-scale bureaucracies are their lack of representativeness, their machine-like rigidity, and, owing to the unknown validity of their procedures, their non-self-correctiveness. As was observed, these interrelated shortcomings may be bearable to the few who command enough power or prestige to benefit from the limited number of exceptions that clerical bureaucracies can apparently accommodate; the same characteristics may also fulfill positive functions for the staff, e.g., insulation from unanticipated demands, control over criteria of achievement, status security, etc. But for the general public the shortcomings of the present situation are not unlikely to outweigh the potential disadvantages of computerized decision-making. Let us examine why this may be so.

Consider two typical classes of problems that the average citizen recurrently encounters in his dealings with bureaucracies: rigidly applied policies, and errors. As in the case of other social events, the extent to which such occurrences may engender social discontent is primarily a function of their interpretation. This interpretation depends on a variety of variables, two of which are of special interest for our present purpose. The first is the process of attribution of responsibility, which under the prevalent social norms makes it incumbent upon the author of a mistake to bear the cost of redressing it. The other is the ubiquitous process of social comparison, which under a declared policy of universalism makes any exceptional treatment of individuals or groups, especially if these have distinguishing socio-economic characteristics, a potential source of feelings of injustice or relative deprivation (see Merton, 1959, especially Chapter 8, where the consequences of feelings of relative deprivation, including their relation to the perceived legitimacy of social structures, are discussed in detail).

These two processes are important reasons for the contemporary discontent with bureaucracies. The average citizen is more likely than not to have to bear the costs (time, negative reaction of the clerks, burden of proof, etc.) of having bureaucratic errors corrected. At the same time, he is quite unlikely to benefit from the limited amount of flexibility of which clerical bureaucracies are capable—either in the form of priority of service, or of a privileged application (or waiving) of rules; as a rule such favors are bestowed upon those who command the proper social connections or resources. Under such conditions, the possibility of a computerized bureaucracy presents at least two attractive features to the general public.

The first is psychological and normative, and one of its aspects has been illustrated by the example of the Tillie in Chapter 8: if services have to be mechanical, then it may be psychologically more appealing to deal directly with a machine than "to be anything but fingerprinted" by role-incumbents for exactly the same service. The necessity of securing the good will of a clerk is a cost that has little justification for most citizens. This is the more so if we take into consideration that because of the logic of bureaucratic operations, this requirement tends to be asymmetrical; indeed, from the point of view of the official, and as opposed to business relations, the customer is an entity with attributes to be categorized, not a free agent endowed with the right to choose. A clerical bureaucracy is therefore currently human more in the sense of the consideration it expects and exacts for its workers, than for what it can or feels obligated to give to its ascribed and choiceless clientele of categorized social entities. For the average citizen the replacement of certain clerical bureaucracies by computerized ones may therefore make little difference in terms of feelings of rigidity and impersonality of treatment. It can be expected, however, to make a significant difference for other feelings that enter into the complex calculus of social preference—in particular those which stem from the processes of attribution of responsibility and of social comparison noted above. Thus, by the logic of its mode of operation, a computerized bureaucracy equalizes the treatment of the powerful and the powerless. Additionally, it removes the need to ask for services to which one is entitled, as if they were favors that a clerk, paid in part with one's tax money, might withhold or delay. Furthermore, it eliminates the kind of unreliability due to routine human errors that is an inevitable part of clerical bureaucracies. On the other hand, a related characteristic of computerized bureaucracies is worth noting: when they do make an error, it is likely to be a systematic one; as a consequence, the mistake generally affects a large number of people, and whatever inconvenience it may cause, an error of this type has at least the advantage of avoiding the individuation of the task and responsibility of redressing it. That is, by sharpening and magnifying the problem, as well as reducing its rate of occurrence, a computerized bureaucracy removes the average citizen from his structural isolation and reduces the necessity and frequency of his having to bear alone the burden of errors or idiosyncratic decisions. In broad terms, therefore, one important psychological appeal of a computerized bureaucracy is its potential ability to get to the heart of the average citizen's feelings of powerlessness vis-à-vis omnipotent clerks and of his feelings of relative deprivation compared to those who, through power, prestige, or social connections, can either influence or by-pass such clerks when need be. The normative and moral advantage of such a transformation, on the other hand, revolves around the marginal loss of flexibility that the computerization of a bureaucracy involves. This seemingly paradoxical consequence can be speculatively derived from the following consideration. Disregarding for the moment the impact of the process of computerization on the staff of a bureaucracy, this type of automation is likely to be regarded as a very dangerous development by various formal and informal elites; indeed, they stand to lose the measure of favoritism and human touch of which clerical bureaucracies are capable. But as far as the general public is concerned, a moment of thought shows that most, if not all, the objections to this feared development apply with equal force to the present situation. Consequently, by exposing the fundamental problems of bureaucratic operations, the issue of computerization is likely to bring about a realignment of interests. This can be expected to follow from the fact that the sharpening of the issue of rigidity and impersonality that computerization perforce brings about makes salient for everyone, including the powerful and the influential, the problems inherent in bureaucratic operations, and leaves no choice but to confront them systematically and directly, for the benefit of everybody. Put differently, the computerization of certain bureaucracies may well become a social issue which can force attention to some of their shortcomings and, in the absence of some other alternative, generate a social demand for the kind of improvement in reliability, efficiency, equality, and for the realignment of social interests, that computerized bureaucracies can bring about—at little or no additional cost in impersonality for most people.

Whether these psychological and normative dynamics of change will actually materialize and gain momentum or not, computerized bureaucracy has in any event an inherent feature which alone might be felt to be of determining importance, and which justifies giving it serious consideration. This is the built-in ability to provide a workable solution to the vexing problem of representativeness. To elaborate this point, it is useful first to return briefly to the discussion of the previous subsection. The major conclusion was that for routine decision-making the task of a discretionary decision-maker should be limited to that of identifying the relevant variables. As the discussion of the cybernetic approach in Chapter 2 has led us to expect, we are therefore faced with the task of retrieving what in this conceptual framework was referred to as the *critical variables,* i.e., those selected aspects of the input which are used by servomechanisms for decision-making. As anticipated, these variables turn out to be few in number and rather simple (paramorphically) in form and, additionally, at the very heart of the procedures that repetitive decision-makers actually use, although, as a rule, without awareness. Because of this lack of awareness, the task of identification requires that the information necessary for the construction of the models be obtained primarily through the analysis of actual decisions. In a computerized bureaucracy this implies that one or more pools of experts or skillful decision-makers must be available to provide by their actual decision-making behavior the data needed for model building. Procedurally, this can be achieved by giving to such experts appropriate decision-making tasks in experimental settings. For instance, man simulations, especially of the in-basket type (cf., Frederiksen, 1962), or the "cognograph" technique (cf., Balke, Hammond, and Meyer, 1973; Hammond and Brehmer, 1973), together with some form of the Delphi method (cf., Roberts, 1976; Linstone and Turoff, 1975; Enzer, 1970), could provide the setting and the means of data gathering required.

For our present purpose, however, the important point is that such pools of decision-makers are not only necessary (at least as long as the field of artificial intelligence has not made a currently unforeseen quantum jump beyond its present stage of development, cf. Dreyfus, 1972), but constitute a completely new function. As such, they create an opportunity for a renewed effort to find more affective solutions to the basic problems of representativeness and validity already noted.

Krislov (1974) points out that the problem of representativeness has a long history which goes back at least to the time of the ancient Greeks; it has never been satisfactorily solved, whether by means of lotteries, selective recruitment, or quotas. The point is that in modern times this problem has been magnified to such an extent that, even without taking into account futuristic scenarios à la Hacker, the challenge of the coming decades may well be nothing less than to avoid stumbling into a new form of tyranny (cf., Steinbruner, 1974, p. 7). This challenge is so complex that at the present time little more can be said in this volume than to point out that the new function will offer the chance of addressing this problem anew. It is probably safe, however, to anticipate that at least two characteristics of the future administrative role under discussion should facilitate the task of structuring it in the appropriate direction. One is related to the fact that the role of a human decision-making "model" casts the problem of recruitment and of appropriate criteria of selection in a new light, and can therefore be expected to afford, if not more degrees of freedom, at least different ones. The other is that such a role is structurally of the task-force type. This fact implies a mode of organization involving some kind of rotation, a principle of organization that is regarded—when feasible—as one of the most effective approaches to the problem of representativeness, especially if it can be geared to an appropriate policy of recruitment.

The contribution that the new functional role can make to the problem of validity is closely related to these characteristics. The substance of this role is to produce enough repetitive judgments in an experimental setting to allow their formalization. The transience and artificiality of such settings, however, immediately reveal the great danger that the indiscriminate incorporation into an actual computer bureaucracy of the freshly retrieved decision rules may present. Note that this is in many ways exactly what currently takes place unobrusively in most bureaucracies, where, in the absence of an appropriate subculture and of validating procedures, rules are de facto routinized on the basis of little more than intuition, "experience," etc. (cf., Chapter 10). But, quite clearly, the issue of mechanization makes it psychologically impossible to evade the problem.

As an illustrative example of the structure (rather than the substance) of the difficulty which must be confronted, consider the task of diagnosing ulcers discussed in Chapter 8. It will be recalled that the lack of consensus between the experts stemmed in part from the fact that the judgmental task turned out to have been at times operationalized by different decision rules. For instance, seven of the nine radiologists viewed small ulcer craters as more likely to be indicative of malignancy than large craters. Moreover, a follow-up study showed that the problem of lack of consensus cannot always be safely resolved by using a majority rule; on the basis of statistical evidence it would seem that it is large craters rather than small ones which are more likely to be malignant (cf., Slovic and Lichtenstein, 1973, p. 45; and for a different example of the problem of illusory correlations, see Chapman and Chapman, 1969).

For our present concern, the point is that validating studies of this kind are naturally triggered by the process of modeling; indeed, the great advantage of this process is that "It is capable of highlighting individual differences and misuse of information as well as making explicit the causes of underlying disagreements among judges in both simple and complex tasks" (Slovic and Lichtenstein, 1973, p. 45). As a result, this process forces attention to the need of having schools of thought, as well as opinions, properly represented, not only for the task of generating enough decisions for modeling, but also for providing the minimum number of alternative models without which a rational selection of those which are to become standard operating procedures is impossible. It further stresses the cardinal importance of actual validation as a decision rule and, by contrast, the danger of having differences resolved by armchair thinking—whether this be done by systems analysts or bureaucrats, alone or in committees. In other words, by bringing out into the open one of the fundamental problems of the bureaucratic mode of operation, the new functional role reveals a pitfall which should be avoided by all bureaucracies. By the same token, however, it suggests that should a misguided computerized bureaucracy allow its officials to select arbitrarily among competing decision rules the set that will be routinized through programming, or avoid altogether to consider alternatives, little would be either changed or lost in comparison with the present situation. Indeed, in clerical bureaucracies as in computerized ones, the solution to the problem rests ultimately on a system whereby alternative procedures are continuously generated and then standardly evaluated, initially to select among them and later to ascertain their continued adequacy.

In sum, then, by objectivizing the existence of inconsistencies and underscoring the importance of planned redundancy as the only valid means of resolving them, the new functional role highlights the inherent shortcoming of procedures which are routinized without a representative sampling of legitimate or reasonable alternatives and without a selection rule based on a process of validation. At the same time, because of its logic such a role provides both an organizational framework for addressing the problem of representativeness and the first element required for attempting to transform bureaucratic organizations into more self-correcting systems. Indeed, one of the functions of the new role is precisely to produce systematically alternative decision-making rules for any new problem. The existence of such alternatives—as of information in general; cf., Chapter 2—does not guarantee, of course, their proper use. But the point is that they are a precondition for such a use, and, should this functional role materialize, it might offer a means not only to increase the validity of bureaucratic operations but also, by a process of reciprocal feedback, to improve the human heuristics on which the continuous development of computerized bureaucracies will depend in the foreseeable future.

To recapitulate, then, because a computerized bureaucracy might come to be viewed by many as psychologically less frustrating than a clerically staffed one, as socially more equitable, as technically more reliable, and because it holds the promise of a partial solution to some of the unresolved problems of representativeness and validity, the notion of an automated bureaucracy may well gain growing support. The actual outcome of these dynamics of change, however, must be anticipated to ultimately depend on the balance of functions and dysfunctions that the transformation will be expected to yield by various segments of the population who can directly either advance or obstruct its occurrence—in particular the employees who may stand to lose their jobs, or at least be displaced. (The other side of the coin is, of course, that an equal number of different or upgraded clerical functions may well in the long run provide a similar number of jobs, as well as improved services, but this is a consideration of a different order, and one which is unlikely to be relevant for those who have a vested interest in the present situation).

Be this as it may, two considerations stand out with some clarity. The first is that the transformation under discussion does not seem to depend any longer on considerations of feasibility, even if one takes into account the present state of the art, which can only be called rudimentary. The second is self-evident: the transformation hinges on the outcome of the dynamics of change at work. In this connection, as Levitt (1976) points out, the problem appears to be primarily one of social values and orientations. What he says of services in general applies with particular force to the special case of bureaucracies.

> Manufacturing has outperformed service because it has for a long time thought technocratically and managerially about its functions. Service has lagged because it has thought humanistically. Since all of us are human, and none machines, that is an unappetizing pill to swallow. Yet regardless of what we would like, it is inescapable that as long as we think in largely humanistic rather than technocratic terms, the service sector of the modern economy will forever lag. So long as we view service as invariably personal—as something performed entirely by personal effort or by the dedication of individuals for the direct benefit of other individuals—it prevents us from seeking alternatives to the use of people. It prevents us from redesigning the tasks themselves; from entertaining revised purposes; from creating new . . . processes, systems, organizations, or controls; perhaps, even, from eliminating the condi-

tions that created the problems in the first place (Levitt, 1976, pp. 92-93).

These remarks, especially in the case of bureaucracies, contain in a nutshell the assumption which underlies the proposition that the conflicting dynamics of change at work will ultimately be resolved in the direction of some form of automation.

THE FUNCTIONALITY-DYSFUNCTIONALITY SPIRAL

In the process of discussing some dynamics of change, I have touched upon one organizational aspect of computerized bureaucracy—the role of the decision-maker "model." In order to anticipate some of the potential strengths and weaknesses of such a system, it is now useful to add some strokes to the sketch of the morphology of an organization of this type.

To concretize the discussion, consider the following digest of an actual case. It is taken from Steinbruner (1974), who relates it to illustrate the "grooved" mode of thinking which is characteristic of clerical bureaucracies:

> A person or organizational entity in such a mode attends to a small number of variables pertinent to the decision problem. Typically, the categories or concepts which the decision maker in this mode uses are determined by ranges of values on the critical variables. . . .
> It will be clear that this process is characteristic of the common bureaucrat. . . . A casually selected newspaper story provides an example: A young, unwed mother gave her baby up for adoption. The adoption agency, following established procedure, matched the baby with a set of new parents on certain characteristics and initiated adoption proceedings. The young, unwed natural father of the child then petitioned to adopt his own child, arguing that he had a job, that his parents would provide shelter and a home atmosphere, and that he had, in fact, cared for the child for several months already. The agency found him unacceptable—he was a man, he was too young, he was unmarried, his job did not pay enough. The young father, the press, and several politicians were outraged. The father struck those who knew him as mature, responsible, devoted to the child and—the critical point—he was the *natural* father. The agency, however, would not budge (Steinbruner, 1974, pp. 126-127).

First, translating the relevant elements of this example into the terminology that we have used, the variables of the heuristic which is involved (or more accurately, of its evaluation function) are evident; they include the sex, age, marital status, and income of the would-be parent. Whoever falls in the proper category, or within the permissible range of variation of these variables, qualifies; whoever falls outside one or more of them does not. However, actual paternity, as the young petitioner found out, is neither included among the variables of the evaluation function, nor is it one of the heuristic's side conditions (see Chapter 4).

With this example in mind, consider now the main classes of tasks that a computerized bureaucracy must perform.

To begin with, it must be able to process appeals to its decisions. It is useful to distinguish between the following (nonexhaustive) categories of appeals:

(1) *Requests for exceptional rulings.* This type of appeal involves a plea for an unusual ruling which need not serve as a precedent, much less as the basis for a standard operating procedure. Rather, it calls for a unique decision on grounds similar to those provided by the legal principal of equity. This kind of appeal may involve one or more of the remedial steps which operationalize the other classes of appeals. In this case, however, their applicability is explicitly deemed to be restricted to a unique case which justifies, for one reason or another, a decision based on the notion of natural justice.

(2) *Recognition of trade-offs.* The aim of petitions of this kind is that trade-offs be recognized between the characteristics which determine the process of categorization. For instance, in the adoption case used as an illustration, had the young father been very wealthy, he could have asked that the income criterion which is part of the standard decision-making procedure by given additional weight (e.g., because of the opportunities that wealth can provide to a child), and be used to compensate for his failure to qualify on one or more of the other criteria; the argument used by the young natural father—the inclusion of an additional criterion—is functionally of the same type.

(3) *Application to border-line cases.* This kind of request differs from the preceding one in that no trade-off is suggested. To illustrate the nature of these appeals, assume that the upper age limit of a couple applying for adoption is set at 45. Prospective parents who have reached the age of 46, but would qualify on all the other criteria, might consider applying for a special exemption which would fall under this heading. Cases of this kind are typically appealed in the hope that the authorities will show some understanding and a measure of flexibility.

(4) *Correction of errors,* is a class of appeals which is self-explanatory.

(5) *Representations related to validity.* This category is made of the appeals which rest primarily on the argument that a given decision procedure is invalid, or even counter-productive. As an illustration, imagine the hypothetical argument that the criteria of adoption in use in fact exclude many potentially supportive parents in favor of conformist homes. It is noteworthy that because issues of validity and of side-effects are researchable, appeals based on such considerations can legitimately be made not only by those directly affected, but also by qualified experts (e.g., social workers, social scientists, etc.).

(6) *Representations related to policies.* These are appeals which question the very goals sought or implied by certain procedures and may raise political issues. For instance, a petition against the denial of the right of single persons to adopt children would be a case in point.

As a side remark, note that this typology, however gross, nonetheless highlights by implication the number and types of arbitrary decisions which are constantly made in clerical bureaucracies, and the corresponding problem of the insidious spread of the tyranny of nonrepresentative administrative decision-making against which the students of various public bureaucracies warn us.

Be this as it may, in addition to processing appeals to its standard mode of decision-making, a computerized bureaucracy must also perform a variety of other functions. These include the capacity to consider requests whose urgency might justify a priority of servicing; the ability to clarify to the general public the system's mode of operation; and the possibility of offering, when need be, explanations related to the input and output of the system. These functions, together with those of policy-making and programming, suggest an overall structure of the kind outlined in Figure 11.1.

The relationship of the public to such a system (in addition to the indirect linkage to the policy-makers through the political process), mainly takes three forms. One is the direct access to the input and output of the computerized module (arrow 2). Another is the possibility to be assisted in this task by a clerical staff fulfilling the type of auxiliary functions listed in the rightmost box (arrow 1). The third is the ability to make appeals and special requests of the kind just discussed (arrow 3).

The growth of such a system can normally be expected to take place through increased automation of the auxiliary functions to which arrow 1 points (by interactive explanations and displays, machine-ready forms, etc.), and simultaneously, but probably at a slower pace, through automation of the other repetitive functions, e.g., validation and programming and especially the handling of special requests. The latter function is conceptually contiguous with that of generating standard operating procedures. As data about the outcome of special requests accumulate, models of the heuristics which operationalize the decision-making process by which they are disposed of should therefore become readily retrievable and formalizable by means of the same methodology that we have discussed, that is, without the need for advances in artificial intelligence that the automation of more creative or unique tasks, e.g., programming, designing ad hoc validating studies, etc., still requires.

The type of computerized bureaucracy which is feasible is therefore a man-machine hybrid which can be looked at in two different ways. It can be regarded as the first stage toward a completely automated system in the

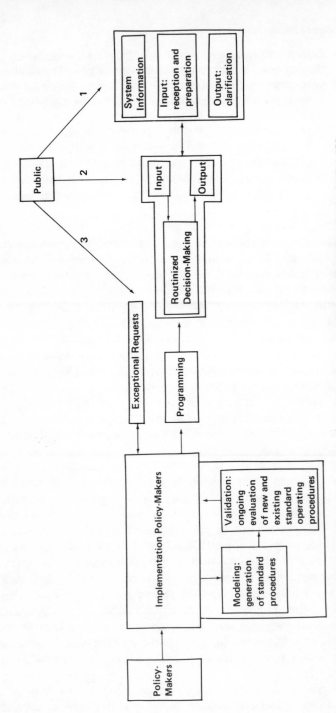

Figure 11.1: OUTLINE OF THE FUNCTIONAL COMPONENTS OF A COMPUTERIZED BUREAUCRACY

making. Alternatively, however, it can also be viewed as a new kind of clerical bureaucracy where the computerized part is an aid to the clerical functions (mostly upgraded) that it retains. Note that in both cases the computerized segment which is currently designable can replace the lower-echelon clerks and fulfill the decision-making functions of the middle management, but little more. This follows from the already noted fact that effective modeling is currently bounded at the lower end by tasks which, although repetitive, require complex pattern-recognition capabilities or sensory-manipulative coordination or both, and at the upper end, by nonrepetitive tasks and creative thinking (cf., Chapter 8; see also Simon, 1960, p. 49; and Dreyfus, 1972, pp. 203-207); these boundaries mark the functions to which arrows 1 and 3 point in Figure 11.1.

This middle-range computerization of the bureaucratic function that recent advances in our (paramorphic) understanding of repetitive human information-processing makes possible has been anticipated from the start (Leavitt and Whisler, 1958; Simon, 1960, p. 49, and also footnote 6, p. 29). The similarly predictable growth of the computerized segment in both directions raises, however, questions which are especially significant when we consider the consequences that might follow the automation of the left hand part of Figure 11.1. When we confront this issue, the question is no longer how we choose to look in the abstract at the man-machine system, but rather which of the two types of possible bureaucracies we would like to help materialize and develop with as few mistakes as possible.

Of all the dangers that a completely automated bureaucracy brings to mind, the one which is possibly the most feared is the implied necessity to submit to the decisions of a robot-like entity, which may in the long run become as monstrous as did Hacker's hypothetical firm. Quite clearly, this might become reality in the future as a function of advances in artificial intelligence, which, however, have still to materialize. But without engaging in such speculations, there is already a more pedestrian pitfall which deserves special attention. This is the danger of a self-defeating remedy to the problem of man's limited information-processing capability, on which part of the rationale for computerizing certain segments of the bureaucratic decision-making process rests in the first place. As Shubik (1975) notes: "A complex computerized model may take on many of the bad aspects of a black box in the sense that when some of the original designers and users have departed there may no longer be anyone around who remembers exactly why a certain system or part of the simulation was built" (Shubik, 1975, p. 282). In other words, the real and immediate danger is not defeat by a computerized bureaucracy's autonomous "will," but more prosaically by our own ignorance, the same limitation which puts the detailed workings of a present-day clerical bureaucracy (which incidentally *does* combine a complex structure with a "will" of its own) beyond our grasp. The danger to avoid, then, at least as long as we have not developed an adequate subculture and effective referencing procedures, is to fall into the trap of insidiously replacing one black box with another. If only for this reason, it would seem very necessary to look in the foreseeable future at computerization as a module for a new kind of clerical bureaucracy and to direct our efforts resolutely toward fostering this kind of development, even if the social forces which are likely to oppose the change-over were not to oppose even more strongly the drastic alternative transformation.

Under the assumption that for both topical and sociological reasons this will indeed be the major path of development of computerized bureaucracies, and that when degrees of freedom are available, it will be prudently preferred, let us now conclude with a renewed look at some of the functions and dysfunctions that one can anticipate such a man-machine system to have.

To begin with functions, consider the integration of an organization of this kind with society. We have already noted a fact that bears repetition: the opportunity created for increasing the representativeness of the system. The role of the people whose function is to serve as "models" for generating standard operating procedures and, even more so, the nature of the task of the officials whose responsibility is to determine the policies of implementation by selecting among these models as well as by handling the special requests, are readily available reminders of the importance of the problem. Yet, it is noteworthy that in clerical bureaucracies the acuity of the parallel difficulty tends to be blurred by the notion that the value premises of decision-making rapidly lose their importance as we move down the hierarchy of the bureaucracy. Somehow, this proposition, in itself valid, often leaves the mistaken impression that in strict hierarchies of this kind, the importance of these premises, and consequently of *individually* developed heuristics, becomes practically negligible immediately below the top level of policy-making. By replacing by a computerized module the middle- and lower-echelon employees, however, a man-machine bureaucracy has the great merit of clarifying both the role of the upper middle management and the issue—as the nature of the decisions called for by the special requests make manifest. One of the functional consequences of a man-machine bureaucracy can therefore be expected to be a renewed and determined effort to find a workable solution to this important problem by simultaneously providing a clear rationale and a structural opportunity.

Another functional effect which can be anticipated is related to the pitfall noted above of perfunctorily replacing one black box with another. This danger might bring about a transient mode of dual organization which might well evolve into a more permanent type of arrangement. As long as a complete and effective referencing system is not developed, the computerized module might be used as a model in the sense discussed in Chapter 10, with the referent clerical bureaucracy remaining full operative. Under such conditions, the computerized segment also being fully operative itself, several possibilities arise.

One is the opportunity to upgrade the model by also modeling actual decision-making behavior rather than its experimentally induced counterpart only. Another is to clarify the potential limitations of creating artificial heuristics for repetitive problems, on the one hand, and, on the other, the irrelevant distortions that organizational life might introduce in those which develop naturally in specific environments.

In terms of its articulation with society, such a dual mode of organization might open an intriguing avenue for a new kind of societal arrangement based on the elimination of some of the monopolistic characteristics of present-day bureaucracies. In particular, the availability of an automated module (for standard decisions) might offer new possibilities for handling illegal strikes and, above all, allow the public to manifest its preference for the kind of service received, without the necessity of an a priori commitment to any single black box. The availability of the computerized module, possibly along the lines exemplified by the operation of the Tillies in banks (see Chapter 8), would indeed allow a continuous and behavioral evaluation of performance by the clientele. Because this evaluation—which might be loosely labeled a "Turing test of satisfaction"[1]—would express itself in actual choice of patronage, it is not unreasonable to expect that it might put continuous pressure for improvement on the system and thus induce a socially beneficial spiral-like process of development (in the sense of dialectic and open-ended).

In short, the potential functionality of computerized modules, either as components of man-machine systems, or as constructs having the potential to force clerical bureaucracies to reflect on the quality of their services and to reform and/or reorganize themselves accordingly, makes the prospect of such a development rationally attractive.

The other side of the coin is, of course, the possible dysfunctions of such a development. One obvious dysfunction is easily predictable. This is the disruption of the job structure and of individual careers that the change-over to one of the possible forms of the man-machine or of the dual type of bureaucracy that we have discussed entails. (The latter is probably the less disruptive as a function of its more progressive rate of transformation. Paradoxically, however, it is not unlikely to be the more frustrating—as suggested by one of the mechanisms underlying feelings of relative deprivation, in this case the comparison with "normal" clerical bureaucracies—see Merton, 1959, especially pp. 236-237.) As noted in Chapter 1, however, this issue, however important, falls outside the scope of this volume.

Another set of potential dysfunctions is related to other socially undesirable consequences, including the possible spread of dehumanized relations, wide-scale mistakes, centralization, etc. These potential shortcomings have been examined in Chapter 8. It will be recalled that they have been shown to be neither necessary nor unique to computerized processes. Moreover, it was observed that there is generally another side to each of these dysfunctions. While it is true, for instance, that the perfect memory of computerized files facilitates the perpetuation of mistakes, it is also true that they have an unmatched capability of totally forgetting whatever information is erased from their memory (for instance, unrepeated juvenile offenses).

This example brings us to a third type of dysfunctions—possible misuses, or what has come to be known as "crime by computer." Indeed, there may be fraudulent erasures, insertions, and modifications, and, in general, unauthorized access to part or all of the system. The mind boggles at the realization of the variety and ingenuity of the schemes already used for perpetrating this new type of crime (see Parker, 1976). By the yardstick of this experience, of necessity limited, one can only wonder about what the future holds in store.

But the critical question, evidently, is how this danger compares with its present-day equivalent, white-collar crime. Such a comparison is unfortunately difficult to make, because while the incidence and cost of crime in general are difficult to evaluate—perhaps as much as 85 percent of it goes unrecorded—the situation is even worse in the case of white-collar offenses. Nonetheless, an estimate, however gross, will prove enlightening. From the rough statistics available, the following picture emerges. In the midsixties the losses from embezzlement, fraud, tax fraud, and forgery in the United States have been evaluated to amount to between 1.5 and 2 billion dollars annually (cf., Parker, 1976, p. 294). By comparison: "The annual white-collar crime losses in the United States were estimated in 1974 by the U.S. Chamber of Commerce to be not less than $40 billion, including only $0.1 billion ($100 million) loss from computer-related crime" (Parker, 1976, p. 294). It would therefore seem that the computer once more dramatizes a pervasive problem to which we have grown accustomed and insensitive in its clerical form. This does not mean, of course, that the dangers of computer crime are illusory. But this does suggest that it is important to keep in mind the alternative, and to put the anticipated difficulty in proper perspective. Parker points out that constant technical, legal, and organizational progress is being made to insure and improve the safety and confidentiality of computer operations. He also speculates that after a peak of crimes and abuses in the nineteen-eighties, safety is likely to start to win out, with a concomitant decrease in incidence, although probably not in scope (cf., Parker, 1976, pp. 293-296). This view does not purport, of course, to be anything else than a reasoned speculation, for nobody can be certain that the dialectic process of abuses and remedies will actually have this time-scale and this form. But the abysmal magnitude of what currently sets white-collar crime apart from computer abuses makes one thing evident: there is ample room for even costly failures before the attempts and experiments which are needed to clarify this issue can be confidently regarded as evidence that in practice computerized processes are indeed at a crime-opportunity disadvantage (relative to the present situation).

The last dysfunction to be considered centers around the paralyzing effect that the break-down of a highly integrated system can be expected to have. This is obviously a very serious problem, and one with which large-scale sudden power failures have already begun to familiarize us. Its closest present-day equivalent would probably be a total, instantaneous, and unforeseen wildcat strike. Not surprisingly, this serious danger has the property of suggesting criminal acts—for instance rendering a system inoperative by kid-napping for ransom part or all of the software—as has already occurred (Parker, 1976, p. 20). On the safety side, the current remedies include the duplication and remote storage of back-up copies of the most important data files and programs (with their operating instructions) and disaster recovery plans (cf., Parker, 1976, p. 281). At present little more can be said about their efficiency than to note that they are built on the sound principle of redundancy, which must necessarily hold the key to the problem—if there is any.

As the foregoing selective discussion suggests dysfunctions are serious, but not necessarily insuperable. Clearly, they should not be underestimated. But if I have been successful in showing the relevance and usefulness of the information-processing approach for the study and reconceptualization of bureaucratic decision-making, these possible dysfunctions might now be regarded as costs which must be rationally weighed rather than as over-whelming considerations against any attempt to computerize the processes of decision-making.

NOTE

1. The Turing test (Turing, 1963, pp. 11-13) aims at allowing one to decide whether or not a machine can be considered "intelligent" (or to "think"). This aim can be achieved by programming a machine to perform a task, say playing chess, and putting it in one of two rooms, the other being occupied by an actual player. The test then runs as follows: A second player—the judge—is placed in a third room, from where he can communicate through typewritten notes with either the machine or the actual player (without knowing which is which). After playing a game with each of his opponents, the judge must decide which was the machine. The experiment is repeated several times. If as a rule the judge's guesses are random, let alone if he is wrong, the machine qualifies as "intelligent."

The logic of this famous test rests on a functional approach to the entity (conceived as a black box) which has to be evaluated for a specific purpose. By a loose analogy, and judging by their popularity, cars can be viewed as better horses than are actual ones; similarly, computerized bureaucracies could be judged to be more satisfactory for some purposes than the actual ones, both systems being evaluated as the black boxes that they are (to the public).

Chapter 12

CONCLUSION: A BEGINNING

Some twenty years ago, Leavitt and Whisler (1958, p. 44) prophesied in their paper "Management in the 1980's" that one of the major effects of the new information technology "is likely to be intensive programming of many jobs now held by middle managers." About the same time, and in a similar vein, Simon expressed the following views in an invited paper in *Management and Corporations in 1985* (Anshen and Bach, 1960):

> The plain fact is that a great many middle-management decisions that have always been supposed to call for the experienced human judgment of managers and professional engineers can now be made at least as well by computers as by managers. Moreover, a large part of the total middle-management job consists of decisions of the same general character as those that have already yielded to automation. The decisions are repetitive and require little of the kinds of flexibility that constitute man's principal comparative advantage over machines (Simon, 1960, p. 43).

In this passage, Simon was commenting on the kind of managerial decisions that could be handled by operations research techniques, e.g., decisions about production rate, product mix, stock management, shipping of goods, etc., and replace those made by middle-management. On the basis of the first results of what has come to constitute the present body of knowledge about human information-processing, he further noted that "there is no longer reason to regard phenomena like 'judgment' and 'insight' as either unanalyzable or unanalyzed" (Simon, 1960, p. 46). Accordingly, he predicted that the same would inevitably hold true within a few years for ill-structured problems of the kind that we have discussed in this book.

Time-wise, Simon's predictions have turned out to be somewhat off; the speed of the development of automation has not been what he anticipated because advances in artificial intelligence and in the theory of general heuristics (see Newell and Simon, 1972), although significant, have tended to remain behind schedule. But the discussion in the preceding chapter has shown that with empirically retrieved heuristics and adequate organizational arrangements the endeavor is nonetheless feasible and can begin to get under way. In general, therefore, and specific mode of implementation aside, what has been said can be regarded as documenting the wisdom of these predictions.

But while part of the discussion points to this likely development, I have noted in Chapter 8 that my core argument is of a more limited nature. To put the whole discussion in perspective, it is useful to conclude with an explicit statement of this argument.

To a large extent the argument is subsumed by the proposition that owing to the characteristics of human information processing, it is in any event useful to construct models of bureaucratic decision-making whether or not automation is contemplated.

This proposition rests on the consideration that in a bureaucracy the overwhelming majority of the decisions are made by routine application of standard operating procedures, whether these are written, normative, or simply habitual (e.g., "discretionary" decisions). Accordingly, the day-to-day operations embody, in effect, the assumption that the standard operating procedures are valid solutions to the problems which evoke them.

Obviously, this need not be the case. Nevertheless, for a decision-making system operating primarily by means of routinely applied heuristics, validity may be the central issue. To a certain extent it may even be functionally equivalent to what profit is for the firm. As the latter is never the only goal of a corporation, neither is the former for a bureaucracy; in both cases a number of additional goals and considerations act as constraints, and the level of profit sought, like that of validity, always represents an explicit or, more often, an implicit trade-off between such considerations as, say, profit and production safety, or validity and the ease with which information can be obtained. A significant difference, however, is that for a variety of egoistic and structural reasons the profit motive can be relied upon for correcting disregards for the primary goal and raison d'être of existing processes of production in economic enterprises—earnings. Validity, the parallel raison d'être of any set of standard operating procedures does not rest on any comparable underlying driving force which can insure continuous efforts to maximize it. The result, as noted in Chapter 10, is that the standard operating procedures of a bureaucracy are characteristically non-self-corrective.

In order to remedy this fundamental deficiency, what is probably required is that both the means and the motivation for doing so be provided by an appropriate institutional arrangement. By the nature of the functions that it can fulfill, the type of model that we have discussed could potentially be a key element in such an arrangement. This follows from the fact that by objectivizing the referent process, such a model provides a strategic meeting ground for administrators to probe their belief system, or for interested parties to whom they are responsible (e.g., the political system) to do so, and for bringing to bear disciplinary research on the decision-making process in the manner discussed in Chapter 10. Models of this kind therefore constitute a natural means to validate both the decision-making procedures themselves and the rationale or rationalization which leads to their repetitive use. While such models are primarily a means of validation in this dual sense, by facilitating the performance of this task and making salient the need to perform it, they might also create some motivation to do so. It is conceivable, therefore, that they could also add some incentive of their own to the more sustained drive that an adequate institutional arrangement must in any case provide if bureaucratized decision-making is to become genuinely self-corrective.

Put differently, the gist is that the same information-processing limitations which make us unaware of the nature of repetitive decisions—a state of affairs which in itself justifies modeling them—also put outside the range of our unaided information-processing capability the adequate understanding of the operation of the system as a whole. A means to overcome this difficulty is therefore needed as a building block for whatever remedy is contemplated.

One major obstacle to the use of models, as of research in general, for such a purpose lies in the logic of the incremental mode of policy-making. As Greenberger et al. note, "Since the prospective costs and benefits of incremental decisions will tend to be relatively small, it makes little sense to invest large amounts of time, energy, and money in the collection and analysis of information to illuminate them" (Greenberger, Crenson, and Crissey, 1976, p. 40).

To the extent that this orientation also prevails at the stage of the routinized implementation of policies with which we are concerned, as there are reasons to believe that it does, a vicious circle is obviously created. Because of uncertainties, lack of knowledge, and information-processing limitations, changes in modalities of policy implementation must tend to be incremental. And because they are so, the development of the means which could help guide the more than incremental changes which might be required, tends to be looked upon as wasteful investments.

As a rule, this vicious circle is regarded as ultimately anchored in the socio-political environment, which makes it unrewarding to act otherwise. But it has also been argued that "the development of public policy and the methods of its administration owe less in the long run to processes of conflict among political parties and social and economic pressure groups than to the more objective process of research and discussion among professional groups" (Don K. Price, quoted in Greenberger, Crenson, and Crissey, 1976, p. 43).

The central thesis of this book rests on precisely such an assumption. It holds that because of advances in a number of subfields, and for the reasons presented in the course of the discussions, an important step towards monitoring and steering decision-making bureaucracies can and probably should now be taken—whether or not automation is also considered.

We must guard against two possible misunderstandings of the nature of this step.

First, the discussion as a whole applies *only* to bureaucratized processes of *decision-making*. To clarify and make as explicit as possible what these processes do and do not encompass, consider the following fairly representative definition of a (public) bureaucracy. By a bureaucracy is meant "a certain kind of formal organization, characterized by a complex administrative hierarchy, specialization of skills and tasks, prescribed limits on discretion set forth in a system of rules, impersonal behavior with regard to clientele, and separation of ownership and control in the sense that the members of the bureaucracy no longer own the tools and instruments with which they work" (Peabody and Rourke, 1965, p. 803). Such a definition encompasses a bank and a hospital as institutions, and policemen on patrol and the officials in charge of hiring them as functions. Moreover, the definition applies to all hierarchical levels and embraces all types of decisions, whether repetitive or not. Under such conditions, and considering that any action can be regarded as a decision and vice versa, it becomes evident that in a broad sense decision-making in bureaucracies is coextensive with bureaucratic behavior.

Obviously, what has been said in this book does not apply to bureaucratic decision-making in anything resembling such an all-embracing sense. Rather, the low- and middle-echelon repetitive decisions with which we are concerned can be specified by considering the following analogy. In any given situation, middle- and low-level bureaucratic decisions can theoretically be partitioned into two classes, one for which Weber's ideal-type of executant would be a responsive and skillful robot, the other a sophisticated decision-making computer. The tasks performed by a policeman or a surgeon, on the one hand, and, on the other, those performed by a registration clerk or a personnel manager in charge of screening job applicants are examples illustrating the nature of this distinction. The point is that there are decisions which express themselves primarily by means of physical actions or sequences of actions, and others whose input *and* output primarily involve documents or information (what is meant by "primarily" is evidently a question which may raise empirical problems of identification in borderline cases, but this is a question with which we need not concern ourselves here). The former class of decisions falls outside the range of decisions with which we are concerned because of the level of sensory-manipulative coordination that they involve (illustrated by the case of the surgeon) and/or because they are usually carried out in unstandardized environments or situations, as typically occurs in the case of policemen on patrol. The class of decisions with which this book deals is therefore made of those primarily characterized by information-processing resulting in information or documents as output.

But this is the parent class. The decisions with which we are actually concerned are only a small subset of this class. This is so because for theoretical reasons it is useful to focus on decisions which are genuinely repetitive—i.e., which are carried out in a relatively controlled environment, a situation to which the bureaucratic in-house standardized or near-standardized form of both the input and output contributes. This strategy allows one to anticipate the existence of stable heuristics within the limits on discretion set forth by the bureaucratic organization and, as empirical research corroborates, to document and model them with the theoretical degree of ease and accuracy expected. In other words, one way to define the bureaucratic decisions to which the discussion applies is to state that *they are the subset of those which involve primarily repetitive tasks and functions of classification and judgment carried out in an office with relatively standardized documents and information as both input and output.* By the nature of this definition, it is clear that a significant part of these decisions and processes is what is commonly referred to by insiders and outsiders as bureaucratic red tape—a not too inaccurate characterization if one considers both the nature of the input and output in which this subclass of decisions is embedded, and the etymology of the term ("from the tying of public documents with red tape"—*Standard College Dictionary,* 1963, p. 1129).

On conceptual grounds this is a small class of decisions. Its significance lies in its theoretical characteristics and in the largely unsuspected importance that such decisions have as determinants of the output of the processes or subprocesses that they govern in various bureaucracies. The strategy we have advocated of resolutely focusing on such decisions as a substantive class of phenomena of great scientific interest in its own right is a direct consequence of these properties.

The second possible misunderstanding which should be avoided is related to the contribution that modeling can make to the validation of individual (discretionary) or code book procedures.

Because the latter are directly available and the former can readily be objectivized and formalized, modeling affords the possibility to link them directly with disciplinary research. To illustrate, imagine a bureaucratized process of recruitment or promotion. The individual or code-book prescribed decision-making rules might include such variables as age, education, experience, etc. Obviously, such decision-making rules can readily be compared with the disciplinary state-of-the-art solutions available, in particular with regard to the attributes and cutting points which should be used. One important advantage of this naturally available linkage between routine bureaucratic decision-making and disciplinary research is that it establishes a potentially useful bridge between the two fields of activity. This bridge might conceivably develop into a continuous process of reciprocal feedback, and as such provide a systematic framework for continuously improving and developing the natural and disciplinary heuristics involved on each side of the feedback loop.

At the same time, however, these possibilities of validation are not and cannot be expected to be a panacea. The reason becomes self-evident if we consider that as a result of the present state of knowledge, many procedures rest explicitly on consensual rather than criterion validation. For instance, it was found that in a number of jurisdictions it is "required that candidates have high school diplomas and two years of experience to qualify as a municipal dog catcher" (Kranz, 1976, p. 217). The arbitrariness of such criteria is obvious. But it is one thing to point out that a set of criteria is arbitrary and quite another to provide a genuinely useful alternative. When criteria or, in our terminology, evaluation functions are required—if only to select arbitrarily among too many possibilities—the only possible solution in the absence of any demonstrably valid procedure is necessarily some decision rule which is consensually regarded as acceptable. But, clearly, in such a situation the type of validating studies mentioned above (and in Chapter 10) cannot even be carried out.

What the kind of objectivization of the process of decision-making discussed can contribute under such conditions is to make salient that many decision rules are consensual in this sense, to facilitate their methodical identification, and to allow the question to be systematically raised: consensual—but in terms of which interests? Note, however, that for this purpose the properties of the decisions with which we are concerned are again a great asset. Indeed, because these decisions are generated either by stable individual heuristics or institutionalized standard operating procedures, and because their repetitive application in a bureaucratic setting is only justified if they have a demonstrably useful instrumental purpose, the rationale or rationalization for their use is either explicit or can be required to be made so on demand (say, by the proper hierarchical authority). It is therefore possible to conceive of a model which in order to be complete would include as comments (in a separate listing) the explicit functions that each of the modeled procedures is believed to fulfill by the persons responsible for their repetitive application.[1] In the case of public bureaucracies, such a listing—which is in effect the beliefs and objectives of the administrators discussed in Chapter 10—could then not only be used for the purposes of validation noted in that chapter, but also for the purpose of providing a public and administrative document that all interested parties could consult and rely on. Quite clearly, the ability of the approach to fulfill this function is of some importance. Avoiding the danger of bureaucratic tyranny requires in part the availability of a systematic means for recurrently validating the procedures whose effectiveness and improvement can be measured by reference to a criterion. In part, also, it requires making explicit the success achieved in doing so and in publicizing the procedures which in the absence of any validation attempts must be regarded—and accepted—as consensual. But while such a dual contribution may be held to be of value, it is by no means a panacea to the problem of validation. The kind of modeling discussed can uncover insufficiencies and point to ignorance gaps; but it cannot by itself bridge them.

To conclude, let us briefly return to the topic of computerized bureaucracies and close the discussion with an issue that it raises.

I have argued that such a development presents advantages which make it likely that the development will actually materialize. The assumption underlying the argument rests, however, on a view of (public) bureaucracies which might be challenged. Kranz (1976), for instance, argues that the purely instrumental view of bureaucracies is erroneous, for they are also a means of participating in the political process and a legitimate source of jobs and economic betterment. On the basis of these premises, he holds that the way to make bureaucracies more representative and more responsive is to staff them so that "the ratio of a particular group in an agency equals that group's percentage in the population in the geographical area served by that office" (Kranz, 1976, p. 79). Kranz argues that this need not affect the quality of the services, because for a multitude of jobs the selection rules used are no less arbitrary than in the example of the dog catchers and consequently bear no demonstrable relationship either to the objective requirements of the jobs or the merit principle.

From the present standpoint, the last argument is noncontroversial. It is precisely because a number of standard procedures, and not only for hiring personnel, may not be related to their declared purposes that the task of objectivization may be so necessary. The proposition that the bureaucratic function can only be controlled by modifying the clerical composition of bureaucracies is, however, a view that it has been one of the aims of this book to qualify and complement. Indeed, this view assumes that the bureaucratic processes of decision-making cannot be distinguished from the clerical mode of implementation. The information-processing approach shows, however, that such a distinction can be made and made usefully. The kind of man-machine system which becomes conceivable can then be made representative by the proper choice of decision-maker "models" and of higher-level officials, according to one's definition of representativeness.

But the increasing feasibility of an automated or semiautomated bureaucracy raises the issue of whether or not the job opportunities that they offer are (or have become) one of the intrinsic justifications of the existence of bureaucracies. For cultural and denotative reasons (e.g., "paper work"), this is obviously a question which is normatively much more controversial in the context of a bureaucracy than if automation is contemplated in an industry, and it is likely that a polemic will develop around this issue sooner or later. To the extent that this volume might be drawn into this controversy, it is important that two things above all be clearly kept in mind.

The first is that the views presented do not imply that the process of computerization be either accepted as desirable or regarded as necessary. All that they do imply is that objectivizing and monitoring certain processes of bureaucratic decision-making has now become possible, and that doing so, perhaps in the manner discussed in Chapter 10, is necessary if the process is to be genuinely controlled. The issue of whether the mode of implementation should or should not remain exclusively or primarily clerical is logically an additional question calling for value judgments in which considerations of feasibility and of anticipated benefits are only one element. My stated belief about what I regard as the social choice to be expected is exactly that—a belief. However, it is because I look upon computerization as not only the most likely development but also one fraught with potential dangers, should it actually materialize, that I have advocated that the dual mode of organization discussed in Chapter 11 be, for a long time, preferred.

The second is that this is a theoretical essay with no original research data to support any of its theses. It goes without saying, therefore, that all the points made, and not only the speculations pertaining to future developments, are legitimately open to question, especially if we consider that advocating a viewpoint often leads—wittingly or unwittingly—to overstatements and omissions. In this sense, as in many others, the argument that I have presented is at best a beginning. But as such, it indicates one possible way to operationalize and adapt to repetitive bureaucratic decision-making the implications of a simple truth: "The difference between scientists and others is not in the working of the human mind, but in the way of dealing with the imperfections of the human mind" (Ben-David, 1973, p. 450).

The time may have come to apply in earnest the implications of this fact to bureaucratic organizations.

NOTE

1. Listings of this kind should be open-ended, for aims can legitimately change, or new ones be added as a result of experiencing with a procedure. In the framework of a self-corrective system, the function of such a listing is not to obtain an immutable list of aims, but to make explicit those which are believed to be pursued and achieved at a given point in time.

REFERENCES

American College Dictionary (1970) Entry "cybernetics." New York: Random House.

ANDERSON, L.R. and M. FISHBEIN (1965) "Prediction of attitude from the number, strength, and evaluative aspect of beliefs about the attitude object: a comparison of summation and congruity theory." *Journal of Personality and Social Psychology* 3, pp. 437-443.

ANDERSON, N.H. (1971) "Integration Theory and Attitude Change." *Psychological Review,* 78, pp. 171-206.

ANSHEN, M. and G.L. BACH [eds.] (1960) *Management and Corporations 1985.* New York: McGraw-Hill.

AXELROD, R. [ed.] (1976) *Structure of Decision.* Princeton, N.J.: Princeton University Press.

BACKMAN, C.W. and P.F. SECORD [eds.] (1966) *Problems in Social Psychology.* New York. McGraw-Hill.

BALES, E.F. (1958) "Task roles and social roles in problem-solving groups." In E.E. Maccoby, T.M. Newcomb, and E.L. Hartley (eds.) *Readings in Social Psychology,* pp. 437-447. New York: Holt, Rinehart and Winston.

BALKE, W.M., K.R. HAMMOND, and G.D. MEYER (1973) "An alternate approach to labor-management relations." *Administrative Science Quarterly* 18, pp. 311-327.

BARNARD, C.I. (1938) *The Functions of the Executive.* Cambridge, Mass.: Harvard University Press.

BAUER, R.A. [ed.] (1966) *Social Indicators.* Cambridge, Mass.: M.I.T.

BECKER, S.W. and D. NEUHAUSER (1975) *The Efficient Organization.* New York: Elsevier.

BEER, S. (1959) *Cybernetics and Management.* New York: John Wiley.

BEN AARON, M. (1975) "The Pötzl effect: corroboration of a cybernetic effect." In R. Trappl and F.R. Pichler (eds.) *Progress in Cybernetics and Systems Research,* Volume I, pp. 247-252. New York: John Wiley.

BEN-DAVID, J. (1973) "The state of sociological theory and the sociological community: a review article." *Comparative Studies in Society and History* 15, pp. 448-472.

BERELSON, B. and G.A. STEINER (1964) *Human Behavior: An Inventory of Scientific Findings.* New York: Harcourt, Brace and World.

BEUTEL, F.K. (1975) "Experimental jurisprudence and systems engineering in determining policy." In S.S. Nagel (ed.) *Policy Studies and the Social Sciences,* Chapter 22. Lexington, Mass.: Lexington Books.

BIDERMAN, A.D. (1966) "Social indicators and goals." In R.A. Bauer (ed.) *Social Indicators,* pp. 68-153. Cambridge, Mass.: M.I.T.

BLAU, P.M. (1973) *The Organization of Academic Work.* New York: John Wiley.
——— (1968) "The hierarchy of authority in organizations." *American Journal of Sociology* 73, pp. 453-467.
——— (1963) *The Dynamics of Bureaucracy.* Chicago: University of Chicago Press.
———, C. McHUGH FALBE, W. McKINLEY, and P.K. TRACY (1976) "Technology and organization in manufacturing." *Administrative Science Quarterly* 21, pp. 20-40.
BLAU, P.M. and R.A. SCHOENHERR (1971) *The Structure of Organizations.* New York: Basic Books.
BLAU, P.M., W.V. HEYDEBRAND, and R.E. STAUFFER (1966) "The structure of small bureaucracies." *American Sociological Review* 31, pp. 179-191.
BLAUNER, R. (1964) *Alienation and Freedom.* Chicago: University of Chicago Press.
BONO, E. de (1971) *The Mechanism of Mind.* Harmondsworth, Middlesex: Pelican.
BORGATTA, E.F. [ed.] (1969) *Social Psychology: Readings and Perspective.* Chicago, Ill.: Rand McNally.
BRAYBROOKE, D. and C.E. LINDBLOM (1963) *A Strategy of Decision.* New York: Free Press.
BREWER, G.D. and O.P. HALL, Jr. (1972) *Policy Analysis by Computer Simulation: The Need for Appraisal.* P-4893. Santa Monica, Cal.: Rand Corporation.
BREZNITZ, S. and A. LIEBLICH (1972) "How to simulate if you must: simulating the dream-work." In M. Inbar and C. Stoll, *Simulation and Gaming in Social Science,* pp. 69-91. New York: Free Press.
BROOKS, R. (1975) *A Model of Human Cognitive Behavior in Writing Code for Computer Program.* Volume I, AD-A013-582. Springfield, Va.: National Technical Information Service, U.S. Department of Commerce.
BROWN, R. (1965) *Social Psychology.* New York: Free Press.
BROWN, T.R. (1970) *The Judgment of Suicide Lethality: A Comparison of Judgmental Models Obtained Under Contrived Versus Natural Conditions.* Unpublished Dissertation: The University Of Oregon.
BRUNER, J.S., J.J. GOODNOW, and G.A. AUSTIN (1957) *A Study of Thinking.* New York: John Wiley.
BRZEZINSKI, Z. (1967) "The American transition." *New Republic,* September 23.
CAMPBELL, D.T. (1975) "Reforms as experiments." In E.L. Struening and M. Guttentag (eds.) *Handbook of Evaluation Research,* Volume I, pp. 71-100. Beverly Hills: Sage Publications.
——— (1971) *Methods for The Experimental Society.* Paper presented at the Eastern Psychological Association, April 17.
CHAPMAN, L.J. and J.P. CHAPMAN (1969) "Illusory correlation as an obstacle to the use of valid psychodiagnostic signs." *Journal of Abnormal Psychology* 74, pp. 271-280.
——— (1967) "The genesis of popular but erroneous psycho-diagnostic observations." *Journal of Abnormal Psychology* 72, pp. 193-204.
CHASE, W.G. and H.A. SIMON (1973) "Perception in chess." *Cognitive Psychology* 4, pp. 55-81.
CHILD, J. (1973) "Predicting and understanding organization structure." *Administrative Science Quarterly* 18, pp. 168-185.
COCH, L. and J. R. P. FRENCH, Jr. (1958) "Overcoming resistance to change." In E.E. Maccoby, T.M. Newcomb, and E.L. Hartley (eds.) *Readings in Social Psychology,* pp. 233-250. New York: Holt, Rinehart and Winston.
COCHRANE, J.L. and M. ZELENY [eds.] (1973) *Multiple Criteria Decision Making.* Columbia, S.C.: University of South Carolina Press.

COLEMAN, J.S. (1976) "Policy decisions, social science information, and education." *Sociology of Education* 49, pp. 304-312.

––– (1973) *The Mathematics of Collective Action.* London: Heinemann.

––– (1972) *Policy Research in the Social Sciences.* Morristown, N.J.: General Learning Press.

COPLIN, W.D. [ed.] (1968) *Simulation in the Study of Politics.* Chicago: Markham.

CRECINE, J.P. (1969) *Governmental Problem-Solving: A Computer Simulation of Municipal Budgeting.* Chicago: Rand McNally.

CRONBACH, L.J. and G.C. GLASER (1965) *Psychological Tests and Personnel Decisions.* Urbana, Ill.: University of Illinois.

CYERT, R.M. and J.G. MARCH (1963) *A Behavioral Theory of the Firm.* Englewood Cliffs, N.J.: Prentice-Hall.

DANIELS, H. and J. OTIS (1950) "A method of analyzing employment interviews." *Personnel Psychology* 3, pp. 425-444.

DAVIS, O.A., and F.H. RUETER (1970) *A Simulation of Municipal Zoning Decisions.* Regulatory Process Workshop Paper No. 1. Carnegie Mellon University (mimeographed).

DAVIS, O.A., M. A. H. DEMPSTER, and A. WILDAVSKY (1966) "On the process of budgeting: an empirical study of congressional appropriations." In G. Tullock (ed.) *Papers on Non-Market Decision-Making,* pp. 63-132. Thomas Jefferson Center for Political Economy. Charlottesville, Va.: University of Virginia.

DAWES, R.M. (1973) "Objective optimization under multiple subjective functions." In J.L. Cochrane and M. Zeleny (eds.) *Multiple Criteria Decision Making,* pp. 9-17. Columbia, S.C.: University of South Carolina Press.

––– (1970) "A case study of graduate admissions: application of three principles of human decision making." *American Psychologist* 26, pp. 180-188.

––– and B. CORRIGAN (1974) "Linear models in decision making." *Psychological Bulletin* 81, pp. 95-106.

DEUTSCH, K.W. (1966) *The Nerves of Government.* New York: Free Press.

DREYFUS, H.L. (1972) *What Computers Can't Do: A Critique of Artificial Reason.* New York: Harper and Row.

DROR, Y. (1968) *Public Policymaking Reexamined.* San Francisco: Chandler.

DUDYCHA, L.W. and J.C. NAYLOR (1966) "Characteristics of the human inference process in complex choice behavior situations." *Organizational Behavior and Human Performance* 1, pp. 110-128.

DUNCAN, O.D. (1969) "Social forecasting: the state of the art." *The Public Interest* 17 (Fall), pp. 88-118.

DUTTON, J.M. and W.H. STARBUCK [eds.] (1971) *Computer Simulation of Human Behavior.* New York: John Wiley.

EDWARDS, W. (1968) "Conservatism in human information processing." In B. Kleinmuntz (ed.) *Formal Representations of Human Judgment,* pp. 17-52. New York: John Wiley.

EHRLICH, J., J.W. RINEHART, and C. HOWELL (1962) "The study of role conflict: explorations in methodology." *Sociometry* 25 pp. 85-97.

EINHORN, H.J. (1971) "Use of nonlinear, noncompensatory models as a function of task and amount of information." *Organizational Behavior and Human Performance* 6, pp. 1-27.

––– (1970) "The use of nonlinear noncompensatory models in decision making." *Psychological Bulletin* 73, pp. 221-230.

ELLIS, D.O., and F.J. LUDWIG (1962) *Systems Philosophy.* Englewood Cliffs, N.J.: Prentice-Hall.

ENZER, S. (1970) *Delphi and Cross-Impact Techniques: An Effective Combination for Systematic Future Analysis*. Working Paper No. 8. Middleton, Conn.: Institute for the Future.

ETZIONI, A. (1975) *Comparative Analysis of Complex Organizations*. New York: Free Press.

FEIGENBAUM, E.A. and J. FELDMAN [eds.] (1963) *Computer and Thought*. New York: McGraw-Hill.

FELDMAN, J. and H.E. KANTER (1965) "Organizational decision making." In J.G. March (ed.) *Handbook of Organizations*, pp. 614-649. Chicago: Rand McNally.

FESTINGER, L. (1957) *A Theory of Cognitive Dissonance*. New York: Harper and Row.

FISHBEIN, M. [ed.] (1967) *Readings in Attitude Theory and Measurement*. New York: John Wiley.

––– and I. AJZEN (1975) *Belief, Attitude, Intention and Behavior: An Introduction to Theory and Research*. Reading, Mass.: Addison-Wesley.

FITZGERALD, J. and A.F. FITZGERALD (1973) *Fundamentals of Systems Analysis*. New York: John Wiley.

FORRESTER, J.W. (1969) *Urban Dynamics*. Cambridge, Mass.: M.I.T.

FREDERIKSEN, N. (1962) "In-basket tests and factors in administrative performance." In H. Guetzkow (ed.) *Simulation in Social Science: Readings*, pp. 124-137. Englewood Cliffs, N.J.: Prentice-Hall.

FREEDMAN, J.L., J.M. CARLSMITH, and D.O. SEARS (1974) *Social Psychology*. Englewood Cliffs, N.J.: Prentice-Hall.

GOLDBERG, L.R. (1976) "Man versus model of man: just how conflicting is that evidence?" *Organizational Behavior and Human Performance* 16, pp. 13-22.

––– (1970) "Man versus model of man: a rationale, plus some evidence for a method of improving on clinical inferences." *Psychological Bulletin* 73, pp. 422-432.

GOLDBERG, L.R. (1969) "The search for configural relationships in personality assessment: the diagnoses of psychosis versus neurosis from the MMPI." *Multivariate Behavioral Research* 4, pp. 523-536.

––– (1968) "Simple models or simple processes? some research on clinical judgments." *American Psychologist* 23, pp. 483-496.

––– (1965) "Diagnosticians versus diagnostic signs: the diagnosis of psychosis versus neurosis from the MMPI." *Psychological Monographs* 79, whole No. 602.

GOULDNER, A.W. (1954) *Patterns of Industrial Bureaucracy*. Glencoe, Ill.: Free Press.

GREENBERGER, M., M.A. CRENSON, and B. CRISSEY (1976) *Models in the Policy Process: Public Decision Making in the Computer Era*. New York: Russell-Sage.

GREGG, L.W. and H.A. SIMON (1967) "An information-processing explanation of one-trial and incremental learning." *Journal of Verbal Learning and Verbal Behavior* 6, pp. 780-787.

GROOT, A. de (1966) "Perception and memory versus thought: some old ideas and recent findings." In B. Kleinmuntz (ed.) *Problem Solving*, pp. 19-50. New York: John Wiley.

GROSS, B.M. (1966) "The state of the nation: social systems accounting." In R.A. Bauer (ed.) *Social Indicators*, pp. 154-271. Cambridge, Mass.: M.I.T.

GROSS, N., W.S. MASON, and A.W. McEACHERN (1958) *Explorations in Role Analysis*. New York: John Wiley.

GROSSMAN, J.B. and J. TANENHAUS [eds.] (1969) *Frontiers of Judicial Research*. New York: John Wiley.

GUETZKOW, H. [ed.] (1962) "A use of simulation in the study of inter-nation relations." In H. Guetzkow (ed.) *Simulation in Social Science: Readings*, pp. 82-93. Englewood Cliffs, N.J.: Prentice-Hall.

GULLAHORN, J.E. and J.T. GULLAHORN (1970) "Simulation and social system theory: the state of the union." *Simulation and Games* 1, pp. 19-41.

HACKER, A. [ed.] (1964) *The Corporation Take-Over.* New York: Harper and Row.

HAMMOND, K.R. and B. BREHMER (1973) "Quasi-rationality and distrust: implications for international conflict." In L. Rappoport and D.A. Summers (eds.) *Human Judgment and Social Interaction,* pp. 338-391. New York: Holt, Rinehart and Winston.

HAMMOND, K.R., C.J. HURSCH, and F.J. TODD (1964) "Analyzing the components of clinical inference." *Psychological Review* 71, pp. 438-456.

HEIDER, F. (1958) *The Psychology of Interpersonal Relations.* New York: John Wiley.

HENCHY, T. and D.C. GLASS (1968) "Evaluation apprehension and the social facilitation of dominant and subordinate responses." *Journal of Personality and Social Psychology* 10, pp. 446-454.

HERNES, G. (1971) *Interest, Influence, and Cooperation: A Study of the Norwegian Parliament.* Unpublished Dissertation, Johns Hopkins University. Ann Arbor, Mich.: University of Michigan Microfilms.

HESS, E.H. (1959) "Imprinting." *Science* 130, pp. 133-141.

HILGARD, E.R. (1957) *Introduction to Psychology.* New York: Harcourt, Brace.

HOFFMAN, P.J. (1968) "Cue-consistency and configurality in human judgment." In B. Kleinmuntz (ed.) *Formal Representations of Human Judgment,* pp. 53-90. New York: John Wiley.

——— (1960) "The Paramorphic Representation of Clinical Judgment." *Psychological Bulletin,* 57, pp. 116-131.

———, P. SLOVIC, and L.G. RORER (1968) "An analysis-of-variance model for the assessment of configural cue utilization in clinical judgment." *Psychological Bulletin* 69, pp. 338-349.

HOLLANDER, E.P. and R.G. HUNT [eds.] (1963) *Current Perspectives in Social Psychology.* New York: Oxford University Press.

HOOS, I.R. (1975) "Reply to technology transfer: another opinion." *Journal of Dynamic Systems, Measurement, and Control* March, pp. 15-17.

——— (1974) *Systems Analysis in Public Policy: A Critique.* Berkeley: University of California Press.

HOVLAND, C.I. (1962) "Computer simulation of thinking." In H. Guetzkow (ed.) *Simulation in Social Science: Readings,* pp. 16-28. Englewood Cliffs, N.J.: Prentice-Hall.

HUMPHREYS, L.G. (1939) "Acquisition and extinction of verbal expectations in a situation analogous to conditioning." *Journal of Experimental Psychology* 25, pp. 294-301.

INBAR, M. (1976) "Toward valid computer simulations of bureaucratized decisions." *Simulation and Games* 7, pp. 243-260.

——— (1969) "Development and educational use of simulations: an example 'the community response game.' " *International Journal of Experimental Research in Education* 6, pp. 5-44.

——— and C. STOLL (1972) *Simulation and Gaming in Social Science.* New York: Free Press.

KAHNEMAN, D. and A. TVERSKY (1973) "On the psychology of prediction." *Psychological Review* 80, pp. 237-251.

——— (1972) "Subjective probability: a judgment of representativeness." *Cognitive Psychology* 3, pp. 430-454.

KAPLAN, A. (1964) *The Conduct of Inquiry.* San Francisco: Chandler.

KATZENBACH, N. deB. [Chairman] (1967) *The Challenge of Crime in a Free Society: A Report by the President's Commission on Law Enforcement and Administration of Justice.* Washington, D.C.: U.S. Government Printing Office.

KELLEY, H.H. and J.W. THIBAUT (1969) "Group problem solving." In G. Lindzey and E. Aronson (eds.) *The Handbook of Social Psychology,* Volume IV. Reading, Mass.: Addison-Wesley.

——— (1954) "Experimental studies of group problem solving and process." In G. Lindzey (ed.) *Handbook of Social Psychology,* Volume II. Reading, Mass.: Addison-Wesley.

KELLY, E.L. and D.W. FISKE (1951) *The Prediction of Performance in Clinical Psychology.* Ann Arbor: University of Michigan Press.

KEMENY, J.G. and T.E. KURTZ (1971) *Basic Programming.* New York: John Wiley.

KERLINGER, F.N. [ed.] (1975) *Review of Research in Education* 3. Itasca, Ill.: F.E. Peacock.

KING, W. (1976) Article in *New York Times,* May 14, p. 81.

KIRK, F.G. (1973) *Total System Development for Information Systems.* New York: John Wiley.

KLEINMUNTZ, B. [ed.] (1968) *Formal Representations of Human Judgment.* New York: John Wiley.

——— [ed.] (1966) *Problem Solving.* New York: John Wiley.

——— (1963) "MMPI decision rules for the identification of college maladjustment: a digital computer approach." *Psychological Monographs* 77, whole No. 577.

KNOX, R.E. and P.J. HOFFMAN (1962) "Effects of variation of profile format on intelligence and sociability judgments." *Journal of Applied Psychology* 46, pp. 14-20.

KORT, F. (1968) "A nonlinear model for the analysis of judicial decisions." *American Political Science Review* 62, pp. 546-555.

KRANZ, H. (1976) *The participatory Bureaucracy.* Lexington, Mass.: Lexington Books.

KRISLOV, S. (1974) *Representative Bureaucracy.* Englewood Cliffs, N.J.: Prentice Hall.

KUHN, T.S. (1964) *The Structure of Scientific Revolutions.* Chicago: University of Chicago Press.

LAND, K.C. and S. SPILERMAN [eds.] (1975) *Social Indicator Models.* New York: Russell-Sage.

LAUDON, K.C. (1974) *Computers and Bureaucratic Reform.* New York: John Wiley.

LAUGHLIN, J.E. (1978) "Comment on 'estimating coefficients in linear models: it don't make no nevermind.' " *Psychological Bulletin* 85, pp. 247-253.

LEAVITT, H.J. and T.L. WHISLER (1958) "Management in the 1980's" *Harvard Business Review,* November-December, pp. 41-48.

LEONTIEF, W. (1968) Book Review in *The New York Review,* October 10, p. 32.

LEVITT, T. (1976) "Management and the 'Post-Industrial' Society." *The Public Interest,* No. 44, Summer, pp. 69-103.

LIBBY, R. (1976) "Man Versus Model of Man: Some Conflicting Evidence." *Organizational Behavior and Human Performance,* 16, pp. 1-12.

——— (1976b) "Man Versus Model of Man: The Need for a Nonlinear Model." *Organizational Behavior and Human Performance,* 16, pp. 23-26.

LIKERT, R. (1961) *New Patterns of Management.* New York: McGraw-Hill.

LINDSAY, P.H. and D.A. NORMAN (1972) *Human Information Processing.* New York: Academic Press.

LINDZEY, G. [ed.] (1954) *Handbook of Social Psychology.* Volume II. Reading, Mass.: Addison-Wesley.

––– and E. ARONSON [eds.] (1969) *Handbook of Social Psychology*, Volume IV. Reading, Mass.: Addison-Wesley.

LINSTONE, H.A. and M. TUROFF [eds.] (1975) *The Delphi Method: Techniques and Applications*. Reading, Mass.: Addison-Wesley.

LORENZ, K. (1966) *On Aggression*. New York: Harcourt, Brace and World.

MACCOBY, E.E., T.M. NEWCOMB, and E.L. HARTLEY [eds.] (1958) *Readings in Social Psychology*. New York: Holt, Rinehart and Winston.

MADDEN, J.M. (1963) *An Application to Job Evaluation of a Policy-Capturing Model for Analyzing Individual and Group Judgment*. 6570th Personnel Research Laboratory, Aerospace Medical Division, Air Force Systems Command. May, PRL-TDR-63-15.

MARCH, J.G. [ed.] (1965) *Handbook of Organizations*. Chicago: Rand McNally.

––– and H.A. SIMON (1958) *Organizations*. New York: John Wiley.

MARX, K. (1906) *Capital*. New York: Modern Library.

McLEAN, R.S. and L.W. GREGG (1967) "Effect of induced chunking on temporal aspects of social recitation." *Journal of Experimental Psychology* 74, pp. 455-459.

McPHEE, W.N. (1963) *Formal Theories of Mass Behavior*. Glencoe, Ill.: Free Press.

MEEHL, P.E. (1959) "A comparison of clinicians with five statistical methods of identifying psychotic MMPI profiles." *Journal of Counseling Psychology* 6, pp. 102-109.

––– and W.G. DAHLSTROM (1960) "Objective configural rules for discriminating psychotic from neurotic MMPI profiles." *Journal of Consulting Psychology* 24, pp. 375-387.

MERTON, R.K. (1959) *Social Theory and Social Structure*. Glencoe, Ill.: Free Press.

–––, A.P. GRAY, B. HOCKEY, and H.C. SELVIN [eds.] (1960) *Reader in Bureaucracy*. Glencoe, Ill.: Free Press.

MILLER, G.A. (1956) "The magical number seven plus or minus two: some limits on our capacity for processing information." *Psychological Review* 63, pp. 81-97.

––, E. GALANTER, and K.H. PRIBRAM (1960) *Plans and the Structure of Behavior*. New York: Holt, Rinehart and Winston.

MONEY, J. (1970) "Matched pairs of hermaphrodites: behavioral biology of sexual differentiation from chromosomes to gender identity." *Engineering and Science* 33 (Special Issue: Biological Bases of Human Behavior), pp. 34-39.

MOORE, C.G. (1968) "Simulation of organizational decision-making: a survey." In W.D. Coplin (ed.) *Simulation in the Study of Politics*, pp. 183-226. Chicago: Markham.

MORGENROTH, W.M. (1964) "A method for understanding price determinants." *Journal of Marketing Research* 1, pp. 17-26.

MORGENSTERN, O. (1963) *The Accuracy of Economic Observations*. Princeton, N.J.: Princeton University Press.

NAGEL, S.S. [ed.] (1975) *Policy Studies and the Social Sciences*. Lexington, Mass.: Lexington Books.

NAYLOR, J.C. and R.J. WHERRY, Sr. (1965) "The use of simulated stimuli and the 'Jan' technique to capture and cluster the policies of raters." *Educational and Psychological Measurement* 25, pp. 969-986.

NEISSER, U. (1967) *Cognitive Psychology*. Englewood Cliffs, N.J.: Prentice-Hall.

NELSON, G. (1965) "A space age trajectory to the great society." Introductory Speech to Scientific Manpower Utilization Bill S.2662. *Congressional Record*, October 18.

NEWELL, A. and H.A. SIMON (1972) *Human Problem-Solving*. Englewood Cliffs, N.J.: Prentice-Hall.

––– (1971) "Simulation of human thought." In J.M. Dutton and W.H. Starbuck (eds.) *Computer Simulation of Human Behavior*, pp. 150-169. New York: John Wiley.

———— (1959) *The Simulation of Human Thought*. P-1734. Santa Monica, Cal.: Rand Corporation.

NEWELL, A., J.C. SHAW, and H.A. SIMON (1958) "Chess playing problems and the problem of complexity." *I.B.M. Journal of Research and Development* 2, pp. 320-335.

NEWTON, J.R. (1965) "Judgment and feedback in a quasi-clinical situation." *Journal of Personality and Social Psychology* 1, pp. 336-342.

New York Times [editorial] (1976) *Crisis in Mathematics*, June 2, p. 36.

OFFSHE, L. and R. OFFSHE (1970) *Utility and Choice in Social Interaction*. Englewood Cliffs, N.J.: Prentice-Hall.

OLSHAVSKY, R.W. (1971) "Search limits as a function of tree size and storage requirements." *Organizational Behavior and Human Performance* 6, pp. 336-344.

ORNSTEIN, R.E. (1969) *On the Experience of Time*. Baltimore, Md.: Penguin.

OSGOOD, C.E. and P.H. TANNENBAUM (1955) "The principle of congruity in the prediction of attitude change." *Psychological Review* 62, pp. 42-55.

OSKAMP, S. (1965) "Overconfidence in case-study judgments." *Journal of Consulting Psychology* 29, pp. 261-265.

———— (1962) *How Clinicians Make Decisions from the MMPI: An Empirical Study*. Paper presented at the American Psychological Association, St. Louis.

PARKER, D.B. (1976) *Crime by Computer*. New York: Charles Scribner's.

PARKINSON, C.H. (1957) *Parkinson's Law and Other Studies in Administration*. New York: Houghton Mifflin.

PATTERSON, C.H. (1955) "Diagnostic accuracy or diagnostic stereotyping?" *Journal of Consulting Psychology* 19, pp. 483-485.

PEABODY, R.L. and F.E. ROURKE (1965) "Public bureaucracies." In J.G. March (ed.) *Handbook of Organizations*, pp. 802-837. Chicago: Rand McNally.

PERROW, C. (1974) *Control and Bureaucracy*. Department of Sociology. Stony Brooks, N.Y., SUNY (mimeographed).

———— (1974b) "Is business really changing?" *Organizational Dynamics* 3, pp. 31-44.

PETERSON, C.R., R.J. SCHNEIDER, and A.J. MILLER (1965) "Sample size and the revision of subjective probabilities." *Journal of Experimental Psychology* 69, pp. 522-527.

PHILLIPS, L.D. and W. EDWARDS (1966) "Conservatism in a simple probability inference task." *Journal of Experimental Psychology* 72, pp. 346-357.

Planning-Programming-Budgeting System (PPBS) (1967) *PPBS: Progress and Potential*. Congressional Hearings, Ninetieth Congress, 1rst Session, September 14 and 19-21, p. 1.

POSNER, M. (1973) *Memory and Thought: An Introduction to Cognitive Psychology*. Glenview, Ill.: Scott Foresman.

PÖTZL, O. (1960) The relationship between experimentally induced dream images and indirect vision." (1917). Reprinted in *Psychological Issues*. Volume II, No. 3, Monograph 7. New York: International Universities Press.

PRUZEK, R.M. and B.C. FREDERICK (1978) "Weighting predictors in linear models: alternatives to least squares and limitations of equal weights." *Psychological Bulletin* 85, pp. 254-266.

QUADE, E.S., and W.I. BOUCHER [eds.] (1968) *Systems Analysis and Policy Planning*. New York, N.Y.: Elsevier.

REIFFA, H. (1970) *Decision Analysis*. Reading, Mass.: Addison-Wesley.

RAPOPORT, A. (1970) *N-Person Game Theory: Concepts and Applications*. Ann Arbor: University of Michigan Press.

––– (1966) *Two-Person Game Theory: Essential Ideas.* Ann Arbor: The University of Michigan Press.

RAPPOPORT, L. and D.A. SUMMERS (1973) *Human Judgment and Social Interaction.* New York: Holt, Rinehart and Winston.

RASOR, J.R. (1969) *Simulation and Society.* Boston, Mass.: Allyn and Bacon.

REITMAN, W.R. (1965) *Cognition and Thought.* New York: John Wiley.

RESTLE, F. (1961) *Psychology of Judgment and Choice: A Theoretical Essay.* New York: John Wiley.

ROBERTS, F.S. (1976) "Strategy for the energy crisis: the case of commuter transportation policy." In R. Axelrod (ed.) *Structure of Decision,* pp. 142-179. Princeton, N.J.: Princeton University Press.

ROSENHAN, D.L. (1973) "On being sane in insane places." *Science* 179, pp. 250-258.

SARBIN, T.R. (1942) "A contribution to the study of actuarial and individual methods of prediction." *American Journal of Sociology* 46, pp. 593-602.

SCURRAH, M.J. and D.A. WAGNER (1970) "Cognitive model of problem-solving in chess." *Science* 168, pp. 209-211.

SECORD, P.F. and C.W. BACKMAN (1974) *Social Psychology.* New York: McGraw-Hill.

SHANNON, C.E. (1950) "Automatic chess player." *Scientific American* 182, pp. 48-51.

––– (1950b) "Programming a digital computer for playing chess." *Philosophy Magazine* 41, pp. 356-375.

––– (1975) *Systems Simulation: The Art and Science.* Englewood Cliffs, N.J.: Prentice-Hall.

SHARKANSKY, I. (1968) "Comments on Crecine's Paper." In W.D. Coplin (ed.) *Simulation in the Study of Politics,* pp. 146-148. Chicago: Markham.

SHAW, M.E. (1958) "Comparison of individual and small groups in the rational solution of complex problems." In E.E. Maccoby, T.M. Newcomb, and E.L. Hartley (eds.) *Readings in Social Psychology,* pp. 564-575. New York: McGraw-Hill.

SHEARER, J.L., A.T. MURPHY, and H.H. RICHARDSON (1967) *Introduction to Systems Dynamics.* Reading, Mass.: Addison-Wesley.

SHELLY, M.W., II, and G.L. BRYAN [eds.] (1964) *Human Judgments and Optimality.* New York: John Wiley.

SHEPARD, R.N. (1964) "On subjectively optimum selection among multiattribute alternatives." In M.W. Shelly II and G.L. Bryan (eds.) *Human Judgments and Optimality.* New York: John Wiley.

SHONFIELD, A. and S. SHAW [eds.] (1972) *Social Indicators and Social Policy.* London: Heinemann.

SHUBICK, M. (1975) *Games for Society, Business and War: Toward a Theory of Gaming.* New York: Elsevier.

––– and G.D. BREWER (1972) *Models, Simulations, and Games: A Survey.* R-1060-ARPA/RC. Santa Monica, Cal.: Rand Corporation.

SHULMAN, L.S. and A.S. Elstein (1975) "Studies of problem solving, judgment, and decision making: implications for educational research." In F.N. Kerlinger (ed.) *Review of Research in Education* 3, pp. 3-42. Itasca, Ill.: F.E. Peacock.

SIMON, H.A. (1976) *Administrative Behavior.* New York: Free Press.

––– (1969) *The Sciences of the Artificial.* Cambridge, Mass.: M.I.T.

––– (1967 and 1969b) "Motivational and emotional controls of cognition." *Psychological Review* 74 (1967), pp. 29-39. Also in E.F. Borgatta (ed.) *Social Psychology: Readings and Perspective,* 1969 (b), pp. 104-113. Chicago: Rand McNally.

––– (1960) "The corporation: will it be managed by machines?" In M. Anshen and

G.L. Bach (eds.) *Management and Corporations in 1985*, pp. 17-55. New York: McGraw-Hill.

——— (1957) *Models of Man*. New York: John Wiley.

——— (1955) "A behavioral model of rational choice." *Quarterly Journal of Economics* 69, pp. 99-118.

——— and A. NEWELL (1963) "Models: their uses and limitations." In E.P. Hollander and R.G. Hunt (eds.) *Current Perspectives in Social Psychology*, pp. 79-90. New York: Oxford University Press.

SLAGLE, J.R. (1971) *Artificial Intelligence*. New York: McGraw-Hill.

SLOVIC, P. (1969) "Analyzing the expert judge: a descriptive study of a stockbroker's decision process." *Journal of Applied Psychology* 53, pp. 255-263.

——— and S.C. LICHTENSTEIN (1971 and 1973) "Comparison of Bayesian and regression approaches to the study of information processing in judgment." *Organizational Behavior and Human Performance* 6 (1971), pp. 649-744. Also in L. Rappoport and D.A. Summers (eds.) *Human Judgment and Social Interaction*, 1973, pp. 16-108. New York: Holt, Rinehart and Winston.

——— (1968) "The relative importance of probabilities and payoffs in risk taking." *Journal of Applied Psychology Monograph Supplement* 78, No. 3, part 2.

SMITH, H.C. and J.H. WAKELEY (1972) *Psychology of Industrial Behavior*. New York: McGraw-Hill.

SPENCER, D.D. (1970) *A Guide to BASIC Programming: A Time-Sharing Language*. Reading, Mass.: Addison-Wesley.

Standard College Dictionary [Funk and Wagnalls] (1963) Entry "red tape." New York: Harcourt, Brace and World.

STEINBRUNER, J.D. (1974) *The Cybernetic Theory of Decision*. Princeton, N.J.: Princeton University Press.

STINCHCOMBE, A.L. (1968) *Constructing Social Theories*. New York: Harcourt, Brace and World.

STRUENING, E.L. and M. GUTTENTAG [eds.] (1975) *Handbook of Evaluation Research*. Volume I. Beverly Hills: Sage Publications.

SUMMERS, D.A. (1968) "Conflict, compromise, and belief change in a decision-making task." *Journal of Conflict Resolution* 12, pp. 215-221.

TANNENBAUM, A.S. [ed.] (1968) *Control in Organizations*. New York: McGraw-Hill.

TAYLOR, D.W., P.C. Berry, and C.H. Block (1966) "Does group participation when using brainstorming facilitate or inhibit creative thinking?" In C.W. Backman and P.F. Secord (eds.) *Problems in Social Psychology*, pp. 299-309. New York: McGraw-Hill.

THOMPSON, J.D. (1967) *Organizations in Action*. New York: McGraw-Hill.

TRAPPL, R. and F.R. PICHLER [eds.] (1975) *Progress in Cybernetics and Systems Research*. Volume I. New York: John Wiley.

TULLOCK, G. [ed.] (1966) *Papers on Non-Market Decision-Making*. Thomas Jefferson Center for Political Economy, Charlottesville, Va.: University of Virginia.

TURING, A.M. (1963) "Computing machinery and intelligence." In E.A. Feigenbaum and J. Feldman (eds.) *Computers and Thought*, pp. 11-35. New York: McGraw-Hill.

TVERSKY, A. (1972) "Elimination by aspects: a theory of choice." *Psychological Review* 79, pp. 281-299.

——— (1969) "Intransitivity of preferences." *Psychological Review* 76, pp. 31-48.

——— and D. KAHNEMAN (1973 and 1974) "Judgment under uncertainty: heuristics and biases." Paper read at the 4th. Conference on Subjective Probability, Utility, Decision-Making. Rome, September 1973. Also in *Science* 185 (1974), pp. 1124-1131.

––– (1973b) "Availability: a heuristic for judging frequency and probability." *Cognitive Psychology* 5, pp. 207-232.

––– (1971) "The belief in the law of small numbers." *Psychological bulletin* 76, pp. 105-110.

ULMER, S.S. (1969) "The discriminant function and a theoretical context for its use in estimating the votes of judges." In J.B. Grossman and J. Tanenhaus (eds.) *Frontiers of Judicial Research.* New York: John Wiley.

U.S. Congressional Report (1970) *Economic Analysis and the Efficiency of Government.* Ninety-First Congress, 2nd. Session, February 9. Washington, D.C.: U.S. Government Printing Office.

VARET, B. (1974-75) "Utilisation d'un ordinateur pour la simulation de cas pathologiques et l'enseignement de la methodologie du diagnostic medical." *Bulletin de Psychologie* 28, pp. 7-8.

WAINER, H. (1978) "On the sensitivity of regression and regressors." *Psychological Bulletin* 85, pp. 267-273.

––– (1976) "Estimating coefficients in linear models: it don't make no nevermind." *Psychological Bulletin* 83, pp. 213-217.

WEBER, M. (1946) *From Max Weber: Essays in Sociology.* Translated and Edited by H.H. Gerth and C. Wright Mills. New York: Oxford University Press.

WEICK, K.E. (1969) *The Social Psychology of Organizing.* Reading, Mass.: Addison-Wesley.

WEISS, D.J. and R.V. DAVIS (1960) "An objective validation of factual interview data." *Journal of Applied Psychology* 44, pp. 381-384.

WHITE, K.P. and D. WRIGHT (1975) "Technology transfer: another opinion." *Journal of Dynamic Systems, Measurement, and Control,* March, pp. 11-15.

WHYTE, W.F. (1961) *Men at Work.* Homewood, Ill.: Dorsey.

WIGGINS, N. and P.J. HOFFMAN (1968) "Three models of clinical judgment." *Journal of Abnormal Psychology* 73, pp. 70-77.

WILDAVSKY, A. (1975) *Budgeting: A Comparative Theory of Budgeting Processes.* Boston: Little, Brown.

––– (1964) *The Politics of the Budgeting Process.* Boston: Little, Brown.

WOODWARD, J. (1965) *Industrial Organization: Theory and Practice.* London: Oxford University Press.

YNTEMA, D.B. and W.S. TORGERSON (1961) "Man-computer cooperation in decisions requiring common sense." *IRE Transactions of the Professional Group on Human Factors in Electronics,* (HFE) 2, pp. 20-26.

ZAJONC, R.B. (1965) "Social facilitation." *Science* 149, pp. 269-274.

––– (1960) "The concepts of balance, congruity, and dissonance." *Public Opinion Quarterly* 24, pp. 280-296.

–––, A. HEINGARTNER, and E.M. HERMAN (1969) "Social enhancement and impairment of performance in the cockroach." *Journal of Personality and Social Psychology* 13, pp. 83-92.

ZAJONC, R.B. and S.M. SALES (1966) "Social facilitation of dominant and subordinate responses." *Journal of Experimental Social Psychology* 2, pp. 160-168.

ZELDITCH, M. Jr., and W.M. EVAN (1962) "Simulated bureaucracies: a methodological analysis." In H. Guetzkow (ed.) *Simulation in Social Science: Readings,* pp. 48-60. Englewood Cliffs, N.J.: Prentice-Hall.

ABOUT THE AUTHOR

MICHAEL INBAR received his Ph.D. in Social Relations from the Johns Hopkins University in 1966. He has taught at the University of Michigan, Ann Arbor, and at the Johns Hopkins University. In 1975-1976 he was a Visiting Scholar at the Russell-Sage Foundation. He returned to Israel in 1977 to become professor of Sociology and Psychology at the University of Haifa. Dr. Inbar was the first editor of the quarterly *Simulation and Games.* His publications include *Simulation and Gaming in Social Science* (coauthored with C. Stoll; New York: Free Press, 1972); *The Vulnerable Age Phenomenon* (New York: Russell-Sage/Basic Books, 1976); and *Ethnic Integration in Israel* (coauthored with C. Adler; New Brunswick, N.J.: Transaction Books, 1977). Dr. Inbar is currently professor of sociology at the Hebrew University of Jerusalem and scientific director of the Henrietta Szold Institute for Research in the Behavioral Sciences.s,